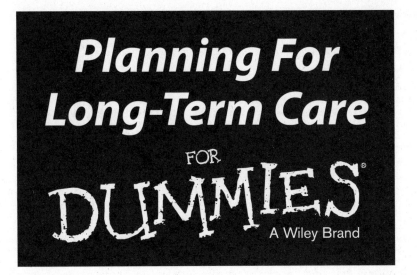

Planning For Long-Term Care

FOR DUMMIES®
A Wiley Brand

by Carol Levine

AARP

FOR DUMMIES®
A Wiley Brand

Planning For Long-Term Care For Dummies®

Published by: **John Wiley & Sons, Inc.,** 111 River Street, Hoboken, NJ 07030-5774, www.wiley.com

For general information on our other products and services, please contact our Customer Care Department within the U.S. at 877-762-2974, outside the U.S. at 317-572-3993, or fax 317-572-4002. For technical support, please visit www.wiley.com/techsupport.

Wiley publishes in a variety of print and electronic formats and by print-on-demand. Some material included with standard print versions of this book may not be included in e-books or in print-on-demand. If this book refers to media such as a CD or DVD that is not included in the version you purchased, you may download this material at http://booksupport.wiley.com. For more information about Wiley products, visit www.wiley.com.

This and other AARP books are available in print and e-formats at AARP's online bookstore, www.aarp.org/bookstore, and through local and online bookstores.

Library of Congress number is available upon request.

ISBN: 978-1-118-72575-7 (pbk); ISBN 978-1-118-75650-8 (ebk); ISBN 978-1-118-75654-6 (ebk); ISBN 978-1-118-75660-7 (ebk)

Manufactured in the United States of America

10 9 8 7 6 5 4 3 2 1

Contents at a Glance

Table of Contents

Part V: Special Populations 231

Chapter 17: Services for LGBT Older Adults. 233

Chapter 18: Planning for Veterans 247

Introduction

*P*lanning for the long term is an important part of ensuring the best possible future for yourself or a parent. (In this book I generally use "parent" to stand in for any older person you care about.) But because you've picked up or downloaded this book, you probably already know that. What you may not know is the broad scope of decisions, services, and choices that planning encompasses. Many people start with a specific question about topics such as buying long-term care insurance or choosing an independent- or assisted-living facility and find that they need to explore many other avenues as they pursue their goals of good health, independence, choice, and quality of life.

As a start, put aside all the negative ideas you may have about what long-term care means. Times have changed, and there are many more options for the long term than there were decades ago. Learning about these options can be challenging, but finding the answers you need and creating a comprehensive and workable plan that fits your needs are well worth the effort.

I wrote this book to offer the broadest possible view as well as to provide information about specific topics. Long-term care in this perspective changes over time and encompasses a range of topics: modifications you can make to your home so you can stay independent and live at home as you age; options for group housing such as independent and assisted living or specially created communities; multigenerational living; personal care and homemaker services as well as transportation and other community services; legal and financial issues such as advance directives and managing money; and the medical care an older person needs, which may be primary care, preventive care, hospitalization, or rehabilitation services. Care for the long term can mean very modest adjustments to your home or full-time residence in a nursing home. Not everyone needs the complete range of options but it is important to know where you or your parent fits or may fit into this spectrum.

In this book I present you with a range of options to consider, always with the caveat that no solution works for everyone. I also include your family, partner, neighbors, and friends — and the community in which you live — as crucial factors in decision-making. Remember too that the emotional aspects of a plan are often underestimated but can determine its success or failure.

This book is different from many other discussions of long-term care precisely because it is so broad in scope. Many professional discussions, while offering valuable analyses, suffer in my opinion from a provider-centered approach rather than one that places the person needing assistance at the center. And consumer-oriented discussions usually take on one subject at a time rather than addressing the whole landscape. Memoirs are valuable testaments but are based on one person's experience. This book is a blend of what I have learned from all these approaches, but it presents the big picture and then zeroes in on the practical, hands-on information that is often difficult to find in one place.

Care for the long term is complex but not incomprehensible. Like any other major decision in life, planning requires weighing risks and benefits, being flexible, and staying open to change. It can be unsettling. Some of your assumptions and preconceptions may be challenged. Even though I have many years' experience in the fields of health policy, aging, and family caregiving, writing this book has given me new insights into the difficulties individuals and families face in planning. I have new respect for their diligence and devotion, and for the painstaking efforts of professionals who assist them.

About This Book

You, the reader, decide how to use this book. It is eminently transparent, organized so that you can easily find the topics you want to know more about and skip the ones that don't apply to your situation. There are many ways to get to various chapters and parts of chapters. You don't need to read the chapters in order, although I would recommend at least skimming the chapters in Part I for an orientation to the book's broad perspective. Of course, you can always come back to these chapters after you have reviewed the areas you want to concentrate on.

Many chapters have separate sections called *sidebars,* which are brief digressions into history, public policy, little-known facts, or other kinds of information that are not essential to the text but add to its depth. You can safely ignore them, but I hope you at least dip into a few.

Every chapter has web links to other resources to help you get more specific information about a particular topic, find information about your state's regulations, or help in other ways. You may note that some web addresses break across two lines of text. If you're reading this book in print and want to visit one of these web pages, simply key in the web address exactly as it's noted in the text, pretending that the line break doesn't exist. If you're reading this as an e-book, you've got it easy — just click the web address to be taken directly to the web page.

This book is meant to serve as a reference, so you don't have to commit any information to memory. It's all there, waiting to be read and re-read.

Additionally, two other *For Dummies* books from AARP — *Social Security For Dummies* (by Jonathan Peterson, published by Wiley) and *Medicare For Dummies* (Patricia Barry; also published by Wiley) — are helpful adjuncts to this book and offer much more detail about those two important public programs.

Foolish Assumptions

This book makes a few assumptions about you, the reader.

- ✔ You probably don't know a whole lot about various aspects of long-term care, such as housing, finances, and medical coverage. And even if you have some professional or personal background in the field, you can benefit from new information and different perspectives.

- ✔ You may be starting to plan long-term care for yourself or your spouse or partner. You probably have some time to plan before the need arises — but don't underestimate how long it may take.

- ✔ You may be starting to plan, or already planning, for an older person such as a parent. The time for planning in this situation is likely to be short, or may follow a health crisis. You need help now. But don't make quick decisions that will be hard to reverse.

- ✔ You may be comfortable using the Internet to find additional resources.

- ✔ You are worried about making the best choice and how to pay for long-term care. Rest easy: You are not alone.

Icons Used in This Book

Throughout the book, you will see several icons that draw your attention to certain kinds of information.

The Tip icon links to an additional resource or offers advice about the topic discussed in the preceding text.

The Remember icon is not a literal order to memorize the information but a word to the wise, a reminder of what you should be considering.

The Warning icon signals important information that alerts you to a potential problem; for example, a fraudulent practice or a scam aimed at older adults.

Technical stuff is just what it sounds like — more detailed information than you absolutely need but may find helpful just the same.

Beyond the Book

As they say on TV, "But wait! There are extras that come with the book."

- ✔ Cheat Sheets (www.dummies.com/cheatsheet/planninglong termcare) are handy online reference tools that you will probably want to use over and over; for example, a list of questions to ask when you visit an assisted-living facility or some easy fixes you can make to your home to prevent falls.

- ✔ Each page that opens a new part of this book includes a link to an online article at Dummies.com that extends the content covered in the chapter. You'll find further information on, for example, creating a will that tells what to do with your digital information. You can go directly to these bonus articles at www.dummies.com/extras/planninglongtermcare.

Where to Go from Here

With all the flexibility inherent in the *For Dummies* format, where should you start? If you know that you want information about a specific topic (for example, reverse mortgages or advance directives), by all means use the table of contents and index to find those sections. If you are still getting your head around the idea of long-term care, then pick a chapter that interests you and dig in. You don't even have to start at the beginning of that chapter. But remember what Maria in *The Sound of Music* told her young pupils: The beginning is a very good place to start.

Part I
Getting Started with Long-Term Care

getting started with

long-term

care

In this part...

✔ Find out how planning for long-term care yet staying flexible can keep you in control and help avoid crises.

✔ Start assessing your current and future needs by creating a personal inventory of your health status, family and friends, personality characteristics, and attitudes about money. All these factors affect your plans, and some may make you think more deeply about your own preferences and values.

✔ Start researching your care options through federal resources, state and local resources, and private groups. Being inquisitive but skeptical is a good approach.

✔ Make decisions a family affair by holding a family meeting. I tell you when it might be advisable to invite an outside mediator and how to avoid or deal with conflict.

Chapter 1

Looking Ahead: The Big Picture

• •

In This Chapter

▶ Defining long-term care broadly

▶ Seeing the changes and new options

▶ Selecting good advisors

• •

*J*ust by opening this chapter, you have become a member of a select group of people who are taking a big step toward a better future for yourself and your family. Most studies show that only a third of Americans have made even the most basic plans for their future care needs. Perhaps you are already facing this dilemma for an aging or sick parent who lacks a plan for the long term and so you know how important it is to consider the future.

Thinking about the many aspects to consider — from finances to health to housing to more — is emotionally difficult, but it is also intellectually challenging because the choices available are often not clear-cut. They may involve complex financial calculations as well as personal and family preferences. But ignoring the question only makes the day of reckoning that much more difficult. In this chapter I help you start to think about long-term care in a proactive and positive way.

Planning for the Long Term Starts with You

Long-term care is different for each individual and ideally should be tailored to a person's needs and preferences. I want to reinforce this notion: Long-term care does not start with a place or a payment mechanism or a set of services; it starts with a person.

Many conventional definitions, however, start with a different focus — what services are included, who provides them, where they are provided, and, most important, who pays (or won't pay) the bill. These factors are obviously important, but they should not overshadow the person at its center.

In addition to being person-centered, planning should start early — at a point when various options for living at home or in a community can be arranged that prolong independence and make it less likely that institutional care will be needed. From that perspective, modifying your home to make it safer and more accessible is part of a long-term care plan. So is considering the possibility of multigenerational living and various forms of group residence in the community. These options are discussed in Part II.

The chapters in Part III take up the important issue of paying for care. Coordinating one's healthcare needs with other kinds of assistance is a critical element because staying healthy is a good way to avoid the need for heavy-duty long-term care, and these topics are discussed in Part IV. Finally, Part V looks at the special issues you may face if you're part of a specific group, such as family caregivers or veterans of military service. Part VI has a chapter on common myths about aging and long-term care and one on using websites with state-by-state information, valuable because so much of long-term care is determined by state, not federal policies. Appendix A is a glossary of terms you may encounter, and Appendix B is a list of resources. Throughout this book I reinforce the idea that a long-term care plan is not just about where you live or what services you get but about how you want to live and how to achieve your goals.

What Is Long-Term Care?

Defining long-term care is, perhaps surprisingly, not straightforward. Many people in the field of aging consider long-term care to be services that are nonmedical, such as personal care (bathing, dressing, feeding) or household tasks (shopping, cooking, transportation). Although these aspects of assistance are essential, in this book I take a broader view to include factors like medical care, housing options, financial considerations, advance care planning, and the community environment. I believe that when considering long-term care, most people should look at the whole spectrum of need rather than only specific segments.

In its 2013 overview of long-term care service providers, the National Center for Health Statistics found that about 58,500 providers served about 8 million people in the United States. These included 4,800 adult day services, 12,200 home health agencies, 3,700 hospices, 15,700 nursing homes, and 22,200 assisted living and other residential care communities. The majority in four of these five sectors were for-profit organizations. Only adult da... mostly nonprofit. While these numbers may seem large, they ... family caregivers who provide unpaid care to the vast majority ... who need long-term assistance. The full report is available at `http:` `cdc.gov/nchs/data/nsltcp/long_term_care_services_20`

As I frame it, long-term care includes the various kinds of assistance ... ...on needs to maintain the highest possible level of health and quality of life over time. As the population ages and increasingly more people face chronic illnesses, which often diminish the ability to function independently, long-term care needs to encompass and integrate a broader range of services to meet complex needs. Some aspects of planning concern immediate or foreseeable needs, for example, for a person with chronic illnesses or disabilities. Other aspects might fall under the heading of long-range planning, for example, considering long-term care insurance or establishing a regular savings plan. Some aspects of planning, such as preparing a will and advance directive, should be done by everyone, even those in excellent health.

Looking at long-term services and supports

As an alternative to the term *long-term care,* another term has entered the lexicon: *long-term services and supports,* or LTSS. This term typically refers to non-medical services paid for privately or by Medicaid, although it can also apply to services such as transportation and homemaker visits provided by community agencies. By replacing *care,* which some people with disabilities see as a negative term, with the more impersonal *supports and services,* the new terminology is intended to stress an individual's independence and control over who provides assistance and how it is organized. Whichever term is used, a person- and family-centered approach is key, and this is something I stress throughout the book.

Noting that "LTSS has traditionally been provided in a fragmented, uncoordinated system of care provided by disparate agencies, each with its own funding, rules, and processes, and which are separate from the healthcare system," the federal Commission on Long-Term Care in its 2013 report to the Congress recommended that individuals and service providers "align incentives to improve the integration of LTSS with healthcare services in a person- and family-centered approach." (The Commission's final report is available at `http://ltccommission.lmp01.lucidus.net/wp-` `content/uploads/2013/12/Commission-on-Long-Term-Care-` `Final-Report-9-26-13.pdf`.)

In this book, I have chosen to use *long-term care* as a general category and *long-term services and supports* when referring specifically to services called by that name.

Using Medicare as a starting point

"Medicare does not cover long-term care." You'll come across this mantra again and again as you research long-term care. Yet I devote considerable attention to Medicare, precisely because many beneficiaries consider it their starting point in thinking about their future care needs. So what will Medicare cover? Understanding its limits is a first step in reality testing. What Medicare covers (after deductibles, coinsurance, and copays), you do not have to pay for; what Medicare does not cover requires additional resources.

Here is Medicare's definition of long-term care, as stated in its 2014 handbook "Medicare and You":

> *Long-term care: —A variety of services that help people with their medical and non-medical needs over a period of time. Long-term care can be provided at home, in the community, or in various other types of facilities, including nursing homes and assisted-living facilities. Most long-term care is custodial care. Medicare doesn't pay for this type of care if this is the only kind of care you need.*

Note the final "if" clause; this creates an opening for custodial care when the person also has a need for skilled care.

And here's Medicare's definition of custodial care:

> *Custodial care: —Nonskilled personal care, such as help with activities of daily living like bathing, dressing, eating, getting in or out of a bed or chair, moving around, and using the bathroom. It may also include the kind of health-related care that most people do themselves, like using eye drops. In most cases, Medicare doesn't pay for custodial care.*

Custodial care, a term many people find demeaning, is often called *personal care,* but it means the same thing. And it is definitely not *nonskilled*, as anyone who has performed these tasks knows.

Navigating the Roadblocks

Aging is a reality. And an undeniable part of that reality is that most people, especially those who live to an advanced age, will need assistance in some aspects of their lives. The Kaiser Family Foundation estimates that 70 percent of Americans 65 and older will eventually need assistance for an average of three years.

Yet what is undeniable in terms of demographics is easily deniable when it comes to our own lives and those of our older family members. A study conducted by the Associated Press-NORC Center for Public Affairs Research in 2013 found that about half of Americans over the age of 40 believe that "almost everyone" is likely to require long-term care at some point, but only a quarter think they themselves will need it.

I can check off quite a few reasons for delaying the planning process, but there are just as many benefits to start now.

Reasons for resistance

It isn't hard to understand why there is so much resistance to thinking about care for the long term. The usual suspects are societal attitudes that glamorize youth and promote ways to erase signs of aging, denial of mortality, fear of dependence, and other anxieties.

Another reason for resistance to planning is the high cost of long-term care, which is usually described in terms of nursing homes or extensive home care services. Search the Internet for "long-term care" and you will be directed primarily to articles on its financial aspects, written by business writers and offering suggestions about financial planning. Paying for long-term care is a major topic (and it comes up over and over again in this book; check out the chapters in Part III), but it is by no means the only topic to consider. Sometimes the focus on the high cost is in itself a deterrent to planning. It may seem impossible to save or obtain that much money, so why try? Again, costs are a reality but should not deter planning.

Only about a third (35 percent) of the respondents in the AP-NORC survey I cited earlier had saved money to pay for long-term care. Moreover, their understanding of costs was wide of the mark, both in underestimates and overestimates. Under a third were able to correctly identify the range of costs for nursing homes, assisted living, and home care aides. And they didn't expect to pay the bill themselves. They expected Medicare to pay for a home health aide or a nursing-home stay, which is covered only for short-term, not long-term care, and then only under certain circumstances. (For more on what Medicare covers, see Chapter 10.)

Benefits of planning

Decisions made in a crisis situation are often hasty and ill-considered. This is true in many aspects of life but is particularly problematic when a person's health and well-being are at stake. Not all crises can be avoided, but when they do occur, having a plan in place reduces the likelihood of the most severe unintended consequences. For example, an important part of a plan is an advance directive (see Chapter 16). In a medical emergency, if you can't speak for yourself, an advance directive and a healthcare proxy (a person legally authorized to speak for you) can make it more likely that you get the types of treatment you want and, even more difficult to achieve, don't get what you don't want. Certainly it can be hard to think about this kind of situation, but the alternative is worse. Without some form of advance directive, no one will know what you want or don't want, and it will be unclear who has the authority to speak for you. If your family can't agree, the decision will be made by strangers, and in the worst-case scenario, there will be litigation. The effort involved in creating an advance directive is minimal compared to the consequences of not having planned ahead.

This example also underscores another benefit of planning — making decisions for yourself instead of leaving them to others or to chance. Having absolute control is unrealistic, and possibly even undesirable, but letting family and other intimates know your values and preferences about long-term care is very important.

Some families are used to discussing and even arguing about all sorts of things, from trivial to significant. Others avoid conversations about serious matters. You can't change family dynamics that have taken years to develop, but you can work within that framework to make your wishes known and to anticipate objections. Sometimes you may have to make some compromises, such as limiting your driving or accepting some help at home. In other situations, your family may have to accept a less-than-perfect living situation out of respect for your wishes. If you and your family can negotiate these bumps, you are all less likely to find yourselves in opposite camps when it comes to making major decisions.

Planning also allows you to investigate more choices more thoroughly. You will still have hard decisions to make, but you will have the benefit of information, discussion, and time. Still, your planning has to be flexible. Try to build in as many alternatives as possible to allow for changes in health, finances, family situations, and all the other elements that can make a difference.

How Care for the Long Term Is Changing

Long-term care isn't what it used to be — and that's a good thing. There are many more options for living at home or in the community, where the vast majority of people want to be. Technology is making it possible to have your healthcare monitored at home and to keep you in touch with family and friends. There is a greater awareness of the importance of a stimulating environment for mental and physical health.

Nursing homes are changing too, as they move toward a more person-centered focus and introduce elements of stimulating activity and participation for their long-stay residents.

Looking at why changes are being made

There are several reasons for the changes in long-term care.

Money is a factor

One reason is economic: Medicaid — the federal-state program for low-income people — is the major payer of long-term care. According to a February 2013 report from the National Health Policy Forum, in fiscal year 2011 Medicaid paid 62.3 percent of long-term care expenditures, with 21.9 percent paid for out-of-pocket, 11.6 percent by other private sources, including long-term care insurance, and a small percentage (4.6 percent) by other public sources, such as the U.S. Department of Veteran Affairs (VA). The report is available at http://nhpf.org/library/the-basics/Basics_LTSS_02-01-13.pdf.

Medicaid's long-term care expenditures are expected to increase from $207.9 billion in 2010 to $346 billion in 2040. To keep this spending in check, Medicaid has tried to move away from what has been called an "institutional bias," which means that the bulk of funding goes toward nursing homes, putting it instead toward more community-based care. In 1995, for example, 80 percent of Medicaid spending on long-term care was for institutional care; by 2011 that percentage had dropped to 55 percent. Community-based care is typically cheaper than nursing home care, which makes it attractive to Medicaid programs faced with escalating costs, and is also preferred by individuals. While this should be a win-win situation, it has proven difficult to implement fully, partly because of the need for more housing options and direct-care workers to provide community care. Another reason is that federal rules require Medicaid programs to provide institutional care but home- and community-based services are optional.

Legal reasons

The federal Americans with Disabilities Act (ADA) is another reason for the change. In 1999, the U.S. Supreme Court held in *Olmstead v. L.C.* that unjustified segregation of persons with disabilities in nursing homes constitutes discrimination in violation of Title II of the ADA. The Court held that public programs such as Medicaid must offer community-based services to persons with disabilities when such services are appropriate, the affected person doesn't oppose community-based treatment, and community-based services can be reasonably accommodated, taking into account the resources available and the needs of others who are receiving disability services from the entity.

In its ruling, the Supreme Court explained that "institutional placement of persons who can handle and benefit from community settings perpetuates unwarranted assumptions that persons so isolated are incapable of or unworthy of participating in community life." Furthermore, "confinement in an institution severely diminishes the everyday life activities of individuals, including family relations, social contacts, work options, economic independence, educational advancement, and cultural enrichment." Although the case that reached the Supreme Court was about two young people with mental disabilities, the *Olmstead* decision applies to people of all ages and all different kinds of disabilities. (Many states, including Georgia, the state where the plaintiffs in the *Olmstead* case lived, have yet to implement fully a plan for moving eligible people from institutions to the community.)

While the *Olmstead* ruling is limited to a defined group of nursing home residents, it acts as an incentive for federal and state programs to develop appropriate community-based alternatives to institutions, which may benefit a larger group of people. It also reaffirms the importance of consumer choice in long-term care.

People want change

In addition to economic incentives and legal rulings, consumer demand has also played a part in moving away from old forms of long-term care to more home-like and person-centered settings. As people live longer — often into their 90s and beyond — the length of time a person needs various forms of care has increased and has required accommodation to various levels of need.

Although the trends of longer lives and person-centered settings are positive, implementation across the country is inconsistent and variable. At best, the system is a patchwork quilt of settings and services, some strong and some weak, with different eligibility requirements and payment sources. But compared to a few decades ago, the quilt itself is bigger because people have demanded better options. In succeeding chapters I describe several of these newer options, with some suggestions about how to find out more about what is available in your community.

Keeping up with insider language

Every industry and service enterprise has its own language. Long-term care is no exception, and the terms are constantly evolving. Those who are fluent in this language sometimes forget that newcomers to the field don't understand their acronyms, short-hand, and jargon. Throughout the book I explain terms as they come up, and I include a glossary in Appendix A. Just to get started, however, here are a few of the terms commonly used in the new world of long-term care that you may encounter. As you move forward, don't hesitate to ask when someone uses a term you don't understand or seems to be using a term in a way that is unfamiliar.

- ✔ **Activities of daily living** are ordinary tasks like bathing, eating, getting dressed, and going to the bathroom that most people don't think twice about but that become difficult for a person who is ill or has a disability. Assistance with ADLs can range from lending a hand, literally or figuratively, to heavy lifting and total responsibility for carrying out the task. (Also see IADLs later in this list.) The number of ADLs is often used as a benchmark for eligibility for long-term care insurance benefits or nursing home or home-based services.

- ✔ **Acute care:** The type of care provided in hospitals to treat an illness or accident that needs immediate attention. Acute care is distinguished from *chronic care,* which treats illness that last for a long time, and *long-term care,* which may involve episodes of both acute care and chronic care. Coordinating care among acute care and chronic and long-term care is often a job that falls to family members or to the person needing the care.

- ✔ **Assisted-living facilities (ALFs):** Even though most people have heard of assisted living, there is no standard definition. States vary in what they call these facilities and how they regulate them, if they do at all. Generally, however, assisted-living facilities are group settings for people who need assistance in ADLs or IADLs but do not require nursing home level medical care. (See Chapter 6.)

- ✔ **Instrumental activities of daily living (IADLs):** These activities are the common household or management tasks such as paying bills, organizing transportation, shopping, laundry, and the like. They often go hand in hand with ADLs because the person who needs assistance with physical care may not be able to drive or shop alone. Even using the phone with all the complicated prompts that one encounters today may be difficult for someone with, for example, severe arthritis. But needing assistance with ADLs or IADLs is not necessarily associated with cognitive decline.

- ✔ **Skilled nursing facility (SNF):** A nursing home that can provide skilled nursing care that can only be provided by a nurse, such as injections, and rehabilitation services, such as physical therapy, and is certified to meet federal and state standards.

- ✔ **Transfer:** Here's a term that has several meanings. In long-term care jargon, it usually means moving a person from bed to chair or the reverse. Someone who is a *two-person transfer* requires not just one but two aides to do the job. This may be because the person is obese, paralyzed, or has another condition that makes it unsafe for both person and helper to manage alone. The second meaning of *transfer* refers to moving a person from one setting to another, such as from an assisted-living facility to an emergency department.

A good place to look up terms that relate to Medicaid and financial issues is the glossary at `http://longtermcare.gov/the-basics/glossary/`. Another resource is the United Hospital Fund's Next Step in Care "Terms and Definitions" at `www.nextstepincare.org/Terms_and_Definitions/`. For medical terms, consult a medical dictionary such as Medline Plus at `www.nlm.nih.gov/medlineplus/` from the National Institutes of Health.

You will find that different people interpret terms differently and that agencies and insurance companies often have their own interpretations of what counts as, for example, *medically necessary,* which is often the trigger for benefits. To keep everything straight, I suggest that writing down the information you're given when it relates to eligibility or another aspect of services along, with the name, title, and contact information of the person who gave you the information. And if you don't like the definition you're given by someone, you may be able to get a more favorable interpretation from a supervisor after you've explained the situation.

Meeting Your Changing Needs

Long-term care is, or should be, a dynamic process. The needs of a person with mild cognitive impairment, for instance, are very different from the needs of a person with advanced dementia. As another example, someone diagnosed with diabetes needs chronic care, that is, doctor or nurse visits, ongoing monitoring, including blood tests, medications, and foot and vision exams. If the diabetic condition deteriorates to the point where the person is unable to walk or perform daily activities independently, then long-term care needs come into the picture. Someone considering moving from house to apartment or assisted living should think about whether this is a move that can satisfy future needs as well as immediate ones. Not everyone moves though the spectrum of needs at the same pace, or even goes through all the same stages.

Some future needs can be anticipated, and others cannot. The goal is not to have a detailed plan for every possible contingency but a general idea of what can reasonably be anticipated and planned for.

Location, location, location

The well-worn real estate adage of choosing a home on the basis of location applies to long-term care as well. In this case, location is not so much an economic asset (although in some cases it can be) as a symbol of personal comfort and satisfaction. Long-term care is not just about services and providers; it is primarily about meeting all your needs, and that includes the social and emotional aspects.

Many people just say, "I want to stay in my own home!" And indeed, that's a reasonable short-term goal, but it may not be feasible in the long run. Beyond their initial statement, many people just stop thinking about it, or assume that their children (or more likely, a particular child) will say, "I'll move in with you so you can stay at home." Maybe that will happen, and maybe it won't. But it certainly requires an explicit understanding between the parties, not just an assumption.

In thinking about location, you want to consider:

- ✔ **The pros and cons of relocation:** Moving to another community to be nearer children, often at their urging, is one solution. You have to consider what you may lose and what you may gain. Someone with strong ties to a particular community, for example, a faith community or club or other group, may miss that connection. On the other hand, you may be able to re-create those ties in another setting. A lot depends on the type of community you would move to, whether you have spent enough time there to be confident you would like it, and whether you will have to depend on your children for transportation and other needs. Being a visitor and being involved in their activities is different from being a permanent resident. Some social groups welcome newcomers, but others closed their ranks a long time ago.

- ✔ **Climate:** It's almost a stereotype that older people want to move to warmer places, but in fact that is one main reason people do relocate. There may be health reasons to move to a different climate, or the upkeep on house and car in a winter zone may be too onerous to sustain. But not everyone adjusts easily to a more or less constant temperature, especially if it's very hot. And although blizzards can create dangerous situations for someone living alone, so can hurricanes and tornados, which generally occur in warmer areas.

- ✔ **Cost of living:** Different regions of the country are more or less expensive places to live. This applies not only to independent or assisted living but also to costs of medical care, food, personal-care services, transportation, and other items that will figure into your plan.

An extended visit to a community you are considering is a good way to find out whether you like it or not. Before or after your visit, you can look online to get an idea of prices for everything from groceries to rentals. You will also see what social, sporting, and cultural events are featured. Think about what you most like to do now and what you would like to be able to do in a new location.

Timing and flexibility

If you are going to make a change, when is the best time to do it? I can't give you the perfect answer. Still, if you are planning to stay where you are for the immediate future, you should start now reassessing your home for safety and accessibility. The mostly minor modifications you can make now (see Chapter 5) will help prevent falls, which are the most common reason for a need for more intense long-term care services. Even if you don't expect to stay in this location permanently, the modifications will add value to your home because they will also make it safer for others, including families with young children.

At the same time, you should begin to investigate alternatives. Without the pressure of family members or doctors insisting that you make a change, you can think about what matters most to you and what you have become used to but can live without.

If a change does fit into your plan, allow enough time to make all the arrangements, and consider all the pieces that need to be reassembled in a new location, whether that is assisted living, a retirement community, or apartment. Moving is one of life's most stressful events, even if it is well-planned and desired. Take your time.

You may not have enough space in your new location for the lifetime of memorabilia or objects you have collected. You may have to donate or sell some possessions. If you are moving from a big house to a smaller house, apartment, or condo, you may have to decide what furniture to keep and what won't work in the new setting. This is a process that stops many people from moving forward, but if you enlist help from family and friends, and if need be, from professional organizers, it can be liberating.

Be flexible. Even if you aren't moving to a different location or a different community, you're entering a new stage of life. Change can be stimulating but also disorienting.

Paradoxically, remaining independent often means asking for help. Asking for and accepting help is often a major hurdle in any long-term care plan. Being willing to acknowledge that you can't do everything alone (and probably you never really did) is the first step toward a person-centered long-term care plan. Family and friends are your first sources of help but they are not the only ones. Neighbors, volunteers from community groups, building contractors, home care aides, and transportation services can all play a part in helping you achieve your goals.

Getting Professional Advice

Among the people you may need to consult in making long-term care plans are professionals such as doctors, lawyers, and accountants. These professionals can help you make realistic plans and avoid costly and potentially damaging errors.

Choosing these advisors can be tricky, however. Your niece who just graduated from law school may offer to help you write a will, but she lives in a different state and doesn't know the law in your state. You have some investments with a local broker, and you have done well with his recommendations. But he has a financial interest in guiding you toward certain choices, which may not serve you well as you contemplate a long-term care plan. And even your doctor, who has taken care of you for years, sees you as you are, not necessarily as you may become. She may or may not be the best person to give you a completely honest appraisal of your health outlook for the future.

All of these people may be competent advisors. It makes sense, however, to consult with others so that you can be sure you are getting objective and accurate information.

For example, you may want to ask for a special geriatric evaluation from a physician who is experienced in caring for older adults whose course of illness and reactions to medications may differ significantly from younger people. An attorney who specializes in elder law has seen the troubles people get into with carelessly written advance directives or wills and can guide you toward creating documents that contain the precise instructions you want. And a financial advisor who charges a fee but does not gain from your investment choices may be a good person to help work out the financial aspects of your plan.

When considering using the services of a specific professional, ask about the following issues before moving forward:

- ✔ Experience with working with clients with similar needs
- ✔ Length of time in practice
- ✔ Recommendations
- ✔ Fees for the service

Even with good advisors, you need to be intimately involved in all decisions (or have a family member do this on your behalf). The investment of your time and money helps ensure that you get the kind of care for the long term you want.

Chapter 2

A Personal Inventory of Needs and Preferences

- -

- -

*L*ong-term care is not the same for everyone. A lot depends on your current health status and anticipated future needs, of course, and your preferences for assistance in managing day-to-day activities. Finances are an important part of the equation as well.

But two people with the same health and financial profile may want to live in different types of settings and receive help in different ways. In this chapter I help you step back from the immediate decisions and think about the kind of person you are and how you want to spend your time. If another person will be sharing this stage of life with you, you should both undertake this exercise. It may reveal some surprises as well as similarities in goals. If you are helping a parent plan, you can encourage them to go through the process with you. You will get to know each other in new and possibly revealing ways as this chapter guides you through finding out what type of long-term care best suits your needs and lifestyle. It also helps you create a long-term plan to steer you in the right direction.

Looking at the Present — and the Future

Imagining what you will be like in 10, 15, or 20 years is hard. But your life so far gives you some clues. What were you like 10, 15, or 20 years ago? Have you changed a lot, or is there a consistent pattern? Have you changed jobs or careers? Have you moved around the country or internationally? Have you been married, divorced, or widowed — more than once? Have your spending or savings habits changed? Or has your life gone along in more or less planned and predictable ways?

These questions are not intended to be value judgments about one way of life or another but simply a way for you to consider your tolerance for risk (or, if you prefer, adventure), need for stability, and comfort with change. In the following sections, I organize the inventory around four categories: healthcare needs; family, friends, and professionals; personality characteristics; and attitudes about money. Each is an important element in creating your personal profile.

Healthcare needs

High among the list of characteristics to consider when planning your long-term care is your health and health behaviors. Although definitions of long-term care tend to focus on nonmedical needs for assistance (as described in Chapter 1), your overall health and any special considerations are clearly important aspects to consider not only on their own but because they will affect many aspects of the nonmedical care you will need.

Here are some questions to ask yourself. Be ruthlessly honest. No one else has to see your list unless you want to share. It is intended to give you a template to think about your healthcare needs and how they would be incorporated into a long-term care plan.

- How would you describe your overall health — poor, fair, good, excellent? Has this status changed in the past few years?

- Do you have any chronic conditions? (Examples are high blood pressure, diabetes, arthritis, and heart problems.) What are they? Are they under control?

- How many doctors do you see regularly? Are your appointments scheduled checkups or as-needed visits? Do these doctors share information with each other and with you?

- Do you see any other healthcare professionals — home care nurse, physical therapist, or chiropractor, for example?

- Do any of your health conditions limit your ability to function at home or in the community?

- Do you use mobility assistive devices of any kind — cane, walker, or wheelchair, for example?

✔ How many prescription medications do you take?

✔ How many over-the-counter (OTC) medications do you take?

✔ Do you have an up-to-date list of all your prescribed and OTC medications?

✔ Does anyone help you with healthcare tasks such as giving injections, monitoring machines like oxygen tanks, or taking care of wounds? If so, who helps?

✔ Have you had your vision and hearing checked in the past year?

✔ Do you need glasses or a hearing aid?

✔ Do you smoke?

✔ Do you drink alcohol or use drugs? How often?

✔ Do you see a dentist regularly?

✔ Do you eat nutritious meals (most of the time)?

✔ Have you fallen in the past year? Were you injured?

✔ Do you have trouble sleeping?

✔ Do you exercise regularly? Or at all?

✔ Do you often feel sad or lonely?

✔ Are you concerned about memory loss?

✔ Do you have clear preferences about the kind of care you would want or not want if you were in a coma after extensive brain damage, or were not expected to recover from an illness?

✔ Have you told anyone about these preferences and documented them in an advance directive?

✔ Do you worry about your health? If you do, what worries you the most?

Even this schematic outline should help you assess your current and potential future needs for healthcare. If you have generally good health and manage your healthcare needs with a minimum of professional involvement, then you should be able to maintain this level of healthcare wherever you are. There are also options for home-based care, which are discussed in Chapter 14. But if you already have serious chronic health conditions that require frequent doctor visits and multiple medications, moving away from your regular source of care may present problems.

For example, a move to assisted living may appeal to you because of the attractive setting, the availability of meals and housekeeping services, and the promised activities. But most assisted-living facilities do not have the capacity to serve the medical care needs of someone with serious chronic conditions, and the location may not be convenient to your usual doctors' offices. On the other hand, you may be able to maintain your current health-care arrangements in an assisted-living facility. It's important to find out.

If you are thinking of moving to a nearby assisted-living facility, where your contact with your regular healthcare providers can be maintained, it is a good idea to let them know of your plans and to ask whether they have any reservations about the idea. If you are thinking of moving far away, then you can ask for referrals to providers in your new location. But remember that assisted-living facilities do not provide medical care, and you will need to build that into your plan.

Family, friends, and professionals

Healthcare may be a critical factor in long-term care, but it's not the only one. Just as important are your values and preferences about the kind of life you want to continue (or begin) to live.

This section asks for an inventory of the people in your life, what roles they play now, and how you would like them to be able to participate if your needs for assistance grow.

✔ Who do you consider your family? The people you include can be spouses, parents, children, grandparents, siblings, cousins, or other relatives. They can also be domestic partners, companions, and other people with whom you have a very close relationship.

- Which of these people do you rely on most for emotional support and comfort?

- Who would you call first if you needed help in making a medical decision? Settling a financial problem? Talk about your will?

- Who lives closest to you? Or with you? Does distance present a problem in getting together regularly or on short notice? You might be able to discuss a problem with someone far away but that person is not going to be able to help out in an emergency.

- Do any of these people rely on you for the same sorts of assistance? For example, financial support? Advice and counseling? Day-to-day assistance?

- How do you currently communicate with your family? Frequent visits? Phone? E-mail? Texts? Or only at special events?

- Are there tensions within your family about money, relationships, obligations, or other factors?

- Are there family members with whom you have no relationships that you would like to involve in your life?

✔ Overall, how important is it to you to be close (geographically and emotionally) to your family?

✔ Beyond family, do you have close friends who in some ways substitute for family or add to family support?

- Could you call on them for the kinds of assistance that might be expected first from family?

- What limits would you anticipate friends might place on assistance?

✔ Do you have trusting relationships with professionals such as doctors, lawyers, accountants, clergy, and others who might be able to advise you on matters relating to long-term care? If not, can you identify people who might fill this role?

Personality characteristics

Having looked at your health status and your available family resources in the previous sections, now take a clear look at your own preferences and values. This is where you can list what is important to you and what doesn't matter all that much. Again, be candid.

✔ Does religion play an important role in your life? If so, does this mean going to religious services regularly and observing religious practices? Or is it a less organized but still significant influence guiding how you live?

✔ If you're still employed, how important is your job to your sense of well-being? Would you miss that role? What in particular do you value?

✔ If you are retired, do you miss any part of your working life? Or are there aspects of working that you are happy to be free of?

✔ Would you describe yourself as shy, outgoing, or somewhere in between?

✔ Do you make friends easily?

✔ Have you made any new friends in the past year?

✔ Do you like everything to be neat and tidy? Does clutter bother you?

✔ If you don't mind clutter, does it result in what some people may call a total mess or hoarding?

✔ Do you like to be around animals? Have you always had pets? Do any particular kinds of animal frighten or annoy you?

✔ Do you like to be part of a group and participate in activities with people you know? If so, what kinds of activities do you most like to share? Some examples are travel, community service, sports (watching or playing), avocations like music or gardening, cooking, or any other leisure time pursuit.

✔ Do you like the idea of being in a group of people you don't know? Would you enjoy meeting people from different backgrounds? Or do you prefer to be around people whose backgrounds are similar to yours?

✔ Do you find the idea of group activities unappealing? If so, what aspects do you dislike?

✔ Do you prefer to do things on your own or with one or two people?

✔ If you are a loner rather than a group person, would you find it hard to adjust to group living, even if you had your own living space?

✔ Do you like to do things on your own rather than relying on others for help?

✔ Even if you ask for help, do you like to be in charge of the details?

✔ Do you have a cooperative nature — that is, do you like to work out problems with other people, or would you prefer to take charge or have someone else take charge of the solution?

✔ Do you value stability and security above the possibility of change, even if it improves your life?

Attitudes about money

Now I come to the most sensitive part of the inventory. (I haven't included sex, but you can add that to your list if you like.) It's money — not just how much you have but how you think about it. Here too the goal is not to make a judgment about your financial-management skills but a way to think about how you will approach long-term care. In nearly every case, long-term care does involve spending money, and much of it will be from your own or your family's resources.

Do you have a philosophy about money? People say things like, "Money is meant to be spent," "A penny saved is a penny earned" (maybe updated to be more than a penny), "It's important to save for a rainy day," and "I'm spending my children's inheritances." Sometimes, of course, these are offhand remarks, but even so they may indicate overall attitudes about money.

Even without an explicit philosophy, many people approach financial decisions within some basic framework of optimism, fatalism, or risk-avoidance. Sometimes this philosophy has developed because of childhood experiences of poverty or difficult times in young adulthood, or the reverse, a lifetime of financial ease or a lack of responsibility. Different people react to financial stress in different ways. Think about your personal financial philosophy as you answer the following questions:

- ✔ Do you know how much money is in your checking account, savings account, investment portfolio, pension fund, and other assets? Or do you leave that to someone else to manage?

- ✔ Do you carry a lot of cash or do you use credit cards for most purchases?

- ✔ Do you buy a lot of products online or from television advertisers?

- ✔ Have you ever regretted a major purchase bought on impulse?

- ✔ Do you like to shop?

- ✔ Are you or have you been in serious debt?

- ✔ Do you know much money you are receiving (or will receive) from Social Security or a pension?

- ✔ Do you know how much money your home (if you own it) is worth in today's market?

- ✔ Do you know how much you pay in taxes and maintenance?

- ✔ Do you have a regular household budget? Do you live within it?

- ✔ Do you like to trade in your car every year or two?

- ✔ Are vacations or travel an important part of your life?

- ✔ Do you have current or future financial obligations to other family members, such as grandchildren's education?

- ✔ Would you be able to maintain these obligations if you start spending more on long-term care?

- ✔ Do you want to be able to leave money to children or grandchildren or other people?

- ✔ Do you want to be able to leave money to cultural, religious, or other institutions that you have supported?

A financial adviser can help you work out just what your assets are worth (you may be surprised to find you are worth more than you think) and create different options for accessing and spending this money. Different housing options have different cost profiles. Setting up a budget based on the costs that different housing options will require is a good way to determine what extra money you may have or how much you may need to trim from your current budget.

You have to be prepared to set priorities and limits. You should be comfortable with the financial plan as a basis for determining how much you can spend on long-term care without jeopardizing other important factors in your life.

Creating a Long-Term Care Plan Based on Your Profile

The personal profile you have sketched, along with other items that are important to you, can offer some guidance as you move forward.

For example, someone who belongs to a number of social and community groups, likes to meet new people, has generally good health, has no dependents (other than, perhaps, a spouse), and has sufficient financial resources to set aside for care may well look into assisted living. The facility may be nearby or in a setting closer to adult children or siblings (who, in this scenario, are financially independent). Check out Chapter 6 for more information on assisted living.

A person with a similar profile may not like group living and would prefer to spend the money on home modifications and home care assistance if necessary.

On the other hand, someone who already needs help with chronic health conditions, is struggling economically, and doesn't have many contacts outside family may find a multigenerational living arrangement worthwhile. In this scenario, the rest of the family could benefit as well from the contributions. This option could also involve a nearby setting or a move, depending on where family members live and who moves in with whom. It may even involve the creation of a new home to match the new household's needs.

For someone with serious health conditions and the anticipation that the needs for care will increase, the options are more limited. More family or paid assistance will be required, either in this person's home or in a nursing home. Home- and community-based services can provide a basis for the needed care, but if 24-hour care or care requiring special expertise is needed, these services will not suffice. A nursing home (or the extended-care section of a continuing-care retirement community) may be the most appropriate option (see Chapter 15).

In between, of course, are many possibilities and options. I consider these in other chapters in this book. But in evaluating specific settings and services, keep the personal inventory in mind as the framework for decision making. Someone else's decision may be perfect for that person. You want to make a decision that is right for you.

Chapter 3

Researching Options for Services

*T*he options for long-term care are varied and sometimes complicated. The good news is that a lot of information about your options is available from many different sources. The bad news is that the information is often incomplete or inaccurate, driven by marketing agendas, and hard to apply to your particular situation.

With some judicious selection and the help I provide in this chapter, however, you can find reliable sources of basic information to get started. Then you can narrow your search to the sources most likely to be helpful. Even then, you need to double check the information to make sure you have accurate facts and figures. All this research can be a lot of work, so ask a friend or family member to help you with this process.

Finding Information and Reading Between the Lines

If you are in the market for a new car or washing machine, what do you do? You probably look online for product information and perhaps user reviews, go to a dealer to see the different models, and maybe ask friends and family for their recommendations. Then you decide to buy a particular model based on price and features. You look at the product, find out what it has and doesn't have, what it costs to buy and have it delivered, and what the manufacturer's warranty covers. This is typical consumer behavior.

Healthcare and long-term care only loosely fit the consumer behavior model. Although some aspects are similar, developing a long-term care plan involves many other considerations, such as what type of person you are and what type of lifestyle you want to have in the future (as discussed in Chapter 2).

For one thing, in healthcare you often don't know the cost until after you've used the product — for example, had a hospital stay or outpatient tests. You may not know that certain hospital doctors are not in your insurance network and will bill you separately. You have a better idea going forward in long-term care, but even then, many costs are hidden. And your choices are more lasting and carry greater weight in your life than that new washing machine.

In your research, finding out what's not included is just as important as learning what is included. Don't take anything for granted; ask and document the answers.

You have to read between the lines or specifically ask about what isn't transparent. For example, a basic fee for an assisted-living facility may not include charges for additional aide services, or if they are mentioned, the likelihood of your needing them may be downplayed. Health-insurance coverage may not include some expensive prescription drugs or assistive devices; its coverage of home health care may be limited. Long-term care insurance may construct barriers to accessing benefits by denying claims and delaying decisions.

One aspect of consumer behavior does fit both the product and long-term care models: the importance of being informed, inquisitive, and at times skeptical. The more you know, the less likely you are to be surprised. Preferably, your surprises should be on the positive side, not the "Why didn't someone tell me this?" variety.

Organizing your research

When looking for options for long-term care, the three major routes are the Internet, phone, and personal visits. Often, you will be searching multiple sites, making numerous phone calls, and visiting various facilities. How can you keep all the information straight?

Here are some tips to help you find and keep the information in an easily accessed way.

✔ **Web searches:**

• Digital filing: If you are technically adept (or have a techie in your family), you can set up a system of folders on your computer to store information in different categories. Or you can bookmark sites that you visit frequently.

- Paper filing: If you're a paper person, set up a notebook or filing system that becomes your information bank. Print out pages from sites you want to save information from. It can be incredibly frustrating to try to find something you know you have read somewhere but can't find it again. Be sure to include the web address on the page printouts for future reference.

When conducting web searches, use different search words to help guide you to multiple sites. And always check that the sponsor of the website is reputable and reliable. Verify the information with an authoritative source. Note whether the article or web page is dated to make sure the information is current.

Web addresses may disappear into cyberspace. If you encounter this problem, try searching for the organization by its name. Unless the organization has disappeared along with its website, you can usually find the new web address.

✔ **Phone calls:**

- Plan questions in advance: If you call an organization for information, make sure you have specific written questions. Write down the answer to each question as you get it.

- Keep a log: After each phone call, mark the date, time, and person you spoke with, as well as contact information and any notes from the phone conversation. Keep these hardcopies in your research files in case you need to contact a person again or want to follow-up.

You may have to go through a number of phone referrals to find the person best able to answer your questions. Be persistent.

✔ **Personal visits:**

- Bring questions: When you visit a facility, bring along a written list of questions. Fill in the questions during your visit and keep the list in your research file. This way you can compare and contrast different facilities at a glance.

- Prepare documents: On your search for long-term care, you will visit different types of facilities. Each place requires certain types of documentation, so plan ahead, make copies of everything you need, and file the papers with the other information you gather about each facility. Make sure you bring all the relevant documents to the meeting.

With these preliminary tips, you can begin your search. The next sections offer information about federal programs; regulations about long-term care services such as assisted-living facilities, nursing homes, and home care agencies; and community-based services. Then I discuss making visits to facilities.

Federal government programs

Federal agencies — primarily the Centers for Medicare & Medicaid Services (CMS), but also other agencies such as the Administration for Community Living, the Administration on Aging, and the Social Security Administration — are a good place to begin. (Medicaid is a federal-state program, so it is important to look at both the federal rules and your state's program.) Throughout this book I refer to specific online links, but here I give an overview of some of the main resources.

- ✔ **Medicare:** Even though Medicare doesn't cover long-term care, it is an important resource for the medical care that people receiving long-term care services and supports need. Some of the short-term benefits, for example, for home healthcare or rehabilitation services, may fill gaps while more viable long-term solutions are arranged.

  CMS, part of the U.S. Department of Health and Human Services, oversees Medicare. Its website, www.Medicare.gov, is the primary resource for beneficiaries and families.

  If you are enrolled in Medicare, you receive by mail a handbook entitled "Medicare and You," which is updated every year. Although the cover says it is "an official U.S. government handbook," the inside cover warns that it isn't a legal document. For legal guidance, you need to go to the relevant statutes, regulations, and rulings, which can be hard to find and tough reading for a non-lawyer. The handbook is also available online and in an e-book format.You can also speak to a Medicare agent by calling 1-800-MEDICARE (1-800-633-4227).

  If you use a smart phone, use the numbers not the letters because the "E" will not connect.

  See Chapter 10 of this book or check out AARP's *Medicare For Dummies* by Patricia Barry (Wiley) for more detailed information. These sources cover the basics, including the differences between original Medicare and a Medicare Advantage plan. If you need help choosing a specific Medicare Advantage plan, you need to do further research on local plans.

- ✔ **Medicaid:** Medicaid is the federal-state program that provides health care and long-term care for people with low incomes and assets or very high medical costs. Eligibility and services vary by state. Much of the information on its website, www.medicaid.gov, is designed for regulators and policymakers, although it includes links to state sites, which have more specific information for residents. This is just a place to start; you will need to dig into the information on the state Medicaid website and other sources. See Chapter 10 for more on Medicaid.

✓ **Administration for Community Living:** In 2012, the U.S. Department of Health and Human Services created an umbrella organization, the Administration for Community Living (ACL), to bring together various federal agency resources to coordinate policy and reduce fragmentation in policies on disability and aging. The main website is www.acl.gov, and ACL has many resources on long-term care at http://acl.gov/ Get_Help/Help_Older_Adults/Index.aspx.

✓ **Administration on Aging:** The Administration on Aging (AoA) is part of the ACL. AoA supports what is often called the *Aging Network* of agencies and professionals. It was created in 1965 with the passage of the Older Americans Act and provides support services, nutrition services, preventive health services, the National Family Caregiver Support Program, elder-rights services, and services to Native Alaskans, Native Hawaiians, and Native Americans. Its website, www.aoa.gov, provides information. Long-term care is specifically addressed at http://longtermcare. gov/. The site includes a Long-term Care Pathfinder, which provides basic information about costs and links to other government sites.

✓ **Eldercare Locator:** The Eldercare Locator, a free service of AoA, is a basic go-to site for locating resources in your community. Its website is http:// eldercare.gov/Eldercare.NET/Public/Index.aspx. You can access an online chat forum, or you can call 1-800-677-1116 for information.

✓ **Area Agencies on Aging:** The more than 600 Area Agencies on Aging (AAAs) provide information and referrals to services such as adult day care and senior-center programs in their region. The National Association of Area Agencies on Aging has a map of AAAs at www.n4a.org/about-n4a/?fa=aaa-title-VI or through Eldercare Locator. Some state associations of AAAs also have maps of their locations within the state.

✓ **Social Security Administration:** The Social Security Administration (SSA) administers Social Security benefits, which may be an important part of the financial side of your long-term care plan. The agency's website at www.ssa.gov lets you check or estimate your retirement benefits online and get other information. All Social Security benefits must now be paid by direct deposit, so if you or your parent or other relative is receiving Social Security benefits, it should be by direct deposit. AARP's *Social Security For Dummies* (by Jonathan Peterson; Wiley) provides more detail on all aspects of Social Security.

✓ **USA.gov:** This site is the main federal government portal. It has a section on senior citizens' resources, which has links to a variety of federal agencies and a separate listing of many state resources, including lesser-known ones such as "Farmers Markets near You," prepared by the U.S. Department of Agriculture.

✓ **National Disability Rights Network** (www.ndrn.org): Every state and territory has one protection and advocacy agency (P&A) responsible for protecting the rights of individuals with disabilities.

State and local programs

Different states assign aspects of long-term care to different agencies. Finding the right state agency for the information you need can be challenging. For example, Medicare is Medicare wherever you are (although there are some local variations in determining payment to providers) and Social Security is one system, but Medicaid in Florida is the Florida Agency for Health Care Administration, and in Wisconsin it is ForwardHealth. More important than the name is the variation in Medicaid from state to state.

After you have located the right agency (and if possible, the right person in the agency), make sure to keep a record of how to find it again. Check out the following list for state agencies that are relevant for long-term care planning:

- ✔ **Departments of aging:** Every state has an agency devoted to services for older adults, often linked to services for people with disabilities. Like Medicaid, however, what the agency is named varies, although not as much. Although the most common name is Department (Office Division, Commission) of (for, on) Aging, other variations include: Office of Elder Services (Maine) and Aging Long-Term Support Administration (Washington). The National Association of States United for Aging and Disabilities has a state-by-state listing of offices at www.nasuad.org/about_nasuad/state_agency_website_links.html. These agencies have information about senior centers, food programs, counseling, and other services, both state-funded and in partnership with federal agencies.

- ✔ **County and city departments of aging:** Many counties and cities also have departments of aging that contract with local community agencies to provide services. It may be easier to get information from a local agency than from the state, although that may depend on the level of staffing. These are the same agencies described in the Federal Program section as Area Agencies on Aging.

- ✔ **Advance directives:** The Federal Patient Self Determination Act, enacted in 1990, requires hospitals and other providers (including psychiatric hospitals and other mental-health providers) and health plans to maintain written policies and procedures with respect to advance directives — documents that spell out what kinds of treatments you do or do not want if you are not able to speak for yourself. The providers must ask whether a patient has an advance directive; in practice this means that if you're admitted to a hospital, someone (probably the admitting clerk) will ask you if you have an advance directive. If you do, that information should go in your medical record. The federal law does not specify what form the advance directive should take; that's up to states (see Chapter 16 for more detail). The advance directive usually includes the name of the person you have chosen to speak on your behalf if you are unable to express your wishes. Caring Connections, an arm of the National Hospice and Palliative Care Organization, has state-specific forms you can download at www.aarp.org/advancedirectives.

✔ **Medicaid:** Every state has a Medicaid program for low-income people that provides a basic package of services as defined by federal law (see Chapter 10 for more details). Each state, however, determines its own optional services and criteria for eligibility for different types of services. Home- and community-based services are optional and may be covered under a waiver from the federal government that allows states to spend their funds for these services or through other approaches. Some programs have long waiting lists.

Federal and state regulations

Both the federal and state governments regulate long-term care services and facilities. The standards are set by agencies that pay for services, monitor quality of care, and establish rules for licensing staff. It is important to understand what standards are monitored and how a particular facility or agency measures up to the requirements. Particularly important, of course, is the number of problems noted by government surveyors or through public complaints.

✔ **Home care agencies:** There are different types of home care agencies with different regulatory oversight. In order for a home care agency to be paid by Medicare and Medicaid, it has to be approved by CMS (Centers for Medicare & Medicaid Services). These agencies provide skilled nursing care, personal care, and therapies from professionals such as physical, occupational, speech, and respiratory therapists. Social-work services are also available. Home Health Compare (www. medicare.gov/homehealthcompare/search.html) is a CMS website that gives you information on specific agencies and how they are doing with meeting federal standards. Many but not all states license home care agencies that provide personal care services. Check the website of your state department of health to see whether all home care agencies are licensed and what they require in terms of background checks and training. See Chapter 14 for more detail.

Most states do not regulate companion agencies that provide nonmedical services such as preparing meals, homemaker services, and personal care, although the number that do monitor them is increasing. You will have to exercise due diligence about the agency's practices regarding background checks of employees, training, and other issues.

✔ **Assisted-living facilities:** The federal government doesn't have standards for independent living or assisted-living facilities. (A final CMS rule of January 2014 sets standards for states that include assisted living facilities in their Medicaid home- and community-based services waivers. States have a transitional period to ensure that they meet the standards.) These facilities are subject to various state regulations, which include building and safety codes. Some are licensed under different categories of congregate living. Because they do not provide medical services (except in a specific nursing unit), they are not generally regulated by departments of health. (See Chapter 6 for more information.)

✔ **Nursing homes:** Nursing homes are subject to federal and state regulation, with specific requirements about staffing, training, prevention of abuse and neglect, reporting incidents of poor quality, and other standards. A CMS website, Nursing Home Compare, allows you to search by facility name (www.medicare.gov/nursinghomecompare/search.html). (See Chapter 15 for more details on nursing homes.) State governments also regulate nursing homes, and many department of health websites also provide information on the results of their surveys. This information is also available on Nursing Home Compare.

✔ **Quality Improvement Organizations (QIOs):** Part of the CMS structure, each state has a designated QIO that is responsible for ensuring and improving quality of care and for reviewing complaints. If, for example, you feel that you are being discharged from a hospital too quickly, you can appeal the decision to the local QIO. Most people don't know about these organizations, but they can be very helpful in resolving problems. A directory of QIOs is at www.qualitynet.org/dcs/ContentServer?c=Page&pagename=QnetPublic%2FPage%2FQnetTier2&cid=1144767874793.

✔ **Long-term care ombudsmen:** Ombudsmen (the term comes from Swedish) investigate complaints and negotiate solutions to problems in nursing homes and assisted-living facilities. You can find a directory at www.ltcombudsman.org/ombudsman.

Although they aren't directly related to long-term care, you may also find the following CMS websites useful:

✔ Comparing hospitals: www.medicare.gov/hospitalcompare/search.html

✔ Comparing physicians: www.medicare.gov/physiciancompare/

✔ Comparing dialysis facilities: www.medicare.gov/DialysisFacilityCompare/search.html

You can see a directory of equipment suppliers that participate in Medicare's competitive bidding program at www.medicare.gov/SupplierDirectory/.

These or other comparison sites are useful as a starting point but they do not provide all the information you need, and the sources on which they base their reviews may be incomplete or outdated.

Community-based organizations

Public programs are important sources of information, but you may find that information from nongovernmental sources answers more of your immediate questions. These sources may be national organizations concerned with issues related to aging, national disease-specific organizations with local or regional chapters, service organizations in your community, and others.

Some organizations do advocacy, some provide services, and some do both. Some are primarily focused on the older person or person with disabilities; others on the person and their family members.

Many of the public agencies will refer you to these local resources, but I recommend doing an environmental scan of your own. A state or city Department of the Aging, for example, may have lists of community agencies that it funds, but its list may not include other organizations, such as faith-based groups or volunteer organizations.

There is no comprehensive list of these organizations, and there are hundreds of them, so you will have to do some detective work (again, a friend or family member can help out). But most of the major national organizations can also direct you to local resources. Some disease groups have several organizations providing information, so you should compare the sites to see which one offers the most relevant information for you.

Here are a few sites to get started:

- **AARP** (www.aarp.org): From the home page you can go to several different subject categories, such as health, work and retirement, home and family (which includes caregiving), and money. Each of these sections provides information and directs you to other resources.

- **Alzheimer's Association** (www.alz.org): This site has links to local chapters, which offer educational sessions, support groups, and other services. The main site has information about Alzheimer's disease and other dementias, including research and treatment.

- **American Diabetes Association** (www.diabetes.org): The website has links to local chapters, information on prevention and treatment, and services.

- **American Heart Association** (www.heart.org/HEARTORG): The AHA has information about heart disease and stroke, treatments, and prevention.

- **Cancer Care** (www.cancercare.org): Cancer Care's website provides free professional support services to anyone affected by cancer. The organization has educational programs for patients and caregivers, counseling services, and limited financial assistance. Services are available online and by phone.

- **National Council on Aging** (www.ncoa.org): Through its BenefitsCheckup tool, NCOA has information for older adults on accessing benefits such as help paying for medications or food. The tool is organized by state or zip code.

- **National Hospice and Palliative Care Organization** (www.nhpco.org): This organization has information about end-of-life concerns and links to help you find providers of both types of services.

A view of media reporting on health

Many people get a lot of their information about healthcare from television or newspapers.

News reports are often orchestrated by big companies and their public relations firms. So, be wary of news reports that use the words *cure, miracle,* and *breakthrough.* The questions most often left unanswered in these reports are whether there are alternative options, whether the treatment is actually available or is still in an experimental phase, the cost, who is promoting the information, and whether there is a conflict of interest. Check with your doctor before buying into these drugs or treatments.

A website that provided expert analyses of news reports, Health News Review (www.healthnewsreview.org), went on hiatus in July 2013, although its founder, Gary Schwitzer, a professor at the University of Minnesota, continues to write a blog on the site. The site has toolkits about interpreting medical studies and other ways to get behind the headlines. Even though the part of the site that analyzes current news stories is down, perhaps temporarily, it does have general advice about a skeptical approach to news reports.

Small organizations may not have staff to respond immediately to your requests. You may have to call back a few times to get the information you need. Be patient but persistent.

This list is only a glimpse into the multiple resources available through voluntary health organizations and advocacy groups. Search the Internet by disease, by area of interest (treatment options, financing, research, and more) to drill down into your specific areas of interest. All the chapters in this book on specific aspects of long-term care (financing, for example, or family caregiving) have many more suggestions.

Don't be misled by sites that promise cures or easy ways to finance long-term care. The Internet is a hotbed of literally incredible offers and fraudulent schemes.

Taking Your Research to the Next Level: Site Visits

One of the most important decisions to make in your long-term care plan is where to live. And, the real test of whether all the information you have collected meets your needs can only come from your direct experience. Websites, brochures, phone calls, and interviews set the stage by giving you basic information about costs, eligibility, services, and the like. But when it comes to deciding whether to stay where you or your parent are and make accommodations to fit your changing needs or to move to another setting, only a site visit will give you that final piece of information.

The chapters in this book on assisted living, nursing homes, and multigenerational family housing, as well as those specifically addressed to the lesbian, gay, bisexual, and transgender population (LGBT) and veterans, all have advice about what to look for in a long-term care setting.

When you visit a facility, ask questions — lots of them. Write down the answers and the name of the person who gave them to you. Whatever your specific questions, try to adopt the attitude of being an interested but not convinced consumer.

But in addition to asking questions, be a good observer. If you are looking at a facility, try to get an overall impression of the place. Borrowing a term from real estate jargon, does the place have *curb appeal* — that is, is it attractive from the outside? This doesn't mean luxurious or showy. Facilities have personalities, just like people, and you can often get a sense of whether that personality is warm and welcoming just from the way you feel when you enter it.

Then focus on individual elements such as the type of accommodation for mobility or low vision, how residents and staff interact, and the noise level both inside and out. Could you see yourself (or your parent) in this place? If so, what appeals to you about it? If not, what bothers you? It is important to speak to current residents and staff to get a true picture of what your experience at the facility might be like. Try not to make snap judgments, but also trust your instincts.

Don't be swayed by one person's opinion. Listen to all the pros and cons, and then make your decision with your family based on all the evidence and your own evaluation.

Chapter 4

Making Decisions: A Family Affair

. . . .

In This Chapter

▶ Discussing plans with your family

▶ Working out fair and acceptable arrangements

▶ Resolving problems

. . . .

*U*nless you live in total isolation, the decisions you make concerning a long-term care plan affect other people — family, friends, coworkers, and others. You may already depend on some of these people, and they may depend on you. Although the ultimate choice should be yours, getting to that point may involve some discussion and negotiation. Compromise is not a four-letter word; it may be the best way to proceed.

Talking through these decisions with other people can sometimes be uncomfortable, but I strongly encourage you to do it sooner rather than later. The decisions don't have to be implemented immediately, and you will be better prepared if you have a road map. You may encounter detours and roadblocks, but if you have a destination in sight, you can work around them.

In this chapter I discuss some of the issues you may consider as you discuss the options with others, and I suggest some ways to resolve disagreements, whether they are based on the current situation or have long-standing roots.

Holding Family Meetings

Perhaps you have held family meetings throughout the years to discuss job changes, divorce, moves, problems in school, budgets, and other family matters. Or perhaps yours is a family where the very idea of sitting down together to talk about a major life change would be a totally new and probably anxiety-producing experience. If so, don't be put off by the novelty of the idea. Planning for long-term care is not a decision that you should make alone, whether the plan is for you or for a parent or other relative.

Who should be included?

If you created a personal inventory as recommended in Chapter 2, you have a list of your close family members and friends. Review it and see if you want to add anyone or take anyone off the list. If you didn't go through this exercise, now is a good time to do it.

This list gives you a starting point for people to include in your plan. But not all of them need to be part of every aspect of your decision making. Limit your initial discussions to the people most directly involved in your life, or the life of your parent or other relative. This is your inner circle, or core group. People who you believe would want to be involved but can only do so on a limited basis form an outer circle. People can move from one category to another as the discussions proceed and as needs arise.

When making plans, involving the person who is at the heart of the long-term care is essential. If it is you, then you are already the center. But if it is a parent or other relative, he or she should be the primary person in every discussion. In some situations, that may not be possible — because of advanced dementia, for example — but for most situations the person himself is the critical factor. That doesn't mean that everything this person says or wants should be accepted at face value; it just means that the discussion should be *with* the person, not just about him or her.

If you have a spouse or partner, of course this person should also be involved. If you have adult children who may provide assistance to you or a grandparent, they should be included as well. Sometimes people who are more distantly related — cousins, nieces, and nephews, for example — are important members of the group. If the person you are planning for is your parent and you have siblings, count them in (even if the relationships between you and them or between them and your parent are not ideal).

Try to keep the inner circle to a manageable number — perhaps five or six. But don't leave out anyone who really should be involved. If you have a large number of children or siblings, they should be included. They may not accept your invitation to participate and you may need to deal with that later on, but the invitation should be open.

When should you get together?

Legions of columnists and other advisers encourage people to have serious discussions about long-term care at holiday times. The rationale is that it is more likely that the whole family will be together at these times. But is this really the best time to have a serious talk about sensitive matters? Remember that holidays are also times when family members are distracted by taking care of children and planning for the next event on the agenda; they may just want to enjoy the occasion. In some families holidays are particularly stressful times when past jealousies and slights come alive again. If alcohol is on the menu, it may be a disinhibiting and unhelpful factor. Instead of burdening a holiday with this discussion, I recommend setting aside a specific time for a serious and thoughtful discussion about long-term care, without any distractions.

With Skype and other technology, it is possible to have a meeting without everyone being in the same room. Businesses do it all the time, and it can work for families too.

If you anticipate disagreements and personality conflicts, consider inviting a neutral observer, such as a clergy member, social worker, or family friend who understands the family dynamics. This person is not a decision maker but can try to make sure that all points of view are heard in a respectful way. He or she can also keep the discussion on target and not let it get into a rehearsal of old family history or perceived injustices. This is not an occasion to debate whether "Mom always loved you best." The goal is not to arrive at a quick decision or to settle old disputes but to reach a consensus about long-term care, even if that consensus is only an agreement to keep talking.

You also need to consider where to hold the meeting. It may be your home or your parent's, someone else's home, or a different place altogether. Whoever is host should supply plenty of snacks. Alcohol is not a good idea. It does loosen the tongue, but with unpredictable results.

What should be on the agenda?

Unless a crisis has occurred to precipitate the meeting, then present it as a preliminary discussion, not a done deal. You may say to your adult children, for example, "This winter has made it clear to me that I really can't keep up the house and grounds the way I used to. I'm thinking about moving — maybe to assisted living, or maybe just to a smaller house or apartment. I've done a little research but I want to get your opinions." Or, "Since your father died, I've been really lonely in this big house. I think it's time to make a move, but I'm not sure what to do. I don't want to move in with any of you but it would be nice to be closer."

Or to your siblings you might say, "You all know that Mom had a few bad falls recently. Her doctor is concerned that the next one might be even worse. Mom wants to stay here in the house she has put so much love into and that we all grew up in. But is that the best choice? Mom can speak for herself but she asked me to start the discussion with you."

You probably don't want to follow a formal agenda and parliamentary proce-dures, but it is a good idea to establish some ground rules. For example,

- Describe the purpose of the meeting and what you hope to accomplish.

- Make it clear that everyone will have a chance to speak and that all views are important.

- Encourage questions and concerns.

- Let participants know that personal gripes and problems are off limits.

- Set a time limit for the meeting. Meetings that go on endlessly are unlikely to resolve issues.

- Near the end of the designated time, sum up (or ask someone else to do it) and make a list of the issues that need to be resolved, who will gather more information, and when you will meet again.

For example, if the meeting is to discuss a change in your own or your par-ent's medical condition, and this may mean additional help is needed, you may want the agenda to include:

- A concise description of the medical condition and recommended treatments (it is helpful to have a doctor's summary as well as a plain-language interpretation).

- Share any preliminary research you've conducted. Don't set yourself up as the expert, but try to counter opinions that you know are not based on fact.

- What the course of treatment will mean in terms of its physical impact on you or your parent and the extra help that will be needed (someone to help with household chores, someone to manage finances, someone to communicate with doctors).

- Likely length of treatment.

- Financial implications (what insurance will cover, what will have to be paid for out-of-pocket).

- What may be down the road, such as the need for full-time help or move to assisted living.

- Next steps and who will take on specific tasks.

The most important part of the agenda is not the specific items you put on it, but the nonjudgmental and open-minded atmosphere you create. Even if no decisions are reached, you will have set the stage for further meetings and discussions. All too often a family meeting is something that happens in a hospital, with professionals guiding the discussion, with a focus on end-of-life care. Better start the process long before that and on your own terms.

Unless you have to make an immediate decision (and you should try to avoid that), one meeting is not going to resolve the issue. The outcome of the first (and maybe the second and third) meeting should be a good discussion of the possible choices, with unanswered questions put on the table. Everyone should have an opportunity to speak and to be heard. Closing off discussion prematurely only causes problems later. Of course, this is easier said than done in families with a history of poor communication, but that is not a reason not to begin.

Although long-term care planning includes consideration of end-of-life issues, such as advance-care planning, in my view it is best to separate these emotion-laden discussions. It is hard to go back and forth between discussing the merits of assisted living and the kinds of treatments one would want in a terminal illness. But both are important, and one can set the stage for the other. Use your judgment and your knowledge of family dynamics to decide where to start.

For more advice on holding a family meeting, go to The Family Caregiver Alliance's guide at `www.caregiver.org/caregiver/jsp/content_node.jsp?nodeid=475`.

Being Considerate of Others

It's tempting to think about a long-term care plan as all about Mom, or Grandma, or oneself. But in reality most plans affect others, either in their implementation or in the ultimate consequences. Be sure to think ahead and include these considerations in the plan.

Time and energy are two big components of helping out an aging relative and are two of the biggest complaints that family helpers have when comparing what they're doing to other family members' contributions. When discussing how a long-term plan should be laid out, make sure to allocate responsibilities and to keep everyone informed. The next two sections go into more detail to help you prevent any pitfalls.

Allocating responsibilities

Knowing who can do what is imperative to making a long-term care plan work.

Making a list of responsibilities

As early as possible, perhaps after the first family meeting, ask each person in the core group to construct a list of what he or she would be able to do to implement the proposed plan. The tasks can be time limited, such as helping you or a parent to clean out a house, sell or donate unwanted items, and plan a move. It could be long-term, such as providing primary care one day a week, one weekend a month, or some other period. It could be monetary, including offering to pay for home modifications, some home care assistance, or a designated amount for the overall budget. Or it could be an offer to have your parent move in with you or to move in with your parent.

Many people are reluctant to get involved because they fear it will become an overwhelming task, as it surely is if only one person is responsible. Limiting participation to specified contributions — whether they are the person's time or money — is a better way to encourage involvement.

When you have everyone's lists, compare them and see if tasks are self-allocated in a generally fair and workable way. The goal is not to arrive at an exactly equal division of labor or financial contributions; this is not like dividing a pizza pie. Rather the goal is a fair distribution of participation, one that takes into account the different participants' other responsibilities, assets, location, and other factors. Some people will draw the line at personal care; others cannot afford to contribute as much money as the others in the group. Everyone should be at least comfortable with the result. And the main person — you or your parent — should also feel that this arrangement is acceptable.

It is possible, and maybe even likely, that the preliminary allocation of tasks doesn't work for some reason — everyone wants the same job, for example, and some jobs are not spoken for. In that case, time limits may be helpful — "If you do the transportation this month, I'll do it next month, and we can work out a schedule after that." Or some jobs may require paid help. Better to spend some money to hire someone, if you can afford to, than to leave the job undone or done by an unwilling person. And in some families there are people who just won't do anything; they may give a reason or they may not. Perhaps a private conversation with this person to try to understand what is going on — which may not have anything to do with the issue at hand — will result in some cooperation. Or it may not. Whatever the outcome, if this person is or should be in the inner circle (a sibling, for example), keep him or her informed about all medical updates, financial decisions, and other key factors. Many good long-term care plans have been derailed by a family member who claims that "Nobody told me what was going on."

Of course, as time goes on and needs change, the agreement may have to be revisited. But if the concept of sharing is well embedded in the arrangement, changes are more likely to be negotiable. Sharing is a concept we are taught as children; it is just as important in long-term care.

Taking on financial responsibility

Whoever has the responsibility of dealing with financial affairs should understand the seriousness of this task. It is more than paying monthly bills and balancing a checkbook. It involves keeping detailed records of how your or your parent's money is being spent. This may seem unnecessary in families with good relationships, but it is prudent in every case. Working with an accountant or another financial advisor, if feasible, set up a way to record income and outlays. Major financial decisions, like taking out a reverse mortgage or buying an annuity, should be discussed with the core family group.

You or your parent should have an up-to-date will, and its provisions should be shared with the core group. The names of the person who is designated as healthcare proxy and the alternate should also be shared. The point of all this record-keeping and sharing of information is not to sow seeds of distrust. In fact, it is the opposite. When everything is in the open, people are less likely to mutter about where the money is going and who might be taking advantage of the situation.

Being the medical record keeper

If one person is designated to accompany you or your parent to the doctor and to monitor health conditions, that person should also share important information with the core group. If possible, you should ask permission from your parent or other relative to share this information with specific people. They do not need to know every test result or blood-pressure reading, but they do need to know about major changes or problems. Without this ongoing medical information, others will not understand the severity of an illness or a cognitive decline. Many family disagreements about end-of-life decisions start from inadequate information much earlier in the course of the illness. Partly this problem comes from some doctors' unwillingness to give bad news, but the person closest to the situation may also be reluctant to accept or share this bad news.

Timely sharing of medical information can also inform discussions of palliative care and hospice and make it more likely that these options are instituted early enough to make a real difference in care.

Bringing in the outer circle

Friends and family members not in the core group can play an important role in a long-term care plan. They can do errands, shop for food, cook or bring meals, provide transportation, and do a million other things that need to be done but are hard to fit into a busy primary caregiver's life. Most of all, they can do what they are best at doing: spending time with you or your parent, revisiting the past, talking about current events, taking walks, watching television, playing cards, listening to recorded books, or doing whatever both people enjoy.

If you or your parent is moving to an assisted-living facility, remember that keeping in touch with people from your prior neighborhood or community is important for health and happiness. Many people have difficulty making friends in a new setting, and some assisted-living residents are reluctant to start new friendships because the time together may be short. It is comforting to see old friends and to introduce them to the new people on your (assisted living) block. They may have a lot in common.

Many people in the outer circle will want to help, but putting goodwill and time together can be a chore in itself. Two websites have systems for organizing the outer circle:

- **Lotsa Helping Hands** (www.lotsahelpinghands.com) has tools and calendars to help organize volunteers to provide assistance.
- **Share the Care** (www.sharethecare.org/index.html) has a handbook and advice about starting a group in your community.

You can also create your own system through a designated website or other means.

For the outer circle, it is important to set limits on what is expected and acceptable and what is not. For example, if someone who comes to read to your parent but has to cancel, that's a disappointment, not a major problem. But if that person has volunteered to take your parent to a doctor's appointment, that's a different level of responsibility. Have a list of alternates, but if someone cancels frequently, don't ask that person to do an essential task.

To be a member of the outer circle in good standing, people have to accept the basic terms of the plan you have developed. Friends may think they are helping by criticizing the way the primary caregiver or the home care aide does things, or telling you that they have read about a miracle drug that will get you back on your feet in no time, or even an investment that will guarantee an amazing return. This is the kind of help you do not need. People who undermine relationships or care systems are using a vulnerable person's needs as an opportunity to display their often misguided expertise. Put them into the outer, outer circle.

Dealing with Conflict

Family conflict is at the heart of the world's great literature, from the Bible to the present. Think of King Lear. How much better off he would have been had he discussed his plans for long-term care with his daughters instead of royally announcing his decision. Few families today have a kingdom at stake, but sometimes high drama can come from very small stakes.

Mediators and counselors

If, after all your preparations and forethought, conflict cannot be forestalled, it may be time to call in a mediator or counselor. This person can be a professional; clergy, social workers, psychologists, family therapists all have training on how to handle conflict. It is important that the person be, and be seen by all, as an objective advisor, not someone hired to convince the others to agree to a plan.

Some mediation techniques are the same as I have discussed for holding a family meeting. They include setting ground rules for discussion (no negative personal comments, no interrupting, and time limits). Talk about feelings is allowed, but only in the "*I*" format. That is, "I felt left out of the discussion," not "You left me out of the discussion."

Sometimes individual counseling can help someone deal with the situation itself and the conflict it has engendered. Often these conflicts have roots in childhood or adolescence. Although you may feel that you have moved on and no longer feel these old hurts, they sustain surprising power over time.

Consensus and compromise

When a family is totally at odds over some aspect of long-term care, whatever the ultimate decision, there should be no winners and losers. If the process has further alienated some family members and made it less likely that there will be a meeting of minds — much less a meeting in person — then everyone loses. And witnessing family fights can be detrimental to younger family members, even to children, who may not understand just what all the unpleasantness is about.

When conflict erupts, as it often does, try to keep the animosity level low. Everyone will have to live with the decision, often for years, as well as their behavior during the conflict. It is about long-term care, after all, and that may mean a very long time. The goal should be consensus and compromise, not victory.

Part II

Long-Term Care in Different Settings

Range of Fees in Continuing-Care Retirement Communities

	A: Life Care	B: Modified	C: Fee for Service	D: Rental
Entry fee/Security deposit	$160,000–600,000	$80,000–750,000	$100,000–500,000	$1,800–30,000
Independent-living monthly fee	$2,500–5,400	$1,500–2,500	$1,300–4,300	$900–2,700
Assisted-living monthly fee	$2,500–5,400	$1,500–2,500	$3,700–5,800	$4,700–6,500
Nursing-care monthly fee	$2,500–5,400	$1,500–2,500	$8,100–10,000	$8,100–10,700

Table source: U.S. Government Accountability Office, "Older Americans: Continuing Care Retirement Communities Can Provide Benefits, but Not Without Some Risk" (June 2010).

web extras

When you modify a home for safety and accessibility, color is more than a decorative choice. Check out a free article at www.dummies.com/extras/planninglongtermcare for some tips on making color work for you.

In this part...

- ✔ Consider all your options for housing and transportation — two major elements in a long-term care plan.

- ✔ Evaluate how you can modify your home for safety and accessibility so that you can *age in place* (stay in the same home).

- ✔ Find out what assisted living or some other form of group living can offer you if staying at home is not an option.

- ✔ Use guides and checklists to help you evaluate your community. Aging in place involves more than the home — a lot depends of what community resources are available.

- ✔ More than one generation living together is an old idea that is new again. Consider the many aspects that make these arrangements successes or failures, including finances and space.

- ✔ Address the touchy issue of driving — when it is time to hang up the car keys — and the alternatives that can keep an older person connected to friends, family, and the community.

Chapter 5

Aging in Place

*W*hen you ask your parents about their long-term care plans, their response may remind you of Jennifer Hudson in the movie *Dreamgirls* singing, "And I'm telling you I'm not going!" Most older adults want to stay in their current home as they age. But the home you or your parent or other relative have lived in for years may not serve well now or in the future. Modifications may be necessary to accommodate changing needs, and you may need people and services to help with many tasks that you or your parents are no longer able or willing to do.

In this chapter, I guide you through some of the options available for home modification and obtaining outside help from family members and services. I also review plans you should have in place to prepare the house and your family for a disaster such as a hurricane or flood or a more common event such as a power outage.

What Is Aging in Place?

Aging in place is a new name for an old idea: staying in your own home until you die. The federal Centers for Disease Control and Prevention (CDC) has a broader and more complicated definition: "the ability to live in one's own home and community safely, independently, and comfortably, regardless of age, income, or ability level." This definition adds conditions to the circumstances under which aging in place should occur. The person has to meet all three conditions — be safe, comfortable, and able to live independently. Living independently may mean living alone without any outside help or it may mean being able to live alone only if outside help is available. The critical element is being able to choose what you do and when you do it.

Sometimes these conditions conflict. Your parent may be quite comfortable at home, but the home may not be safe. Or the home may be safe, but she cannot manage on her own. Or all those conditions may be met, but you or your parents don't have enough income or assets to support the arrangement.

The CDC's definition also includes living in your community as part of its standard. This adds another layer of complexity. What exactly is a community? What if the home is safe but the neighborhood is not? What if the person does not have a community of people nearby who are able to help out as needed? Living alone should not mean living in isolation. So what seems to be a straightforward definition turns out to be complicated. You can do a lot to make sure all these elements are in place, but of course some things are beyond any individual's control.

This chapter focuses on ensuring that the home is safe and comfortable and on accessing home-based or local services routinely and in emergencies. I save larger issues related to the community and options for community-based services for Chapter 8.

Dealing with Two Major Hazards

An important first step in deciding whether aging in place can work is taking a hard look at your own or your relative's home. Looking past a cherished home's attractive features and focusing on its flaws and hazards can be hard to do. Having someone with fresh eyes with you as you survey the premises can be helpful, preferably someone with experience in home modification for older people, such as a physical or occupational therapist, a geriatric care manager, or a contractor who has done similar jobs. If you are trying to improve the home for an older relative, be aware that older people often downplay concerns about safety and resist change. Be tactful but firm. Safety is not the only issue, but it is a prerequisite to enjoying a good quality of life.

The two issues I cover in this section are falls and burns. They aren't the only sources of injury at home, but if you address these two, you'll likely prevent other kinds of injury as well.

Preventing falls

Your first priority should be preventing falls. Falls are among the most common accidents in homes. Older people are at risk for falls because keeping your balance as you age is more difficult, and it's also harder to readjust your feet to regain your balance if you slip. Arthritis can limit your range of motion. Many older people suffer bone loss, or osteoporosis. Hips are the most likely joints to be injured because people tend to fall on their sides.

Falls are often the first step in a cascade of decline that ends up with a hospital stay and eventual placement in a nursing home or death. Fortunately, many fall-prevention measures are easy to take and are not expensive.

Here's a checklist for falls prevention adapted from the National Center for Injury Prevention and Control, a division of the CDC. The full list is available at www.cdc.gov/ncipc/pub-res/toolkit/checklistforsafety.htm.

✔ **Floors:**

- When you walk through a room, do you have to walk around furniture? If so, make a clear path by moving the furniture.

- Are there throw rugs on the floor? If so, remove them or use double-sided tape or a non-slip backing.

- Are there papers, books, towels, shoes, magazines, boxes, or blankets on the floor? Pick them up and keep them off the floor.

- Do you have to walk over or around wires or cords (like lamp, telephone, or extension cords)? Coil or tape cords and wires next to the wall. You may need an electrician to put in another outlet.

✔ **Stairs and steps:**

- Are shoes, papers, or other objects on the stairs? Remove them.

- Are some steps broken or uneven? Have them repaired.

- Does the stairway have a light? An electrician should install an overhead light and light switch at the top and bottom of the stairs. (Use an energy-saving type of light bulb so it doesn't need to be changed as often.)

- If there's carpet on the stairs, make sure it's firmly attached to every step.

- Make sure that handrails are not loose or broken and that they're on both sides of the stairs.

- To make seeing the stairs easier, paint a contrasting color on the top edge of all the steps. For example, use a light color paint on dark wood.

✔ **Kitchen:**

- Are often-used items on high shelves? Move them to lower shelves (about waist level).

- Is the step stool unsteady? If you must use a step stool, get one with a bar for support. Never use a chair as a step stool.

✔ **Bathroom:**

- Tubs and shower floors are often slippery. Put a non-slip rubber mat or self-stick strips on the floor.

- Install grab bars inside the tub and next to the toilet. Make sure you have this done by someone who knows how to place them correctly and securely. The screws should be installed in the studs in the wall, not in the tiles, or the grab bar will pull loose.

✔ **Bedroom**

- Is the light near the bed hard to reach? Make sure a sturdy lamp is close to the bed.

- Is the path from the bed to the bathroom dark? Put in a night-light, preferably one that turns itself on after dark.

Dealing with clutter and hoarding

Your survey of the home may have uncovered an unpleasant secret. Your aging relative has accumulated piles of unread newspapers and magazines, the refrigerator is full of rotting food, or the cats have taken over the bathroom. This behavior is not just difficult to look at, it is also a fire and safety hazard. Some of this accumulation is clutter. Bending down to pick up papers may be difficult for a person with arthritis, or a person with vision problems may not be able to read the sell-by date on foods. But sometimes the accumulation of stuff rises to the level of hoarding, which is a more serious problem.

Hoarding interferes with ordinary life by making it impossible to use the space as intended and impedes access in an emergency. You may be tempted to overlook the problem because one good cleaning would get rid of the worst of the mess. But it's not something that should be ignored, and if you get rid of the piles of what you call junk and your relative considers priceless, he or she will only refill the space as quickly as possible.

There are many theories about what causes this kind of behavior, which may be related to depression, anxiety, prior losses, or other mental-health issues. Dealing with hoarding requires consultation with experienced mental-health and home-organizing professionals who can negotiate the cleanup in nonjudgmental ways. The Hartford (CT) Hospital has a useful website on compulsive hoarding: www. harthosp.org/InstituteOfLiving/ AnxietyDisordersCenter/ CompulsiveHoarding/default. aspx.

Preventing burns

Burns are another common problem in the home. Even a minor burn can lead to infection and serious consequences. Older people literally have thinner skin that's more susceptible to scalding from hot water or burns from electrical appliances. To keep older people safe from burns in their home, make sure that you

✔ Replace electrical cords that are broken or cracked.

✔ Replace electronic devices, heaters, or appliances that overheat, spark, or smoke.

✔ Use a power strip instead of an extension cord.

✔ Keep electrical appliances away from water.

✔ Unplug small appliances such as toaster ovens and coffee pots when not in use.

✔ Keep a three-foot zone of safety around the stove, oven, and microwave.

✔ Use microwave-safe cookware.

✔ Set the water temperature to a maximum of 120° F (this may be a job for a plumber or building staff).

✔ Use a humidifier that sprays cool mist instead of hot steam.

✔ Have smoke alarms installed and change the batteries twice a year. You can use time changes as your reminder.

Smoking in bed is still a common cause of fires. Do everything you can to prevent this really bad habit.

A comprehensive brochure with guidelines for preventing burns from the Hearst Burn Center at New York Presbyterian Hospital is available at `http://nyp.org/pdf/burn_center/Burn_Safety_Prevention_Older_Adults_englishWEB.pdf`.

Modifying a Home for an Aging Person

When you've completed your safety checklist and made all the easy fixes and repairs, you may still find problem areas still exist. Some may be unsafe conditions, but others may be barriers that make it difficult for you or your relative to move about freely and to enjoy the comforts of home that make him want to stay put in the first place. This section covers modifications that can be made to an aging person's current home to allow him to continue his present living arrangement.

For more information on this topic, check out the *AARP Guide to Revitalizing Your Home: Beautiful Living for the Second Half of Life* by Rosemary Bakker, at `www.aarp.org/RevitalizingYourHome`.

Categorizing types of home modifications

Many houses and apartment buildings were constructed before universal design features were common or in some cases required by guidelines for remodeling and new construction under the Americans with Disabilities Act (ADA), passed in 1990. Ramps in public places, doors marked for wheelchair entrance, and buses with lifts and special seating for people with disabilities have become so common that they are scarcely noticed (unless of course you're the person with a disability who needs these accommodations). Yet the need for similar accommodations in private homes is less visible although equally important.

The Rehabilitation Engineering and Assistive Technology Society of North America (RESNA) puts home modifications into three categories:

✔ **Accessibility:** Accessibility modifications allow a person in a wheelchair or with disabilities to move easily throughout a structure, such as with widened doorways, lowered countertops and sinks, grab bars in the tub or shower, and light switches and electrical outlets at waist height.

✔ **Adaptability:** Adaptability covers changes that can be made more quickly, without having to completely redesign the home or use different materials for essential fixtures.

✔ **Universal design:** These features are usually built into a home, including appliances, floor plans, and fixtures that are flexible, sturdy, reliable, and easy for all people to use. See the AARP description of universal design for a list of some basic features at `www.aarp.org/home-garden/home-improvement/info-09-2009/what_is_universal_design.html`.

These categories are important because they involve different levels of planning, implementation, and cost. For example, adapting a home is the least complicated type of modification. Grab bars and outdoor ramps are examples. Making a home accessible, however, may involve structural changes and complying with building code and ADA requirements. Universal design may come into play when you are completely remodeling a home or building a new space.

Checking out accessibility

General home safety issues (which I cover in the earlier section "Dealing with Two Major Hazards") are important for all older people living on their own. But other specific features can make the home easy to use — or not — for people who have disabilities or who are aging. Start in the kitchen and bathroom and think about the particular problems you or your parent may face in accessibility.

✔ Are cabinet knobs or pulls easy to use? Pulls are generally considered easier to use than knobs.

✔ Are stove controls easy to use and clearly marked?

✔ Are faucets easy to use? Universal design faucets have one lever, not two knobs to turn. This makes mixing hot and cold water easier.

✔ Can the oven and refrigerator doors be opened easily? Is the freezer easy to reach?

✔ Is the kitchen counter height and depth convenient? Most kitchen counters are too high for a person in a wheelchair.

✔ Is there room to move around the bathroom and a place to put towels and shampoo in easy reach?

✔ Is the shower faucet easy to use? Turning on the shower and getting the right temperature can be difficult. A new shower head or faucets may be needed.

✔ Does the height of the toilet seat make getting up difficult? A raised seat may help.

In closets and storage spaces, check on the following:

✔ Does the closet contain items that have just been put there to get them out of sight? Move them so that the closet is easier to access for coats, hats, umbrellas, and boots.

✔ Can items in the closet, like a coat on a hanger, be removed and replaced easily?

✔ Could the use of storage space be improved with closet shelf systems?

Doors and windows may need the following updates:

✔ Are the doors wide enough to accommodate a walker or wheelchair? 36 inches is the standard for a wheelchair. Most door openings are much narrower.

✔ Are the doors and windows easy to open and close?

✔ Are the door locks sturdy and easy to operate?

Evaluate the electrical outlets and safety devices:

✔ Are electrical outlets easy to reach?

✔ Is the area around outlets free of clutter?

✔ Are the outlets properly grounded to prevent shock?

✔ Can you hear the doorbell in every room?

✔ Is the telephone readily available for emergencies? A land line may be more reliable in an emergency than a cellphone.

✔ Is there an alarm system? If so, it is easy to use? If not, consider whether one is needed.

This is only a partial list. The National Center on Supportive Housing and Home Modifications has a Safety Checklist and Assessment Instrument at www.homemods.org. Rebuilding Together, Inc., has an extensive home-modification checklist at http://rebuildingtogether.org/wp-content/uploads/2012/06/RT-Aging-in-Place-Safe-at-Home-Checklist.pdf. Also see the AARP Home Fit Guide at www.aarp.org/HomeFitGuide.

Some items that need correcting can be done by you or a friend or family member, but if you have determined that major changes are necessary — for example, widening doorways or replacing kitchen cabinets or appliances — you probably need to find a contractor to tackle the modifications. Head to the next section for advice on finding the right person for the job.

Remodeling is a messy and often frustrating experience. The first phase, demolition — even if it's limited to one room or area — is unsettling. Delays are common. It may be a good idea to move your relative to another setting while the work is being done, especially if you expect a lot of dust, noise, and disruption.

Finding a contractor

How do you find a reliable and knowledgeable contractor? If you have already worked with a contractor and were pleased with the results, then you have a head start. Ask this person to go over the problem areas with you, suggest fixes, estimate the cost, and tell you how long it will take to do the work.

Most people with accessible homes have neither built their own houses nor undergone extensive remodeling. Ask for recommendations from friends or neighbors who have had similar work done. Check online referral sites for recommendations. Then ask a few contractors for estimates and for people to call for references. Some home builders work with certified aging-in-place specialists, a program developed in partnership with AARP. Visit www.aarp.org/home-garden/home-improvement/info-03-2004/caps.html for more information.

Before hiring a contractor, check with the local Chamber of Commerce or other agency to see if any complaints have been filed against him. Make sure the contractor is licensed to perform the work and can obtain any building permits required. Finally, ask for a written agreement that stipulates a small down payment and schedule of payments, with the final payment to be made only when the work is completed and approved.

 One of the most frequent scams carried out against older people occurs when a "contractor" scans a neighborhood for a likely target and offers to do needed (or unneeded) repairs or home modifications. The person asks for a large down payment and either disappears or does only a token amount of work. If you are thinking of home modifications for older relatives, be sure to warn them about this scam. No one should do any repairs without your approval.

 Attempting any major repairs, especially if they involve climbing ladders or using power tools, is dangerous. Some people want to save a few bucks by doing the jobs themselves, but they need to be reminded that the cost upfront is much less than the aftereffects of being injured.

 If you or your relative live in an apartment building or housing complex, you need to contact the management to make some changes, particularly in corridors and stairways and even within the apartment itself. Co-op or condo residents may be required to obtain approval from their governing board as well.

Getting help paying for home modifications

Many home modifications, such as ramps and lighting replacements, are relatively inexpensive. But when you start widening doors and installing new kitchen equipment like a refrigerator with side-by-side doors, the costs add up. In the bathroom, installing a roll-in shower can be costly although important for someone who cannot move from wheelchair to tub. Eldercare Locator, a federal agency funded by the Administration for Aging (AoA), suggests these resources for financial assistance:

Not covered under Medicare

Don't look to Medicare for help in covering remodeling costs. According to the Medicare Rights Center, "Medicare will never cover home modifications (like the installation of a stair lift or grab bars near the toilet or tub) or assistive devices (like large-button telephones or flashing doorbell signals for the hard-of-hearing)." However, the services of an occupational therapist to teach a person how to use the devices or modifications may be covered.

✔ Some funds for home repair may be available through Title III of the Older Americans Act. They are distributed through the local Area Agency on Aging (AAA). You can find your nearest AAA by calling Eldercare Locator at 800-677-1116 or going online at www.eldercare.gov. These funds are likely to be limited, however, and best suited for relatively small jobs.

✔ Rebuilding Together, Inc., a national volunteer organization dedicated to assisting low-income seniors, may be able to direct you to a local affiliate. You can contact it at www.rebuildingtogether.org.

✔ Some types of home modification — those determined to be medically necessary — may be covered by Medicaid (for eligible low-income people), depending on the state you live in. For example, a roll-in bathtub or shower for a person in a wheelchair may be covered. A doctor's order may be required, and some Medicaid programs limit eligibility to certain diagnoses or ages. Check your state's Medicaid office for details.

✔ If the home is mortgaged and has substantial equity, a home equity loan may be available from the bank. However, this loan will increase the mortgage payment.

Whether major improvements and their associated costs will substantially improve your or your relative's safety and quality of life is a personal decision. You may decide that aging in place is not really feasible after all and that a move to assisted living or another setting is the best choice (see Chapter 6). If you do decide to stay, by going through the important process of evaluating your home and making those small changes that can prevent accidents, you or your parent will have a much safer home.

Seeking Help at Home

Creating a safe and comfortable environment is only one factor in aging in place. Many older adults need at least some help at home. Some people need just a little assistance with transportation and shopping, for example, while others need a lot of help with personal care such as bathing and dressing. People with complex chronic conditions usually need help with managing medications, operating medical equipment, monitoring symptoms, and similar tasks. In the following sections, I help you consider whether family members or paid professionals can provide those important services.

Allocating tasks to family

At least 80 percent of long-term care assistance is provided by unpaid family members. A first step for providing help at home is to allocate tasks to family members and/or friends. Talk to them to find out who's available and willing to help and what limitations they have. If several cooperative family members are involved, the tasks can be divided. One person may be able to spend several afternoons a week shopping and preparing meals, while another can manage medications and doctor visits. A friend may be able to pick up prescriptions from the pharmacy or drive to religious services.

When you arrange a plan for allocated tasks, make (or have someone help you make) a master list of family helpers, their phone numbers, their tasks, and the schedule. Put the list in an easy-to-find place, such as on the refrigerator, to help the person being assisted remember who is coming when. Also be sure to distribute the list to family and helpers so everyone knows what tasks are being taken care of.

Community-based agencies such as volunteer groups, social-service agencies, and faith-based groups have services that are often helpful. These arrangements can be complicated, but if everyone is willing to be flexible, the necessary tasks can be accomplished. Chapter 19 offers some guidance for family caregivers in these situations.

Searching for services

When family members and friends cannot provide all the help that is needed, paid home health or companion services provided by agencies or hired privately can fill the gaps. One factor in your decision to age in place may be the availability — and affordability — of these services. Home care comes in many varieties and from many different sources.

Medicare (original Medicare and Medicare Advantage plans), Medicaid, private health insurance, and long-term care insurance have their own rules and criteria for providing services. Some people are covered by more than one policy. Chapter 14 covers the details of home-care services and working with insurance plans, but as an introduction, here are a few key points to remember.

✔ Medicare home healthcare is intended to be part-time or intermittent (not constant). The goal, according to Medicare, "is to provide treatment for an illness or injury." The Medicare home health benefit "pays for you to get certain healthcare services in your home if you meet certain eligibility criteria and if the services are considered reasonable and necessary for the treatment of your illness or injury." See "Medicare and Home Health Care" at www.medicare.gov/pubs/pdf/10969.pdf.

To be eligible for this benefit, you must have a need for skilled nursing; that is, the kind of care provided by a nurse or physical therapist. Personal care provided by an aide is included only when this need exists.

✔ Medicaid for low-income people provides long-term home healthcare, including aide services, but eligibility and availability vary by state.

✔ Private insurance generally follows Medicare rules.

> ✔ Home-care services are generally available through long-term care insurance but vary by policy, and there may be waiting periods and other limitations.
>
> ✔ Hiring workers privately is also an option that gives you more flexibility but also more responsibility.

Having reliable, competent, and friendly home-care workers can make a big difference in someone's ability to age in place, but working out a suitable arrangement takes time and effort — and often money.

Finding help for other chores

In addition to paid home-care workers, you or your relative may need additional help in taking care of pets, maintaining the yard, cleaning the gutters, taking trash cans to the curb, and all the other chores that are now difficult to do. If these regular maintenance tasks are not taken care of regularly, the home can quickly deteriorate, leading to safety problems as well as expensive repairs. Serious problems, such as a leaking roof or frozen water pipes, can create havoc. Chores that involve climbing, shoveling, heavy lifting, and other strenuous activities are best done by someone younger and stronger.

Some community agencies and religious organizations have volunteers who will help out with these chores. Ask the organizations you belong to or senior centers for suggestions. Local schools or universities may also have community service programs for students. Some heavy or risky chores should only be performed by trained workers. If you hire people to help, make sure that they give references and do the job competently.

Putting technology to use

Technology is all around us, and *assistive technology* — devices and adaptations that are designed to help people who are aging or have disabilities function independently — can make a big difference in a person's ability to age safely in place. Assistive devices come in all sizes and shapes and can be cheap or very costly. I have already mentioned some common assistive devices — grab bars, handrails, and raised toilet seats. Other common devices are hand-friendly tools for opening jars or gardening, TV remote controls with big numbers, and Personal Emergency Response Systems (PERS), the kind immortalized and satirized in the TV commercial, "I've fallen and I can't get up!" In the healthcare world, telehealth — distance monitoring of chronic conditions like daily weight checks on a person with heart failure — is growing, especially in rural areas.

How far you're willing to go to bring assistive devices into your life is a personal choice. Inventors and investors have identified people aging in place (and their adult children) as a huge market for these products. The products include mattresses that sense every movement and can relay information about how many times the person gets up to go to the bathroom or the kitchen, monitors that track a person's movements in the home, and GPS devices that can locate a person with dementia if she wanders. A robot that can make a bed, cook a meal, and even carry on a conversation is not yet on the market, but if there is a demand, it will certainly be produced. The movie *Robot and Frank,* which described an aging man's reluctant adaptation to a robot, is a fantasy, but fantasies are sometimes early glimpses of reality.

Buying an assistive device is only the first step. You have to learn how to use it and perhaps teach an older adult or an aide how to use it.

Some devices that seem simple are not. For example, a cane is probably the most common assistive device. Yet it has to be the right length and used on the correct side of the body. (Hint: It's not the side where the pain or injury is.) And as you move up the scale toward devices with moving parts and controls to set, the need increases for adequate instruction and someone to call when there are problems. Constant monitoring means constant responses, most of which will turn out to be false alarms. If you're the responder, it can become all too easy to ignore that flashing red light or annoying beep.

Looking for technological solutions to the problems of aging overlooks a basic human need for contact with other people. And while technological devices offer to provide peace of mind, the devices themselves can fail and at best require someone to respond whether there is a real emergency or just a faulty sensor. That in itself can be a major responsibility.

Consider assistive devices by all means, but focus on the ones that will actually make a difference and that don't add burdens to your life. Abledata.com (www.abledata.com), a project of the National Institute for Disability and Rehabilitation Research, has information about products and resources.

Preparing for an Emergency

Disasters happen — hurricanes, floods, heat waves, blizzards, tornadoes, fires, power outages, building collapses, acts of terrorism. An aging person, even one who can live safely at home in ordinary circumstances, is particularly vulnerable when the home environment is threatened and when water, power, gas, or telephone service is interrupted. People who live alone are at particular risk, especially if they are isolated from their neighbors or community agencies. Quite simply, they are more likely to die because nobody checks up on them because no one knows who they are.

Preparing for a disaster is a major part of aging safely in place. The Federal Emergency Management Association (FEMA) and the Red Cross have lists of ways to prepare, which you can see at www.ready.gov/make-a-plan and www.redcross.org/prepare/location/home-family.

The first step is to create a personal support network, a list of people and agencies you or your parent can call on for help in an emergency. The list should include more than one person — preferably three — and each one should know what the particular problems you or your parent might have, such as getting down stairs if there is no elevator. If a home care agency is providing workers in your or your relative's home, the agency should know about the emergency plan. The members of the support network should live or work close to the older person, and they should know who the other people on the list are and how to reach them. Communication in an emergency is often disrupted, and the more people who are in contact, the more likely help is to be forthcoming.

If you or your parent lives in apartment building or housing complex, let the management or superintendent know that in case of an emergency, you would need certain help (back-up oxygen supplies, for example). Many buildings keep lists of people with special needs (and their pets) just for that reason. Some communities suggest that people with disabilities or age-related problems register with the local fire department or police station.

Read on to find out how to put an emergency plan in place and how to create a disaster kit should disaster strike.

Making an emergency plan

FEMA and the Red Cross advise people to create an emergency plan that includes:

- ✔ **A location for you and your relative to meet.** This spot may be right outside the home, if it's safe, or in a more distant location. Finding each other in a disaster can be difficult without a destination. Generally community centers and schools are the most easily identified meeting places. If your community has designated shelters for emergencies, those are good places to reconnect.

- ✔ **Contact information for family members, members of the support team, home care aides, and others.**

✓ **Escape routes and safe places.** Knowing how to get out of a building safely and quickly is essential in some kinds of emergencies. Just as a flight attendant informs passengers to identify the nearest emergency exit (which may be behind you), identifying the safest way to get out of a home is essential. There may be specific instructions for some types of emergencies, such as going to the basement or closet with no windows in case of a tornado warning.

✓ **A plan for pets.** Take them with you if you have to leave, but be aware that emergency shelters may not be able to accommodate them. The support network should include someone who can board the pets temporarily.

Power outages are not as dramatic as major disasters when evacuation is necessary, but they are more common and can create serious risks. It's not just that the lights are out and the TV doesn't work; toilets can't be flushed and food in the refrigerator may spoil. Here are a few tips:

✓ If you or your parent depends on electricity to operate home medical equipment, have a back-up system ready to use.

✓ Have several working flashlights on hand as well as extra batteries.

✓ Don't use candles.

✓ If there is a severe storm warning, fill the bathtub with water so that if the power goes out, there will be water to flush the toilet.

✓ Keep the refrigerator door closed.

✓ Keep your land line, since it may work in storms when cellphone service is not available. And keep your cell phone charged. If possible, have both means of communication available to call for help or to check on service restoration.

For more tips, see the American Red Cross brochure, "Disaster Preparedness for Seniors by Seniors," prepared by 12 seniors in Rochester NY after their experiences during a two-week power outage. It is available at www. redcross.org/images/MEDIA_CustomProductCatalog/m4640086_ Disaster_Preparedness_for_Srs-English.revised_7-09.pdf.

Putting together a disaster kit

A key part of a disaster plan is preparing a kit of essential items that can be easily located and taken with you. The basic items can include but are not limited to

✔ Bottled water and nonperishable food items

✔ Flashlight and extra batteries

✔ Battery-powered radio

✔ First-aid kit and manual

✔ Photocopies of health insurance and other identification cards

✔ Prescription medications, eye glasses, and hearing-aid batteries

✔ Sanitation and hygiene items (moist towelettes, toilet paper)

✔ Clothing appropriate for the climate

Both the kit and the plan should be reviewed regularly and changed if needed.

Fortunately, disasters are relatively rare, but they can be catastrophic. Preparing for these events is no guarantee but can make the chances of survival and safety much greater.

Chapter 6

Independent and Assisted Living and Other Group Settings

*I*t's a common problem: Your house is too big and costly to maintain. Or your kids live halfway across the country. Or you are the "kid" and your parents need more help than you can give them. But no one wants to give up privacy and independence. Whatever your situation, assisted living may seem like a very good solution. And the ads stress how pleasant and easy life can be in a place called, say, Gracious Living Manor. But you have a lot to think about before taking such a big step.

When choosing whether assisted living is the way to go for your situation, there are many considerations. This chapter guides you through all that comes with assisted living: the services, options, costs, and more. I also cover pitfalls to steer clear of and alternative group-living arrangements. But first, it helps to know exactly what assisted living is, so read on.

What Is Assisted Living?

Assisted living is a term that is often used as though everyone understands it in the same way. But that's not the case. Assisted living is just a generic term like *hotel* or *automobile* that covers a lot of options. Before getting into the specifics, I like to start with a simple definition: Assisted living is a residence where groups of people share meals and other activities and where individuals can receive personal assistance to maintain their independence. People who choose assisted living typically would have difficulty living completely on their own but do not require constant medical attention.

You can also think about assisted living as an intermediate step in long-term care. It is in the middle of the spectrum of long-term care, which often goes from independent living to assisted living to nursing-home care. Independent living can be in your own home, as described in Chapter 5, or the entry level of assisted living or in special housing for older people. About 70 percent of residents in assisted living come to the facility from their own home or apartment.

In this section I cover a more formal definition of assisted living, what services are included, which healthcare options may be provided, and tips for finding a facility to provide a broader understanding of all that assisted living covers.

Interpreting industry and government language

Most definitions of assisted living come from industry or government sources and emphasize different aspects of this long-term care setting. It's important to keep the source in mind when you gather information. For example, the Assisted Living Federation of America, a trade organization, says: "Assisted living is a housing and health-care option that combines independence and personal care in a residential setting." This is a good definition as far as it goes, but it doesn't tell you what personal care means and what healthcare services are likely to be offered.

The Eldercare Locator (www.eldercare.gov), a free service connected with the federal Administration on Aging (AoA), has an even more specific definition: "Assisted-living facilities offer a housing alternative for older adults who may need help with dressing, bathing, eating and toileting but do not require the intensive medical and nursing care provided in nursing homes." This definition, while accurate, doesn't include younger adults who may need the kinds of services available in assisted living. It also underestimates the importance of the social aspects of assisted living.

Living with a congenial group of people with whom to share meals, activities, and conversation is a potential benefit. Remember, though, that it is sometimes hard to make new friends in assisted living because they see a lot of turnover. According to the 2010 National Survey of Residential Care Facilities (assisted-living facilities), most people stay in assisted living for only 22 months. Nearly 60 percent move on to a nursing facility, a third die, and the rest move home or to another location.

State governments, which license group residences, call assisted-living facilities by different names. Some examples of the state licensing categories are *residential care facilities for the elderly* (California), *residential facilities for groups* (Nevada), and *personal care homes – assisted-living facilities* (Pennsylvania).

You may also come across the acronym *ALF* in your search. It is shorthand for assisted-living facility, not the old TV character. Similarly, *ALP* is assisted-living program, not a mountain.

Owners of assisted-living facilities tend to shy away from that term in the name, preferring more appealing names like *village, community, manor,* or any phrase that evokes a secure and invigorating lifestyle.

Your state's name for assisted living is not as important as its licensing requirements and its monitoring activities. Some states have detailed standards about what counts as assisted living and what must be provided, as well as building and safety regulations. They may require training for staff, background criminal checks, and other safeguards. Regulations in other states are less definitive. The National Center for Assisted Living, a provider organization, has state-by-state information about regulations and licensing requirements, as well as legislative or regulatory changes you should know about. You can look up your state at www.ahcancal.org/ncal/resources/Pages/AssistedLivingRegulations.aspx.

When you check out your state's regulations, find out whether it has a bill of rights for assisted-living residents. Most states have such a document and generally require facilities to post it and give copies to residents. These documents may be lengthy. Some of the items include the right to privacy, to confidentiality of personal and medical information, to have private communications with a physician or attorney, to practice the religion of one's choice, and to be given notice about transfers or fee increases. Some are negative rights, such as the right not to be coerced or required to perform work. However, not all the documents tell residents how to complain if they feel their rights have been violated. One way is to contact the state's long-term care ombudsman, who is responsible for investigating complaints in nursing homes and assisted-care facilities. You can find the ombudsman in your area at www.ltcombudsman.org/ombudsman. Or you can contact the National Consumer Voice for Quality Long-term Care at www.theconsumervoice.org.

Getting to know what assisted living offers

All assisted-living facilities, however defined, offer three main components:

- **Shelter:** Residents are given a place to live, usually a private unit or apartment.

- **Meals:** Food is provided, although not necessarily three meals a day.

- **Staff:** The facility staff provide the assistance that comes with the name. In addition to managers and activity directors, most facilities have aides or attendants to help with bathing, dressing, getting around with a cane or walker, and other daily tasks.

When it comes to services provided by staff, you may hear the term *ADLs* frequently. It stands for *activities of daily living,* which are the actions people take for granted until they can't do them by themselves anymore — dressing, bathing, going to the bathroom, and feeding themselves. ADLs have a companion term — *IADLs,* or *instrumental activities of daily living* — that includes tasks like making phone calls, managing money, managing medications, shopping, and cooking. People in assisted living, may also need help with these responsibilities.

Assisted-living facilities may be located in cities and look like ordinary apartment buildings. Some are in suburban locations with lots of open space. There are fewer assisted-living sites in rural areas.

Some assisted-living facilities are luxurious and provide a wide range of services and amenities. At the other end of the spectrum, some facilities have small staffs and offer limited assistance.

When you are considering an assisted-living facility, be sure to ask about staffing (how many, training, special skills, and background checks). If the management seems evasive, probe further. The response will give you an idea of whether this is a place you want to consider further or avoid.

Assisted-living facilities may be large or small. About a third of all facilities are considered large (26 or more beds), but they have more than 80 percent of all assisted-living residents. About 82 percent of all facilities are run by for-profit organizations, some of which are national or regional chains. The rest are run by charitable or religious organizations or by state, city, or local governments.

Assisted living: Born in the 1990s

Before the 1990s, you would have had a hard time finding an assisted-living facility. The forerunners of today's facilities did exist, but they were generally called *board and care homes* and were run by religious or fraternal organizations. The big growth of assisted-living facilities in the mid-1990s stemmed from a downturn in nursing-home placement, the desires of an aging population for a housing alternative that stressed independence, and entrepreneurial opportunities in filling this residential gap.

An AARP Public Policy Institute report found that in 2010 the United States had more than 53,000 facilities with more than 1,000,000 beds. (The terminology of *beds* probably stems from nursing home or hospital usage.) Not all facilities are fully occupied, however. Assisted-living facilities are spread unevenly across the country, with largely rural states having the lowest capacity. In the past few years, growth has slowed somewhat as some older people have been unable to sell their homes to pay for assisted living and some operators expanded too quickly and misjudged the market.

In general, larger facilities have more staff and can offer more activities. This benefit may be offset by frequent staff changes and a more impersonal management style. Your preferences about small-group living versus a large residence should be part of your decision. If you or your parent have always lived in a private house with few close neighbors, it may be difficult to adjust to large-group living, even if you have your own apartment. Or a new environment may be just what you are looking for.

Checking out healthcare services

The healthcare services offered in assisted living vary considerably. Most common is assistance with administering medications. Some states require staff with specialized training to help with this task. Some assisted-living facilities have medical staff, usually a nurse, available 24/7 on site; others have a part-time nurse or someone on call.

Compared to practice 20 years ago, assisted-living facilities are now enrolling people with more serious chronic conditions. The National Center for Health Statistics, a government agency, reported in 2010 that 82 percent of assisted-living facility residents had Alzheimer's disease or dementia, high blood pressure, heart disease, or a combination of those conditions. Some assisted-living facilities have adapted to the greater healthcare and assistance needs of these residents, while others have not.

If you have a chronic condition that requires frequent monitoring and check-ups, be sure to ask whether you can continue to see your own doctor or what alternatives will be available, especially if you are moving to a new area.

Alzheimer's disease and dementia are conditions that require specific care and are a huge factor when making a long-term plan. A 2012 MetLife Mature Market Institute survey of long-term care costs found that about half the assisted-living facilities provided Alzheimer's and dementia care, but 61 percent of them charged an additional fee. Sometimes the special units or programs within a facility are called *memory care,* perhaps to avoid the stigma of dementia. If this consideration is important in your plan, be sure to ask about the staff qualifications and training, types of programs available, and opportunities for interaction with other residents. Also ask whether behavioral interventions are used instead of psychoactive drugs, which should generally be avoided. And care for people with dementia should be more than keeping them from wandering; it should include activities designed to stimulate their minds and keep them active.

Finding more information on assisted-living facilities

Your goal is finding the right assisted-living situation, one that offers the right balance of independence and privacy with the kinds of assistance you need now and may need later. Now that you know more about assisted living, you can begin your fact-finding process.

You can get information about specific assisted-living facilities from many sources. A lot of marketing information stresses the *living* aspect of assisted living and glosses over the *assisted* part. It's hard to find out how friendly the staff is, whether management is responsive to concerns, and all the other quality-of-life questions that matter so much. You have to ask about and observe these aspects for yourself. But you can learn a lot from some basic resources, including the following:

- ✔ **Eldercare Locator:** This federal resource (`www.eldercare.gov`) is a good place to start. It directs you to your nearest Agency on Aging for assistance.

- ✔ **State websites:** State websites are important because you can generally find which assisted-living facilities have a lot of health and safety violations or don't offer what you are looking for. You can then eliminate these from consideration. Some states also have good consumer information, specific to that state, on their Office of Aging or Health and Human Services websites. Note, though, that these agencies have different names in different states.

- ✔ **Your state's long-term care ombudsman:** This individual looks into complaints about assisted-living facilities and nursing homes. Check with that office, usually located in the State's Office on Aging, to find out about any complaints about a specific facility and how they have been addressed.

- ✔ **The Commission on Accreditation of Rehabilitation Facilities:** This nonprofit organization lists continuing-care retirement communities that meet its survey standards about business practices, philosophy and physical environment, and some aspects of assisted living. You can contact it at `www.carf.org/ccrcListing.aspx`.

- ✔ **The Assisted Living Federation of America:** A membership organization of assisted-living providers, this group has a website (`www.alfa.org`) where you can search for its members in your area.

- ✔ **Internet sites:** When you search on the Internet for "assisted living," you can find ads for specific facilities as well as companies that offer to help you find a facility in your area. Sometimes these companies are endorsed by celebrities, which is not a guarantee of quality. Personal assistance from "care" or "family" advisors may be available. Facilities on these lists typically pay to be included, so not all options may be offered to you.

- ✔ **Friends or relatives:** People you know who are currently in or have lived in assisted-living facilities are a good resource for information on local facilities. Remember, though, that one person's good or bad experience may not convey the whole picture.

✔ **Doctors and other healthcare professionals:** Talk to doctors and nurses with experience in providing care to assisted-living facility residents.

Use more than one resource, because no single one is likely to have all the options. Be aware of the criteria for including the assisted-living facilities and the sponsorship of the list. And none of these resources can tell you what it's really like to live there. You should address questions about quality of life in your visits to various facilities. I suggest some specific questions in the "Beyond the Brochure" section later in this chapter.

Evaluating the Cost of Assisted Living

Now the big question! How much does assisted living cost? And no surprise, this question is not easy to answer. But it's important, because you or your family will have to pay most of the costs of assisted living. There are two big costs to consider: the entry fee and monthly costs. Here is a brief description of each:

✔ **Entry fee:** The entry fee is the upfront cost of admission. This cost varies considerably across the country and by type of apartment or unit and other factors. A starting point may be $100,000, but this fee can be much higher. Many people use the proceeds from the sale of their homes to finance the entry fee.

✔ **Monthly fee:** Monthly fees fall into a range, but on average the cost of assisted living currently is around $3,500 a month, or $42,000 a year. Genworth Financial, Inc., an insurance holding company, conducts an annual comprehensive survey of assisted-living costs. In 2013, Genworth found that the national median rate for a one-bedroom, single-occupancy facility was $41,400 a year, a five-year cost increase of 4.26 percent. A 2012 MetLife Mature Market Institute survey came up with a similar number — $42,600 a year.

The median figure, of course, includes both higher and lower rates. For example, in the Genworth survey the annual cost of assisted living in Georgia was $32,430; in Texas, $40,035; in Washington State, $51,000; and in Alaska, $72,000. (Everything is more expensive in Alaska and Hawaii.) Genworth's data for each state and within states for major regions or cities is available at www.genworth.com/corporate/about-genworth/industry-expertise/cost-of-care.html.

Assisted living is largely private pay, meaning that you have to come up with the money on your own. Some specific services are exceptions, which I talk about in Chapter 10 on Medicare and Medicaid, and long-term care insurance (Chapter 11) may cover some costs. You may be able to obtain some financial assistance. But for the most part, your own dollars will pay for assisted living. Some portion of the fees may be tax-deductible, so check with your accountant.

Choosing from the menu of cost plans

Stand-alone facilities typically have a selection of plans that are based on the type of services included. While the cheapest option may be attractive for many, the additional costs, particularly for added personal care, can become burdensome. Be realistic about what you or your parent may need. Keep in mind that additional services may be added when needed rather than being included upon entry to the facility.

If the assisted-living facility is part of a continuing-care retirement community, which provides a wide range of living arrangements on one campus, then services and costs will probably be tiered. Generally they fall into the following three categories. (A fourth model, which is essentially a rental agreement, may also be available.)

- ✔ **Type A, extensive or life-care contracts:** This service plan provides housing, residential services, and amenities, including unlimited use of healthcare services, at little or no increase in monthly fees as a resident moves from independent living to assisted living to nursing-home care. The tradeoff is usually a higher entry fee.

- ✔ **Type B, modified contracts:** Often with lower monthly fees than Type A contracts, these plans include the same basic services, but only some healthcare services are included in the monthly fee. The resident pays for additional services beyond a minimum, perhaps at a discounted rate.

- ✔ **Type C, fee-for-service or à la carte contracts:** These include the same basic services as Type A and B contracts but require residents to pay for all health-related services on an as-needed basis. These contracts may have lower entry and monthly fees for the independent living portion of the stay, but there is a risk of higher nursing-home expenses.

Check the facility's financial history

Whether the assisted-living facility is a non-profit or a for-profit organization, find out about its financial history and stability, planned improvements or needed maintenance to the physical plant, possible mergers with other organizations, or other economic factors that might affect your decision. Some assisted-living chains have gone into bankruptcy as a result of inadequate capital investment and ongoing financing. You should ask for an audited financial statement and ask your accountant or financial advisor to help you interpret the information. CARF, a private accrediting organization, has a free "Consumer Guide to Understanding Financial Performance and Reporting in Continuing Care Retirement Communities" at www.carf.org/WorkArea/DownloadAsset.aspx?id=22420.

The more you pay as an entry fee, the more likely it is that monthly charges will not increase. And of course the reverse is also true.

Which plan to choose depends partly on your current and foreseeable needs but also on your emotional and financial tolerance for risk. With Type A and Type C contracts you get the same apartment and same basic services but the difference will show up if — more likely, when — you need more assistance.

To get some idea how these options vary, Table 6-1 shows the range of fees by contract type for a selected group of continuing-care retirement communities.

Table 6-1	Range of Fees by Contract Type			
	A: Life Care	*B: Modified*	*C: Fee for Service*	*D: Rental*
Entry fee/ Security deposit	$160,000– 600,000	$80,000– 750,000	$100,000– 500,000	$1,800– 30,000
Independent living monthly fee	$2,500–5,400	$1,500– 2,500	$1,300–4,300	$900– 2,700
Assisted living monthly fee	$2,500–5,400	$1,500– 2,500	$3,700–5,800	$4,700– 6,500
Nursing care monthly fee	$2,500–5,400	$1,500– 2,500	$8,100–10,000	$8,100– 10,700

Table source: U.S. Government Accountability Office, "Older Americans: Continuing Care Retirement Communities Can Provide Benefits, but Not Without Some Risk" (June 2010).

Part of the entry fee may be reimbursed after you leave or die. This may vary by type of contract. Make sure it's spelled out in the contract.

Asking questions to create a monthly budget

After you have narrowed your search to a few likely possibilities, you should ask for more specific costs. Here are some basic questions suggested by the National Center for Assisted Living:

✔ What is included in the basic monthly cost? Ask for written information.

✔ Does the residence have a written schedule of fees for extra services? If so, request a copy.

> ✔ Under what circumstances might the fees change? How much notice is given for fee increases?
>
> ✔ Is a security deposit and/or an entrance fee required? What is the refund policy?
>
> ✔ Can service agreements and/or contracts be amended or modified?

With this information you can create a budget for monthly costs that includes

> ✔ Basic services, whatever model you choose
>
> ✔ Potential additional services, such as
>
> > • Personal laundry
> >
> > • Medication assistance
> >
> > • Recreational field trips
> >
> > • Transportation
> >
> > • Telephone
> >
> > • Cable television
> >
> > • Internet service
> >
> > • Beauty shop or barber
> >
> > • Special diets (if available)
> >
> > • Other charges

In coming up with a budget, be sure to consider what costs you will no longer be paying (snow removal, gardener, housekeeper) and what costs will simply be transferred to a new provider (telephone, cable television). Most meals will be provided (depending on the plan), but you may still want to eat at a restaurant occasionally.

Don't forget that costs are more likely to go up than down. This is especially true as more personal care and medical services become necessary.

Beyond the Brochure: What To Look For When You Visit

Of all the steps you can take in looking into assisted-living facilities, the most important is your visit. Actually, I should say your *visits,* because you should go more than once, both on planned visits and on unannounced drop-ins. An unplanned mealtime visit can give you essential information, not just about the food but also about the atmosphere in the dining room. What you see, hear, taste, and smell can tell you more about how the facility actually runs than a whole folder of brochures, lists, and websites. Above all, talk to the residents. If the management discourages this, it's a bad sign.

Ask as many questions as you can think of. But also trust your instincts. Is this a place you can see yourself (or your parent) living? Do you get a good feeling from the residents and the staff? Don't ignore small warning signs that may alert you to bigger problems. And don't be rushed into a quick decision.

The following sections walk you through what to look for when visiting an assisted-living facility, both in the common areas and in the individual residential units, as well as noting how a continuing-care concept works.

Making notes about the common areas

The staff member who takes you on a tour will be sure to point out the highlights of the furnishings, the dining room, the grounds (assuming it's not in the middle of a city), and all the available amenities. These things are important, but also take a close look around the public areas to find the answers to the following questions:

✔ Are they clean and litter-free?

✔ Are the bathrooms clean and well stocked?

✔ Do the walls look freshly painted?

✔ Is there good natural light?

✔ Is the temperature comfortable?

✔ Are there comfortable seats for residents and visitors?

✔ Are all the areas accessible for people with mobility problems?

✔ Are there elevators?

✔ Do you see residents with canes, walkers, and wheelchairs? If not, you may assume that none of the residents need this equipment, but it may be that people with disabilities stay in their rooms and don't feel welcome in the public areas.

✔ Are exits clearly marked?

✔ Can you eat when you want or are meal times set?

✔ Is there an easy give-and-take between staff and residents?

✔ Do you feel welcome as a visitor?

✔ If you or your parent is used to ethnic foods or has religious restrictions about foods, can the facility provide appropriate meals?

Checking out the residential units

You should also visit a typical apartment or unit. Make sure you see more than the model apartment, which may have special amenities that are not always part of the basic package. The residential unit is where you or your parent will spend a lot of time, so you want to be sure that it is big enough and can accommodate the personal items you will want to bring. Also find out the answers to these questions:

✔ Is there a 24-hour emergency call system that is easy to use?

✔ Is there space in the bathroom for someone to assist with bathing?

✔ Is the kitchen (if there is one) well laid out and easy to use?

✔ If there is no kitchen, is there a place to keep food?

✔ Are the telephone and television easy to operate?

 AARP has a good summary checklist of questions to ask when you visit and spaces to note the answers and your reactions. A nice feature is that the checklist allows you to enter comments about more than one visit. You can find it at `http://assets.aarp.org/external_sites/caregiving/checklists/checklist_assistedLiving.html`.

Investigating continuing care

Assisted-living facilities may be stand-alone sites or be affiliated with a hospital or nursing home or integrated healthcare system. Many assisted-living facilities are part of a continuum of care that starts with independent living and moves through assisted living to nursing-home care, called a continuing-care retirement community, or CCRC.

The CCRC promise of never having to leave to go to a separate nursing home temporarily (for a minor illness or accident) or permanently may seem like an attractive option. However, many people fail to investigate the nursing-home level of care as extensively as they do the entry level of independent or assisted living. The management may not be as eager to show you the nursing-home setting as the dining room or activity center, but ask to see it anyway. One thing to observe: Are there visitors from the assisted-living section? Sometimes people moved to the nursing home become isolated from their friends still in assisted living.

Pitfalls to Avoid

When deciding whether assisted living is the right place for you or your loved one, there are some common problems to watch out for. After you make the commitment to locate to an assisted-living facility, make note of the pitfalls in the following sections and have a plan ready.

Unnecessary trips to the ER

Assisted-living facilities are understandably concerned about responding appropriately to medical emergencies. But that doesn't mean that every fall or fever requires an ambulance trip to the emergency room, with a long wait and then a likely ambulance ride back to the facility. These episodes are stressful and frustrating. Often the problem could be monitored or treated in the facility with a doctor visit the next day.

Everyone at the facility should have a clear understanding of your preferences about going to the ER, whom to contact should you be unable to communicate, and under what circumstances you would want cardiopulmonary resuscitation (CPR) to be administered if your heart stops. You should ask your doctor about the risks and benefits of CPR for someone with your or your parent's health conditions. Your wishes should be documented. All staff should be aware of your preferences. Most states allow an out-of-hospital do not resuscitate (DNR) order, if that's what you want. Without this document in place, an ambulance attendant is required to perform CPR.

Additional costs or discharge from the facility after a hospitalization or change in condition

Sometimes a hospital stay is necessary, and sometimes a resident's condition changes. Often when older people are discharged from a hospital, they need additional time and help to recover. The hospital stay itself can lead to a temporary loss of function and cognitive problems, especially if you have been on pain medication or had anesthesia. Some assisted-living facilities insist that the resident hire a private aide to help, or even suggest that the resident can no longer stay in the apartment and must move to a nursing home. The circumstances under which this can take place should be spelled out in the contract and should allow for an independent medical assessment. This process may also be part of the state's bill of rights for residents.

According to the federal Fair Housing Act Amendments Act of 1988, which prohibits discrimination against people with disabilities, facilities should make a "reasonable accommodation" to the new needs. However, some may refuse, citing state regulatory requirements, and courts may agree. You can seek legal help from a consumer advocacy group or a private attorney. A court may require the facility to continue to provide services while the case is being decided.

Exclusion from social activities or dining room seating by other residents

One of the most difficult situations in any group-living arrangement occurs when one group of residents bands together to exclude another, perhaps because he or she is showing signs of dementia, has poor table manners because of a neurological disorder, is unable to participate fully in some activity, or for no clear reason at all. Staff have to be sensitive to these situations and try to negotiate an acceptable balance. This may never happen to you or your parent, but it would be helpful to know how staff handle these situations.

Failing to read the contract

Read the contract. Really read it, fine print and all. Ask your attorney, financial advisor, or a trusted friend or family member — or all three — to read it. This is your chance to ask any final questions and to make any final changes. Probably the most common mistake people make when signing up for assisted living is to fail to read the contract very carefully. Don't be one of them.

Consider adding your state's bill of rights for assisted-living residents to the contract. And certainly read both to make sure that nothing in the contract contradicts what is in the bill of rights.

Other Options for Group Living

Perhaps the idea of living with a group of strangers, whose backgrounds may or may not be similar to yours, does not appeal to you. You would rather spend time (and there will be lots of that) with people who share some aspect of your history or experiences.

What options are there? You have a few, but finding the right one is often a challenge. The five main choices are independent living for seniors, affinity communities, cohousing arrangements, house sharing, and group homes. In general, none of them have the same range of services as in most other assisted-living facilities, but exceptions exist. These alternative settings vary, depending a lot on the organization that started them.

Independent living for seniors

Independent living covers a wide range of options – including Naturally Occurring Retirement Communities (NORCs) and Villages (Chapter 8). Most definitions of independent living include any housing arrangement designed or adapted for people aged 55 or over. Some are low-income or subsidized senior housing, and some are high-end retirement communities, complete with golf courses and other amenities. In a continuing care retirement community, independent living is the first level. Whatever the arrangement, the emphasis is on providing a safe and barrier-free environment where basic services are provided to people who can manage with little or no assistance.

Affinity or niche communities

Affinity or *niche* communities are for people who have common backgrounds, usually because of prior employment. There are approximately 100 of these niche communities around the country. The most famous is the Motion Picture & Television Country House and Hospital in California. In existence since 1940, it has been the last residence of many film legends. The 2012 movie *Quartet* depicted a fictional version of a residence where aging musicians continued their craft and personal friendships and disputes. Like its real-world California counterpart, it faced continuing needs to raise funds.

Some affinity communities are based on more typical kinds of employment. For example, there are communities for volunteer firefighters, unionized letter carriers, university professors and administrators, and others. Costs are generally lower because they are subsidized by the founding organizations. The best way to find out if you would fit into one of these communities is to ask the union or professional organization that represents the interests of retired workers to guide you.

Affinity communities may be based on other shared interests beyond employment, such as travel, sports, or hobbies. Ask yourself: Is this connection really important to me? Do I want to spend most of my time with people who feel the same way I do, or who worked in the same industry? It may be a wonderful match, or a little too much of one thing.

Special types of affinity communities exist for lesbian, gay, and transgender individuals (LGBT), discussed in Chapter 17, and for military veterans (Chapter 18).

Cohousing arrangements

Cohousing is a community-development effort as well as housing arrangement. It may be initiated by a group of neighbors or friends. Some cohousing projects are started by housing developers. Cohousing is different from NORC discussed in Chapter 8. In NORCs, people have aged in place, and service programs can be created around their existing neighborhood. The Village concept, also discussed in Chapter 8, is similarly built around existing communities. Cohousing is a designed community.

An idea that started in Denmark, this option involves a group of friends or neighbors who live in separate houses and manage their own finances but work together to design and manage their own community. According to the Cohousing Association of the United States, cohousing has six defining characteristics: participation in the planning process, neighborhood design, common facilities, resident management, nonhierarchical structure and decision making, and no shared community economy (members are not paid for their contributions to the community). There are entry fees and monthly charges.

The potential benefits include the mutual support that members can provide and the village-like atmosphere that is part of the cohousing philosophy. Opportunities for multigenerational living are also important for some families with grandparents or other older relatives. There are, of course, downsides. Cohousing can be expensive, especially if you do not use all the common services. Privacy is limited, and the community may have more or less stringent rules, especially about selling property.

The Cohousing Association's website has a directory of communities by state. These sites are concentrated in Western states like California and Washington but there are some examples throughout the country. And if you are energetic, you can start a cohousing project yourself. To help guide you, check out www.cohousing.org/what_is_cohousing.

House sharing

On a more informal scale, sometimes friends get together and say "Let's live together and take care of each other as we get older." There are even websites for older people looking to share housing. While this idea may be appealing, it takes a good deal of organizational and management skills to make it work. It also depends a lot on each person being mentally sharp, reasonably healthy, and cooperative in nature. This may be true at the outset, but people and circumstances change. Before entering a house-sharing arrangement, have everyone agree in writing on the basic house rules such as how the common rooms will be used, when and how to pay bills, and any special considerations such as allergies, pets, and visitors. So far this idea seems to appeal mostly to women who are single or widowed, although historically men who were separated from their families because of work or illness organized themselves into similar arrangements.

Group homes

Called, variously, residential-care homes, adult family homes, adult foster care, personal-care homes, and board-and-care homes, these are houses in residential neighborhoods that can usually accommodate a small number of people. Typically the residents have a bedroom but not additional private space. The owners provide meals and some assistance with ADLs (activities of daily living). These homes are much less expensive than assisted living, but they don't provide the same range of services. In some states, Medicaid may pay for a group home for eligible people. If you're considering this option, make sure the home is licensed by the state.

Investigating this type of housing involves many of the same steps as looking at assisted living or other group setting. However, these are formerly private homes, operated by private individuals, and their reputation, credentials, and training are particularly important. As in assisted living, visits at different times of day are crucial. Some questions you may want to ask are about food preferences and special diets, whether pets are permitted, television and telephone access, and whether and when guests are permitted. See the Eldercare Locator booklet "Housing Options for Older Adults" at `www.eldercare.gov/Eldercare.NET/Public/Resources/ Brochures/docs/Housing_Options_Booklet.pdf` for a list of questions to ask about group homes.

Finally, remember that you or your parent are looking for a home, not a hotel or a temporary place to stay. Whether the ultimate choice is assisted living or some other group arrangement or to age in place, it should be a decision that is based on your needs, preferences, and resources.

Chapter 7

Under One Roof: Generations Living Together

In This Chapter
▶ Evaluating whether multigenerational living is right for you
▶ Thinking about various housing options
▶ Making the move happen

Remember the Waltons, the large fictional family from the 1970s TV show? Whatever struggles they faced in an isolated rural community in the Great Depression of the 1930s, their strong three-generation family ties saw them through. Viewers saw multigenerational living through a lens of nostalgia and loved it.

An option for families is to mimic the Waltons and consider living together as part of a long-term care arrangement. (If your family can't get through Thanksgiving dinner without hurt feelings or an argument, then this chapter may not be for you.) Multigenerational living is becoming more common, and it can work. But it takes considerable thought, planning, and negotiation. Some of the aspects you will have to consider are space, money, and personal boundaries. This chapter guides you through the key decision points.

Multigenerational Living: Everything Old Is New Again

If you were born after 1940, you probably grew up in a nuclear family: mother, father, 2.3 children. Maybe grandparents or other relatives lived nearby but not under the same roof. Although the nuclear family seemed the norm for middle-class Americans, it was actually an aberration lasting only a few decades. For most of human history, family members of all ages lived together and continue to do so in much of the world. In the United States, large social and economic changes have not only redefined family — think of blended families, same-sex marriages, children born to surrogate mothers — but have also revived multigenerational living with some modern adaptations.

Why different generations are living together

Each family is different and has its own story, but several reasons contribute to the appeal of generations living together.

Economics is probably the major driver of multigenerational living. Unemployment, loss of housing, credit card debt — all the ills of the economy have driven many families together to share resources and space.

Another reason to share a home is the changing needs of aging relatives. By simply living closer together, the strain of helping to maintain one's own home and that of a loved one is removed. The needs of older people who cannot live safely by themselves often can be addressed more easily and economically in a shared household than if they lived in a separate home. And as a benefit to the younger generations in the house, older people can contribute to the household economy and help out with some tasks, particularly child care.

On the flip side, prolonged education and poor job prospects have created the *Boomerang Generation,* young people who have not chosen to or been able to establish households of their own, are unmarried, and have returned to feather their parents' formerly empty nest. This generation includes those who have married and divorced, or who had children while unmarried, and move home with the grandchildren in tow. This way, younger people have a place to live and can help their aging parents at the same time.

Looking to other cultures for insight

As immigration from Asia and Latin America to the United States has increased, cultural traditions from these regions have encouraged families to live together just as immigrants of earlier generations from Eastern and Southern Europe did. For some families, the arrangement is a matter of economics. For others, the older generation may not speak English well and may need assistance in many areas, especially healthcare. Many want to live in multigenerational families because they value older generations' wisdom and traditions. Although living together across generations is a cultural norm for many, it is not without problems as the younger generation takes on more Americanized habits and beliefs.

Defining family households by generation

The Pew Research Center, which studies social and demographic trends, identifies several different types of households. Which one describes your family now and which one would describe it if you all lived together?

- **One generation:** A one-generation household consists of people of the same age group: a married or cohabiting couple, a single person, siblings, or roommates. These people are not necessarily young. A married couple may be in their 80s, and older siblings may live together.

- **Two generations:** A two-generation family household includes a parent or parents and their child or children under age 25. It may include stepchildren from different marriages. A two-generation household can also be made up of a person over 60 and a parent in his or her 80s or 90s.

- **Multigenerational:** A multigenerational household can include

   - *Two generations:* Parents or in-laws or adult children aged 25 or older; a person from either generation can be the head of household.

   - *Three generations:* Parents or in-laws, adult children (and spouse or children-in-law), and grandchildren.

   - *Skipped generations:* Grandparents and grandchildren whose parents are dead or unable to care for them.

   - *More than three generations:* The ages in the household can range from infancy to extreme old age.

The growth of multigenerational households

In 1940, one quarter of Americans lived in households with at least two adult generations, usually parents and grandparents, as well as minor children. By 1980, that share had declined to 12 percent — the intervening decades were the high point of the nuclear family. But in 1980, that trend started to reverse, and since then the share of all Americans living in two-generation households has increased 33 percent. According to the Pew Research Center, an estimated 51 million Americans, or 16.7 percent of the total U.S. population, lives in a household that contains at least two adult generations or a grandparent and at least one other generation. The Pew Center attributes this growth to the rising share of immigrants in the population and the rising median age of first marriage. Although this shift affects all ages, it is particularly significant for the elderly and the young. About one in five adults aged 65 or older now lives in a multigenerational household, as do one in five adults aged 25 to 34. Another measure of this change: In 1900, only 6 percent of people 65 and older lived alone, whereas 27 percent currently do. However, people are living much longer than they used to but with many chronic health conditions. Older people who live alone are less healthy and often feel more depressed than their counterparts who live with a spouse or others.

The more generations living together, the greater the opportunities for sharing knowledge and history. Many families find that they enter the arrangement for economic or caregiving reasons but remain in it because they enjoy the closeness of family interactions. But possibilities for friction and dissension also exist. The multigenerational households of older times were not necessarily happy with the arrangement or unaffected by intergenerational or interpersonal strife. Who inherited the family farm in 19th-century America could be just as contentious as current disputes over non-landed assets. Addressing early on the ways in which everyone's needs will be met and everyone's responsibilities clearly stated will go a long way toward ensuring a cooperative arrangement. In later sections I suggest specific ways to accomplish this.

Considering family reactions before making a decision

A move to intergenerational living typically involves more than two people. If you are planning to bring your parent to live with you, think of how the other people in your life — spouse, children, siblings — are affected by this decision. Having an in-law or a grandparent living in your home is not the same as having them visit. Whether you are having an aging parent move in with you or you are the older person about to move into your child's home, ask yourself the following questions:

✔ Will the other people in my life have to give up space to accommodate another person?

✔ Will children still feel free to bring friends home?

✔ Will my spouse (or your adult child's spouse) have additional responsibilities?

If you're considering bringing a parent into your home, how your siblings react is a particularly sensitive issue. A lot depends on your prior relationship and their relationship with your parent. One sister may feel relieved not to have to take on the responsibility; a brother may worry that being in your home may undermine his relationship with your parent. Money — a topic that I will discuss later in the chapter — is often a contentious issue between siblings. When dealing with siblings, consider the following questions:

✔ Who is going to be financially responsible?

✔ Will a parent's contribution to buying a home or supporting a household take money away from an expected inheritance?

✔ If the move involves the sale of the parent's home, how will the proceeds be used?

These issues are all best addressed at the outset, although they may have to be revisited as circumstances change.

If you are the older person moving in with an adult child, ask yourself

✔ What are my main concerns?

✔ Will constantly being around grandchildren and their high-energy behavior annoy me?

✔ Will I be able to accept the help that is part of the package?

✔ Am I concerned that my son or daughter has never been a good money manager and may not use my financial contribution wisely?

These issues are best discussed before you make a move.

Perhaps the most important question you need to ask yourself before going further in your fact-finding is: Is this something I want to do or something I feel I should do? If it's something you want to do, and the primary person you are concerned about also wants to do it, then you have a good beginning. If it's something you feel you *should* do, that doesn't mean it's a bad idea, just that you're starting with some worries and negative feelings that may affect the outcome. You may be making some assumptions about what it will be like that won't be borne out. Talk to others in this situation to see how they have handled the changes. A trusted family friend or counselor may be able to help you sort out your feelings and to help allay your concerns. But if this honest appraisal results in increasing your anxiety rather than relieving it, this may be the time to acknowledge that the arrangement is not going to be successful.

Where Should We All Live? Considering the Options

Sometimes the choice seems obvious: You live in a big house with plenty of room, and your parent or other relative has only a limited amount of space. Of course your mother will come to live with you. Or the reverse may be true. Your mother is the one rattling around in a big house, and you desperately need more space.

But if the move (by either of you) involves not just living in a different home but in a different part of the country, there may be difficulties leaving everything familiar and adjusting to the new location. A trial period may help determine whether this option is reasonable for the long term.

Another option may be for both of you to find a new home that has more accessible features and is in a convenient location for everyone. Some adult children and parents sell their homes and pool their money to buy a new home with room for both generations. A new home gives everyone a fresh start and minimizes some of the difficulty in adding more people to an already established household.

Some builders are responding to this market by offering homes that have separate entrances, two master bedroom suites, a den or family room that can be converted to a bedroom and bathroom on the first floor, and other flexible areas. Universal design features, such as wide doorways and few steps, are often part of the package, appealing to both the older generation and younger families with small children.

No solution is perfect, and the advantages and disadvantages for each family vary. Before you make a decision, consider all the pros and cons of each option. In the following sections I guide you through the considerations of having a parent move in with you, moving in to your parent's home, and the financial matters you'll need to arrange.

Having a relative move in with you

When the right choice seems to be having a parent or other older relative move into your home, considering how the space will work and how family roles will change is paramount to making the decision.

Organizing the space

If you are thinking about bringing a parent or other relative to live with you, making sure that the space in your home is adaptable should be a priority. Features of the home that are second nature to you — steps down to the laundry or up to the bedroom, a front door that is hard to open, kitchen cabinets that are hard to reach — may be difficult for an older person to navigate. The lighting may be fine for you but not for a person with poor vision. Following are some other aspects to consider:

- ✔ Is there enough available space for all the equipment and personal belongings that your parent may bring? Review all the things that will have to come to your house before the move and try to keep big items to a minimum. The grand piano or massive armoire may have to go, but try to accommodate prized possessions such as collections, artwork, or other valued items.

- ✔ Does the floor plan allow sufficient privacy for everyone? An open floor plan is conducive to family togetherness but also limits the space available for each individual to find a special spot to read, write, watch TV, or take a nap.

✔ Are modifications needed for safety or accessibility? This is discussed in Chapter 5, so look at those suggestions.

✔ Are pets going to accompany your parent? If so, how will you integrate them into your household, especially if you already have animals to care for? Your dog and your mother's cat may get along very well, but don't count on it.

✔ Is there sufficient space for you to have meals together, at least some of the time? Sharing mealtime is one of the benefits of multigenerational living, but given today's hectic schedules and limited space, it may be difficult to arrange. Having a dining space that is easy to use makes it more likely that meals will be shared with one or more family members, even if everyone is not available.

Remodeling your existing home to accommodate an older person may be a possibility. Some modifications can be relatively modest, such as providing an entrance with no steps or creating an open floor plan. So-called mother-in-law apartments or accessory units have been around for a long time and can be added or incorporated into the existing structure. This allows the older person to have private space, often including a kitchen, but still be part of the family. Remodeling can be expensive, however, and may not add to the home's resale value. It may also be useful for a limited time if the older person needs more help or cannot be left alone. Making minor modifications to the home for safety and accessibility may be more affordable than a larger renovation project.

One variation on this idea is a self-contained structure that is built on the premises but not connected to the main house. Informally called *granny pods,* these units come in small, medium, and large sizes (a typical size is 12 feet by 24 feet) and can be set up in a backyard. They have water, plumbing, and electricity. The selling point for many people is the incorporation of technology, which can monitor the person's vital signs, filter air contaminants, and do all sorts of other activities. The prices range from $85,000 to $125,000.

Zoning regulations and building codes may place some restrictions on both accessory dwellings and granny pods. Check with the municipal office on land use and a contractor to find out the rules and the process to apply for a variance if necessary.

For more information on making room, see "When Generations Share Space," at `www.aarp.org/relationships/grandparenting/info-03-2009/ goyer_grandparents_moving_in.html`.

Changing family roles

With all the best intentions, bringing an older family member to live with you requires some major adjustments as family roles and responsibilities change. The Family Caregiver Alliance, a nonprofit agency, offers some valuable suggestions at: `http://caregiver.org/caregiver/jsp/content_node. jsp?nodeid=849`. Here are some key points to consider.

✔ Think about how comfortable you are with becoming the head of house-hold when the household now contains the parent who has always been in charge. And how will the parent feel about ceding control?

✔ Be prepared for resistance from a parent who may no longer feel (or be) in control and may fear losing independence. Involving your parent and all other affected members of the family in decision making is a good strategy, but not everyone will express their views candidly in a family meeting. Some one-on-one conversations may be necessary.

✔ Consider how your parent can contribute to the household, apart from financially. Child care is one common opportunity (as long as the parent is able to keep up with the child). Another is preparing special meals on occasions. Some older people have special skills that can be drawn upon — perhaps minor repairs, gardening, mending clothes, or keeping scrap-books up to date. Most older people want to feel useful, and giving them an opportunity to help out is usually appreciated.

✔ Devise ways to accommodate your parent's interests, routines, and food preferences without unnecessarily disrupting your own lives. If the move involves joining a different religious congregation, make the introductions early. Find out about community activities that your parent can attend.

✔ Be especially sensitive to how your children react to having a grand-parent or older relative in their home. Many children are enormously enriched by living with a grandparent, learning family history and asking about "the old days." At the same time, they may be embarrassed in front of friends by their grandparent's old-fashioned ideas or attitudes. If the older person has symptoms of dementia, explain what is going on to the children and give them tips about how best to respond to repeated questions or other signs of memory loss.

Preparing to move into your parent's home

Instead of having your older relative move in with you, you may consider moving in with that person. You may be struggling to pay the rent for a small apartment while your parent has plenty of space. This may be a more viable option if you live near each other and you would not have to move to another community, perhaps even to another part of the country.

Most of the consideration that I discuss in the preceding sections apply to this kind of move as well, so be sure to consider how they apply in your case. Here are some additional factors to think about:

✔ Moving more than a short distance may require you to give up a job or personal relationships. Is this something you are prepared to do?

✔ Moving in with a parent involves a different psychological adjustment than is the case when your parent moves in with you. If you are moving back to the home you grew up in, the relationship with your parent may start to repeat those earlier times, even though you are now an adult.

✔ If this potential move is prompted by a parent's illness or accident, you may assume that the move is temporary, but it may be difficult to alter once you are in residence.

✔ If you will be moving with partner and or children, consider how they will adjust to the new situation and how your parent will adjust to them.

If, after considering all the implications, the move seems like the right thing to do for all or you, then you need to plan carefully considering all the features that have to be in place.

Making fair financial arrangements

Depending on your financial circumstances and personal relationships, arranging to pay for the additional costs of a multigenerational family may be easy or difficult. For most people, it's a matter of considerable sensitivity and may bring up deep-seated feelings about what is valuable, what is not, and what expenses should be assumed by one or another party. If you are the adult child, you may feel it is your responsibility to pay for everything, even if you don't have the resources to do it or you have competing demands. Your parent may feel the same way or quite differently. Many older people say that they don't want to be a burden, and they often mean that as a financial burden. And then there are your siblings, often living at a distance and watching this arrangement with both relief and suspicion.

 The advice from financial planners, social workers, attorneys, and others is consistent: Make money matters transparent and as equitable as possible. This doesn't guarantee that there won't be conflict, particularly with your siblings, but it does help to minimize it.

Here are some specific steps you can take:

✔ **Determine a set contribution.** Sit down and figure out how much your parent can or is willing to contribute toward household expenses and whether that money will be designated for a specific purpose, such as rent, food, utilities, or household help. Having at least most of the parent's contribution as a fixed sum makes the arrangement more predictable and less threatening to someone who may be accustomed to saving every penny for a rainy day. If you are moving into your parent's home, clarify what you are going to contribute financially and who is going to pay bills and monitor expenses. Be sure to put the agreement in writing. This will help avoid misunderstandings later. The agreement can always be changed.

✔ **Set aside fun money.** Make sure that the parent's contribution allows for some personal money to spend on small luxuries, clothing, or gifts for grandchildren, or any other purpose. This is not an allowance, because it is your parent's money and she has discretion to save it or spend it.

✔ **Set up bill paying.** Set up an efficient and reliable way to pay bills, whether that is online or by check. Some recurring bills, such as rent or mortgage payments, can be deducted from your account automatically. Monitor the accounts carefully. Your parent may have paid all the bills before or that may have been a spouse's job. Your role should not be to take away all financial responsibility, unless the parent is unable to do any independent financial management. You should discuss any major financial adjustments or needs.

✔ **Consider power of attorney.** If your parent agrees, you may want to obtain power of attorney (POA) for financial affairs. This can cover all financial matters or be limited to specific needs. Consult an attorney for advice. Even if your parent is fully able to manage money now, an unexpected medical event may occur in which a POA would be important.

✔ **Check on Social Security.** Make sure Social Security payments or pension payments are deposited automatically in your parent's bank account.

✔ **Watch out for scams.** Older people are often the targets of phone or Internet scammers who announce sweepstake winnings that never happened, solicit money for charities that don't exist, and offer other once-in-a-lifetime opportunities to cash in. Warn your parent about these scammers, and if one happens to slip through your warning net, alert authorities and the bank or credit card company about it.

✔ **Fill in family members on the arrangements.** Involve siblings or other relatives such as nieces and nephews in a discussion about financial arrangements. Let them know what you are paying for (in general, not necessarily in dollar amounts) and what your parent is contributing (again, in general). If they offer to contribute or to take over your responsibilities for a vacation period, make sure there are no strings attached. Also make sure they really understand what they will have to do if they take over your job, even for a week or two. If you feel that other relatives will use this time to pressure your parent for money or changes in the arrangement, then don't accept the offer.

✔ **Consider a personal-care agreement.** If you have to give up your job or cut back on hours to accommodate your parent's needs, consider consulting an attorney about setting up a personal-care agreement. This is a document that sets out the amount your parent will pay you and the hours that will count toward your salary. But understand that it's not a substitute for your regular salary, and no benefits are attached. Some courts have looked askance at agreements that pay family members their prior or even higher salary as a way to transfer assets without incurring tax penalties. The amount should be consistent with what you would pay to a paid home care worker.

✔ **Update the will.** Make sure your parent has an updated will with clear instructions about the disposition of any property or assets as well as items such as jewelry, artwork, or other pieces that may have sentimental as well as monetary value. Sometimes older people promise the same item to several different people, forgetting what they have said to another person.

✔ **Designate a healthcare proxy.** Along with a will, the older person should have an updated advance directive and healthcare proxy naming someone to make healthcare decisions in case she cannot do so herself. You can find more about healthcare proxies and advance directives in Chapter 16.

Making the Move

You've decided. Multigenerational living, with all its caveats, is a good solution to your needs. You've done all the planning, designing, remodeling, and negotiating. Now it's time for the move. Moving is one of life's major stressors, way up there with illness and divorce, so take time to organize this event.

The Family Caregiver Alliance has a helpful and exhaustive checklist for downsizing a home in preparation for a move. You can find it at www. caregiver.org/caregiver/jsp/content_node.jsp?nodeid=2633, but in the following sections I cover some key points from this checklist.

If your parent has accumulated lots of stuff over the years and is determined to keep it, you may have to deal with a hoarding problem. For advice, see the section in Chapter 5 on hoarding.

Most of the moving process is the same steps you would go through if you were moving to a new home, new town, or even overseas. If the move is a parent moving from a familiar place to the unknown, giving up all the familiar surroundings can be hard, even if the move is welcomed and appreciated. Be patient and sensitive to feelings of sadness and the memories associated with the home and its contents. If this move means you are moving in with a parent, the same advice applies. Allow yourself time to do things right for yourself and your parent.

Getting started

Start the process of decluttering well ahead of the move. Doing it in small steps — a few hours a day — makes it less upsetting and reduces the chances that important items will be discarded by mistake. Do the following to make the process go smoothly:

✔ Shred cancelled checks and other unneeded papers. Check with an accountant about what records need to be retained.

✔ Toss outdated food or medications.

✔ Take unused or expired medications to a pharmacy for instructions on safe disposal. Some pharmacies have postage-paid bags you can use to mail the drugs for proper disposal.

✔ Donate clothes or household items that will not be needed in the new home.

✔ Collect all important papers and keep them in one place. These may be deeds, wills, birth certificates, passports, discharge papers from the military, or other legal documents. These are hard to replace and may be necessary to obtain benefits or for other reasons.

✔ If siblings or others have used the home as a storage unit for their high school or college textbooks, memorabilia, and other items with meaning only to them, ask them to reclaim and remove them. They may decide that these things are not so valuable after all and add them to the discard list, or they may be thrilled to have them back again.

Planning ahead

The more you do ahead of time, the easier the transition will be down the road. Be sure to

✔ Start a notebook or computer file folder for the move. Include to-do lists, phone numbers, appointment times — anything that you may forget but will need at some point.

✔ Get estimates from moving companies. Better rates are available for non-peak times (middle of the month, for example).

✔ Make a floor plan of the new home, with accurate measurements and placement of doors and windows, so that you know exactly how much space there will be.

✔ Measure any big pieces of furniture (bed, chest of drawers, tables) and decide where they should be placed by the movers.

- ✔ Make plans for pets to be moved and accommodated in the new home.

- ✔ Refill prescriptions in advance.

- ✔ Obtain or order any medical equipment that will be needed so that it is delivered and in place when the move happens.

Sorting and packing

Use these tips to help the packing stage of the move easier and quicker:

- ✔ Go through one room at a time, starting with the easiest. Sort the items into piles: definitely save, possibly save, donate, and discard. You and your relative may have disagreements about what goes where. Try to compromise but make sure that all truly unneeded and unusable items are discarded.

- ✔ Making packing an event to bring family and friends together. Having a group together takes away some of the anxiety and also creates a positive atmosphere.

- ✔ Label everything with its destination.

- ✔ Make sure you keep all the items needed during the move in one place: keys, mediations, clothing, legal documents, checkbook, cellphone, first-aid kit, cash, and your moving notebook (which I recommend in the preceding section).

Settling in

New connections will have to be made: membership in a new congregation; a new doctor, dentist, dry cleaner, and barber or hair stylist are all important to making your parent feel comfortable. Introduce your parent to your neighbors and friends. Or, have your parent introduce you to people that they know. Take a tour of your community. Walk around the shops and point out your favorite stores for groceries.

After all the boxes have been unpacked and the furniture rearranged, take some time to get accustomed to the new arrangement. What didn't work out exactly as planned? What adjustments need to be made? Don't try to do everything at once.

Checking In over the Long Haul

Finally, check in with everyone a least once a month and perhaps more frequently to see how the new arrangement is going. What is working well? What is not? What unexpected challenges have arisen? Living with extended family means paying attention to each person's needs and feelings so that the family bonds are strengthened, not shredded.

Dealing with all the changes that can occur as a person ages and as family needs change requires frequent reappraisals. Open communication is the key to identifying problem points and taking appropriate steps before they escalate. Sometimes multigenerational families live in harmony for many years. And sometimes, with all the best intentions, this solution just doesn't work out. If that happens, it should not be considered a failure but recognition that sometimes living apart may bring families closer together than living under one roof.

Chapter 8

Beyond Your Home: Living in a Community

. . . .

In This Chapter

▶ Knowing the value of community

▶ Evaluating your community for aging in place

▶ Considering communities that are specifically for older people

. . . .

*Y*oung families starting out look often carefully at communities before buying a home or making a move. They investigate schools, recreation, shopping, parks, safety, commuting, and the ambience of a neighborhood. Although some of the elements may differ, people who are planning for long-term care should look just as carefully at communities. Sometimes, however, the importance of a community is overlooked, precisely because it may be very familiar. Living in a community at one stage of life does not prepare you for what may be needed at a later stage.

This chapter is an overview of the strengths and resources that communities may offer and helps you decide whether your community has enough or the right kind of resources for you or your parent or other relative. Finally, it describes special communities that have been developed around the needs of older people.

Understanding Why Community Matters

Community is one of those words we tend to use freely but without being clear about what it means. Community can be a town or city or a neighborhood. It can be a legal designation for zoning, garbage pickup, or voting. It can be the members of a congregation, people who are the same age, or people of any age who share some important characteristic like a disease or a commitment to a social or political cause. Community can be used in a good way, to support shared goals, or in a negative way, to exclude people or beliefs perceived to be less worthy in some way.

When considering where to live, *community* is the physical structures and services of a place and the interactions of people who live there. Both are important in thinking about what older people need. The ability for you or your loved one to live alone or with extended family may depend on the availability of community services, and the quality of life can depend on the ease with which you can interact with other people. Without community, isolation becomes an almost inevitable outcome.

Communities that encourage older people to stay active, connected, and engaged are called *age-friendly* or *livable communities.* These places have evolved naturally or have been redesigned to make getting around easier for older people and to provide essential services for them. This evolution has become necessary as communities have changed and as the population has aged.

Defining age-friendly communities

Cities around the world are facing similar challenges of aging populations, inadequate services, and deteriorating infrastructure like roads and bridges. The World Health Organization (WHO) has surveyed a number of cities to find common solutions. WHO's report on the subject (which you can view at `http://whqlibdoc.who.int/publications/2007/9789241547307_ eng.pdf`) defines age-friendly cities as those that

- ✔ Recognize the wide range of capacities and resources among older people
- ✔ Anticipate and respond flexibly to aging-related needs and preferences
- ✔ Respect the decisions and lifestyle choices of residents
- ✔ Protect people who are most vulnerable
- ✔ Promote the inclusion of people of all ages in and contribution to all areas of community life

These elements are designed to make communities work for all ages, not just older adults.

AARP has a similar definition: "A livable community has affordable, appropriate housing; adequate transportation; and supportive community features and services. Once in place, these resources enhance personal independence, allow residents to age in place, and foster residents' engagement in the community's civic, economic, and social life." (You can find out more from AARP about livable communities at `www.aarp.org/research/ppi/liv-com2/policy`.)

These broad goals can be met only by concerted community effort. State policies regarding land use, transportation, and housing may need revision. In cooperation with the National Conference of State Legislatures, AARP conducted a survey of state policies on these issues and identified which states have made progress. You can find the results at `www.aarp.org/home-garden/livable-communities/info-11-2011/Aging-In-Place.html`. In addition, AARP has an extensive evaluation guide, available at `http://assets.aarp.org/rgcenter/il/d18311_communities.pdf`, intended to be used by a coalition of community partners to identify problems and plan action. There are sections on walkability, housing, shopping, recreation and cultural activities, transportation, and healthcare services. This would be a good project for a citizens' group, but if you are looking at the community as an individual, the surveys alone can tell you a lot about what is available and what problems exist. For example, the survey on walkability asks questions about sidewalk maintenance, curb cuts, and similar issues. You can fill out the surveys of interest to you and take the result to your municipal government, which is responsible for maintenance. Just reading through the surveys will give you new insight into the many aspects of community that you may have never thought much about.

Looking at livable-community initiatives

More than 300 livable-community initiatives are underway across the United States, and more are being planned. Here are three examples:

- ✔ **New York City:** New York City and Portland, Oregon, currently are the only two cities to join the WHO Global Network of Age-Friendly Cities. Although most people would not consider New York a likely candidate for age-friendliness, many aspects of living in a big city are actually conducive to community support. Among the 59 specific initiatives in New York City are Safe Streets for Seniors, which was designed to improve pedestrian safety by lengthening the time given to cross streets and adding pedestrian "refuge islands" so that people crossing a wide street don't have to do it all at once.

- ✔ **Atlanta:** The region's Lifelong Communities Initiative has initiated several projects. One in Dekalb County aims to develop more sidewalks and a local shuttle transit system so that older people don't have to drive. In Mableton, another suburb, a farmer's market was created to operate in the mornings, rather than on crowded Saturdays or a busier time of day, making it easier for older people to take time shopping without having to deal with crowds.

✔ **Philadelphia:** Of the ten largest U.S. cities, Philadelphia has the highest proportion of people aged 60 or over, with more than half of them foreign-born or members of a minority group. The Philadelphia Corporation for Aging developed Age-Friendly Philadelphia to make sure older people's concerns are part of community planning. These efforts include working to revamp the zoning code to include public-health concerns and strengthening neighborhood centers. They are trying to establish a better mix of commercial and residential zones to help people feel more connected to their neighborhoods.

If you don't live in these or other cities with similar initiatives, you can still do your own independent evaluation of age-friendliness. The next two sections get you started.

Taking a Walk Around Your Community

Walking around your community is one of the best ways to find out what it offers and what it lacks. Take a stroll and bring a notebook and camera. Document what you find.

Making a map of your community will help you understand how roads and buildings connect — or don't. The guide from the United Hospital Fund's NORC Blueprint project (available at `www.norcblueprint.org/uploads/File/Community%20Mapping%20Guide%20revised%20050510.pdf`) shows you how to use tools like Google Map and GPS positioning to create a picture of your community's resources.

Looking at sidewalks and surrounding areas

Here's what to look for when checking on sidewalk safety and places where you can rest:

✔ Are the streets clean? Are trash bins provided at regular intervals?

✔ Are the sidewalks smooth and level?

Falls outside the home can be as dangerous as falls at home, so take particular note of sidewalks and streets that may be dangerous. Call your local agency in charge of streets and buildings to report any particularly bad spots.

✔ Are there traffic lights in frequently crossed areas? Are the lights programmed to allow for older pedestrians' slower speed of crossing?

✔ Are crosswalks well marked?

✔ Are there curb cuts (areas cut out of the edges of a sidewalk) at intersections, making it possible to move a wheelchair or walker without having to lift it up? Do both sides of each crossing have curb cuts? Are the curb cuts visible to people with low vision?

✔ In cold climates, are there regulations about snow removal from sidewalks? Who is responsible for keeping sidewalks free of ice and snow?

✔ Does the neighborhood have leash laws for dogs and requirements for removal of dog waste? Are they enforced?

✔ Are vehicle traffic rules enforced so that pedestrians do not have to dodge cars turning into a lane or speeding up to go through an intersection?

✔ If there are bicycle paths, are they clearly marked and do bicyclists and skateboarders pay attention to older people crossing the street?

✔ Is any outdoor seating provided? It could be in parks, at bus stops, on traffic islands, or any place someone may want to pause and sit before moving on.

✔ Does the neighborhood have well-maintained and safe green spaces?

✔ Are there any public restrooms? Are they wheelchair accessible? Are they clean and conveniently located?

✔ Are streets and public spaces well lit at night?

✔ Is there a visible police presence?

✔ Is the noise level high?

Checking for places to stop, shop, and chat

In the good old days, not all that long ago, you could say, "Let's walk around downtown and have lunch." Not so easy today. As shopping areas have moved from downtown to malls and shopping centers outside the center of the community, it has become more difficult to find places for people to meet naturally in the course of their daily routines. The coffee shop where everyone met for lunch or a snack has been replaced by a fast food counter, where lingering to chat is not encouraged.

So when you're evaluating the opportunities for social interaction in a community, here are some suggestions of what to look for.

✔ Are there places to eat that are easy to get into (ramps or no steps), have comfortable seating (tables that are not crowded together), and that have rest rooms on the same floor?

✔ Are there places where people can get together just to talk or take part in activities? Senior centers, libraries, YMCAs, and other public buildings can serve this purpose.

✔ What shopping options are there? Are there grocery stores, stationery stores, pharmacies, dry cleaners, shoemakers, beauty salons, barbers, and banks within walking distance?

✔ Are there a lot of liquor stores and bars in one area? If so, there may be a lot of noise at night and heavy traffic.

✔ Are there places to window shop?

✔ Are there a lot of boarded-up stores? Does the neighborhood feel abandoned or on the way up? Many downtowns are being reinvigorated, but some are still in a stage of decline.

✔ Perhaps most important, is this a place you want to come back to again and again? Do people seem to be moving as fast as they can to get away, or are they moving along at a pace that allows them to enjoy their outing?

Rating your community

Now that you have mapped, surveyed, walked, and looked at your community from a fresh perspective, what conclusions can you draw? Try this simple technique: Create a list of all the important topics you have reviewed and rate them on a scale of 1 to 10, with 1 being the best and 10 the lowest ranking. Leave a space for notes about why you came up with this rating.

Add up the ratings and see whether on average your rankings were at least above 5. Most likely your review will be a mix of good and bad points. If, however, the bad clearly outranks the good, then perhaps this community is not now and will not likely be a good place to grow old.

Even if the good outweighs the bad, the neighborhood could probably still use some improvements. Are there ways you can improve the lower rankings? For example, can you work with others to improve bus transportation for older people? Or complain to the municipal government about the lack of restrooms? Enlist others to help you; this is not a one-person responsibility or task. Considering what you liked about the higher-ranked areas may give you ideas.

Finding Community Services

In addition to what is visible within a community, an important part of an evaluation is what you can't see: the availability of services designed for older people. Some of these services are

✔ Adult day programs

- Social programs (offer meals and activities)

- Medical day programs (provide assistance with healthcare needs as well as social activities)

- ✔ Case management (coordination of medical needs)
- ✔ Group meals for seniors in a senior center, community center, or church
- ✔ Exercise and physical fitness programs
- ✔ Friendly visitor programs
- ✔ Home-delivered meals
- ✔ Hotlines
- ✔ Legal services
- ✔ Minor home repairs
- ✔ Nutrition counseling
- ✔ Telephone reassurance
- ✔ Support groups
- ✔ Transportation

Not every community has all these services, and they are particularly sparse in rural areas. You or a family member will have to investigate what is actually available and what restrictions are in place. Some publicly funded services called *home- and community-based services* are available only to people eligible for Medicaid (see Chapter 10 for a discussion of eligibility requirements). Other services are open to everyone but have waiting lists. Many services are free, but others charge.

The best place to start is your local Area Agency on Aging, which may be a city or regional office. This agency probably has information on all the publicly funded services available in your community.

Some medical facilities and home-care agencies may have a staff person who can make referrals to community-based agencies. Often this person becomes involved after a hospitalization because of the high risk of readmission if services are not in place to keep the person at home.

Beyond publicly funded services and medical referrals, many religious and charitable organizations offer services. Volunteers work with many agencies to visit older people at home, do minor repairs, shovel snow, pick up prescriptions from the pharmacy in bad weather, and just be a good neighbor. People who receive home-delivered meals often look forward to the delivery person's visit as much as they do the food itself.

Disease-specific organizations, such as the Alzheimer's Association or the Parkinson's Disease Foundation, have local programs that offer training, support groups, and other activities to people with the disease and their family members. The United Hospital Fund's Next Step in Care website has a guide to these resources as well as some helpful tips about finding out what is available. Go to www.nextstepincare.org/Links_and_Resources to find out details.

Before you call an agency, write down specific questions to ask the agency representative, and be as concrete and detailed as possible. Take advantage of the fact that you have a real person on the line to talk to you. If you find this person helpful, get his or her name and ask to speak with him or her if you need to call again.

Think broadly about community resources. A museum may offer special classes or tours for older people or people with disabilities. Colleges and universities may have performances, classes, or other opportunities to stay engaged. Community centers offer programs for all ages and may have special events for older people.

Professionals called *geriatric care managers,* who are usually social workers or nurses, may be able to advise you on what services are available and how they have worked out for other clients They charge fees, generally by the hour. The National Association of Professional Care Mangers has a referral service at `http://memberfinder.caremanager.org/`. You can also ask local agencies for referrals. Geriatric care managers are particularly useful when you not on the scene all the time, because they can keep tabs on the workers you have hired and make sure all is going smoothly.

Can you hear me now?

One of the least-addressed aspects of government and community services is the way they communicate with the people they serve, particularly older adults. The World Health Organization (WHO) guide to age-friendly cities has an age-friendly communication and information checklist. Following are some of the key points, applicable to many settings:

✔ Oral communication accessible to older people is preferred, for instance through public meetings, community centers, clubs, and broadcast media.

✔ People at risk of social isolation get information from trusted individuals with whom they may interact, such as volunteer callers and visitors, home care workers, hairdressers, or doormen.

✔ Printed information should have large lettering, and the main ideas should be shown by clear headings and boldface type.

✔ Telephone answering services should give instructions slowly and clearly and tell callers how to repeat the message at any time.

✔ Bank, post office, and other service machines should be well-lit and easy to use.

✔ Most important: Plain language is best — use familiar words in short, straightforward sentences.

Creating Special Communities for Older People

As the popularity for people wanting to age in place and in their familiar communities has increased, many communities have been taking on new characteristics. They have organized in various ways to meet the changed needs of the aging residents. These communities differ from assisted living, which is a form of group living created to provide personal care and other help. They are also not cohousing arrangements, which are newly designed developments. Unrelated people who choose to live together as they age do form their own small community, but that option is not the same as aging in place. See Chapter 6 for a discussion of these options.

The most common forms of special communities are naturally occurring retirement communities (NORCs) and Villages. They are different approaches to a common desire to age not only in one's own home but also in one's community. NORCs have a longer history than Villages, but both models are evolving.

With the information in the following sections as a starting point, you can make a more informed choice about aging in place in the community you know. If these options don't work for you, then consider one of the group-living arrangements described in Chapter 6.

Navigating NORCs

Many people who are aging in place live near others at the same stage of life. They may have bought their homes in the suburbs when they were starting out as young families, or they may have taken advantage of union- or government-supported apartment housing and never left. These communities are called *naturally occurring retirement communities,* or *NORCs.* No one planned these communities. The residents created them simply by aging in place.

Defining a NORC

The United Hospital Fund's Aging in Place Initiative describes a NORC as "a community that was not originally built for seniors, but that now has a significant proportion of older residents." Just what that proportion is varies by locality, but generally to be considered a NORC for government or philanthropic funding, a community must have at least 40 percent of its households headed by someone 60 years or older. There may be a minimum requirement of 200 people in that category.

The demographic designation is only a start. To be able to serve residents, the NORC has to offer services through a NORC program. Although the first NORC, established in 1986, was in a moderate-income housing complex in New York City, NORCs are now found in suburbs, rural areas, and small towns. Following are the two main types of NORCs:

✔ **Housing-based NORCs:** Also called a *classic, closed,* or *vertical* NORC, these are located in a single age-integrated apartment building, a housing complex with multiple buildings under common management, or an area where a number of apartment buildings are clustered together.

✔ **Neighborhood-based NORCs:** Also known as *open* or *horizontal* NORCs, these are typically one- and two-family homes in age-integrated neighborhoods.

NORC programs and what they offer

NORC programs make the difference between a demographic description and an innovative model of aging in place. NORC programs coordinate a broad range of social and medical services to support the residents in the NORC designated area. They build on the strengths of a multidisciplinary team of social-service and healthcare providers, housing managers or representatives of neighborhood associations, and community residents, especially older adults. They may be affiliated with healthcare organizations in the community. NORCs do not charge for services and are funded by a mix of government funding and charitable grants.

The social service, healthcare, and housing partners such as an apartment complex management agree to organize and develop a mix of on-site services and programs that respond to the residents' changing needs and promote community change in support of successful aging.

The NORC philosophy builds on involving residents in their own healthcare and engaging them in community resources so that they remain active and productive. Some of the on-site services that NORC programs provide include

✔ Social work and case-management services

✔ Nursing services, especially for adults managing chronic conditions

✔ Educational and recreational activities

✔ Health prevention and education activities

✔ Opportunities for community engagement

NORC services are not covered by Medicare or Medicaid, although social workers can help residents gain access to the services they are entitled to under these programs.

NORC programs exist in at least 25 states, but there is no central database of NORC programs. Check with your local Area Agency on Aging (call Eldercare Locator at 1-800-677-1116 for the number) or your state or city's Office of Aging for NORC programs in your area. And much more information can be found on the United Hospital Fund's NORC Blueprint website, `www.uhfnyc.org/initiatives/aging-in-place/norc-blueprint`.

Living in a Village

Villages are organizations that bring together the aging residents of an existing neighborhood to share resources. The residents continue to live in their own homes in their old neighborhoods but are connected by an organization that serves their needs.

Village background

The Village Movement started in 2001 in Boston's Beacon Hill neighborhood. Residents who were getting older but didn't want to move got together and decided to pool resources so that they could obtain services more cheaply. They also wanted a way to connect socially. They created an independent nonprofit organization and set membership dues that are used to leverage their buying power. They hired an executive director to respond to members' individual requests and to develop discount agreements with external preferred service providers. They called their new arrangements *Villages* to emphasize the old notion of people living in small communities helping each other and banding together to meet common needs.

There are now more than 85 Villages in the United States and more than 120 in development. Each Village is independent and develops its own services and activities. The Village to Village Network (`www.vtvnetwork.org`) shares information with the participating members, and the website has a map with the locations of existing Villages.

In 2012 Rutgers School of Social Work conducted a national overview of Villages to find out how they're organized, who the residents are, and what services are provided. Sixty-nine Villages responded. Most had been in existence for three years or less. Over three quarters had at least one paid staff member. Not surprisingly, the survey found a high level (nearly 90 percent) of older adults who were very or extremely involved. Most Villages are free-standing organizations. A few were part of a private social-service agency, a continuing-care retirement community or housing provider, or part of a care consortium.

Services provided by Villages

Volunteers play a large role in Village management by assisting with group activities or administrative tasks. Staff provide some services, such as monitoring phone requests, coordinating requests for professional services, and organizing recreation and social events. The most likely services to be referred to outside providers are home maintenance and repair, home health and personal care, housekeeping, and legal and financial assistance.

All but three of the 69 Villages in the Rutgers survey reported charging a membership fee. An average annual fee for an individual was $430.75 and for a household was $586.91. Some discounted memberships were available with income thresholds. Most of the villages are located in predominantly urban or suburban areas and serve high or middle-to-high income areas.

The typical Village has 96 members, predominately white women over the age of 65. About half of the members live alone, and a quarter need help with household chores. If needed, the Village can help with referrals to physicians and home health aides, but the primary emphasis is on the buying power of the group for non-healthcare services and the social support of the members.

Chapter 9

Getting Around: Transportation Options

*W*hen most people refer to "The Conversation," they mean talking about end of life. But there is another conversation that is equally stressful: talking about whether driving is still safe for someone getting older. Getting a driver's license is a rite of passage to adulthood, and many older adults see losing the right to drive as a return to childlike dependence. The loss isn't just symbolic. In many places transportation options are limited, although communities are beginning to respond with more age-friendly services.

This chapter approaches the touchy question of safe driving with some practical advice about warning signs and technological adaptations for cars. It outlines some alternatives to automobiles, such as various forms of public transportation, paratransit, volunteers, and paid drivers. Most of the material in this chapter assumes you are the person concerned about an older driver, not that you are concerned about yourself. But as you read, think about your own driving habits as well. Every driver can use some of these tips.

Judging Whether Driving Is Still Safe

Talking about safe driving to a parent who may have taught you the rules of the road is not easy. But it should happen, and better before an accident than after one.

Older drivers are by and large safe drivers. They are more likely to wear seatbelts than younger drivers, and they are not as prone to speeding, driving under the influence of alcohol or drugs, or risk taking. They are not as likely to text or talk on the phone while they drive. But these are only the most obvious reasons for accidents. And when older drivers are involved in accidents, they are more likely than younger drivers to suffer serious trauma and to die.

The reality is that aging changes reaction times, vision, and distance perception. Medications that older people take may affect their driving ability. The label on the pill bottle may warn, "Do not operate heavy machinery while taking this drug," but some people do not realize a car is the ultimate heavy machinery.

Many older drivers adjust their own driving habits to take account of these changes. They drive less at night, don't go as far from home, and drive more slowly (too slowly, other drivers may complain). Even with these adjustments, older drivers may be at risk not just from their own driving but also from other drivers who create situations that require quick thinking and rapid responses. Think of how many near misses you have experienced or witnessed as drivers zip through stop signs or make left-hand turns without checking for oncoming traffic.

Watching for warning signs for older drivers

The Hartford Center for Mature Market Excellence created a checklist of 29 warning signs for older drivers. You can use the items on the checklist to observe your parent's driving over time and monitor it for a pattern of warning signs and an increase in frequency. The full list is available at `http://hartfordauto.thehartford.com/UI/Downloads/FamConHtd.pdf`.

Here are what I consider to be the top ten warning signs that someone shouldn't be driving anymore, culled from the 29 signs:

- Difficulty turning to see when backing up
- Riding the brake
- Signaling incorrectly
- Parking inappropriately
- Hitting curbs
- Failing to notice traffic signs
- Having trouble navigating turns

> ✔ Moving into the wrong lane
>
> ✔ Getting confused at exits
>
> ✔ Confusing the gas and brake pedals

The last item on my list — confusing the gas and brake pedals — is frequently cited as the cause of serious accidents involving older drivers, often resulting in injury to pedestrians and property damage.

If you see any of these signs (or even if you don't so far), a conversation about safe driving makes sense. The next section helps you open that touchy subject.

Starting the conversation and evaluating needs

No one wants to get involved with police officers. Getting pulled over for traffic violations or for being involved in an accident can feel shameful, and this kind of incident is in fact what the conversation on driving safety is intended to prevent.

This talk is best done in a nonjudgmental and nonthreatening way. A trusted person, whether it's a family member or someone else, can initiate this conversation. A spouse or adult child may be a good choice (or not, depending on the relationship). Other than family, older drivers seem to respond best to doctors. The strength of the trust between the two people is what counts.

Here are some ways to open the conversation:

> "With so many bad drivers on the road, I worry about your safety. Can we talk about what you can do to stay safe?"
>
> "I know you are on some new medications. Have you talked to the doctor about whether they affect driving?"
>
> "Do you think you might need new glasses? I noticed that you almost missed the exit sign."
>
> "Are you getting enough sleep? You seem to be easily distracted on the road."

Of course, your very clever parent may see through even this fairly gentle approach and react defensively. Unless the situation is really an accident waiting to happen, use the opportunity to talk about adapting the car, which can be a less emotional topic. I come back to the question of what to do when an older person absolutely refuses to make any adjustments later in the chapter.

If your parent is open to concerns about his or her abilities in the driver's seat, you may be able to set up a driving evaluation. A comprehensive driving evaluation can be arranged through a local occupational therapy driving rehabilitation specialist. Occupational therapists are able to identify the physical, visual, and cognitive challenges the individual faces and can recommend ways to limit risks. Visit the American Occupational Therapy Association web page to find a specialist in your area: www.aota.org. A comprehensive driving evaluation can also be arranged through your state's department of motor vehicles. However, many older drivers are wary of going to the DMV because it has the power to revoke a license.

An option may be a driver safety course, such as the one offered through AARP Driver Safety, offered in classrooms and online at www.aarp.org/drive. Taking the course with a friend (or you) may reduce resistance; present it as an educational experience, not a punishment.

For more advice on how to assess your loved one's driving and for tips on how to discuss the topic with loved ones, AARP Driver Safety offers a free seminar called "We Need to Talk," developed based on information created jointly by The Hartford and MIT AgeLab. The seminar is available in both English and Spanish and can be viewed online at www.aarp.org/weneedtotalk.

Adapting a Car for Older Drivers

You can't make an aging body young again, but you can fix a car to accommodate physical and cognitive changes created by aging. The car your parent or other relative drives may benefit from a checkup. The mirrors may not be adjusted properly, obstructing rear and side vision. Reaching the gas and brake pedals may be difficult, and operating them may cause muscle strain and reduce reaction time. The driver's seat may be too close to the wheel.

CarFit, an educational program developed by the American Automobile Association, AARP, and the American Occupational Therapy Association, can help educate drivers to become safe and comfortable in their cars. CarFit organizes community events at which technicians and volunteers discuss safe settings to make the car fit the driver. The service takes approximately 20 minutes. Go to www.car-fit.org/carfit/EventMap for a map of events around the country.

Take the opportunity to have your own car checked out. It may reveal some problems you were not aware of and may also make the experience more acceptable to your parent.

Some adjustments, such as pedal extensions or other adaptive equipment, may require technical assistance. The American Occupational Therapy Association has a directory of driving rehabilitation specialists at `http://myaota.aota.org/driver_search`. Also see the website of the Association for Driver Rehabilitation Specialists, `www.driver-ed.org`, for professionals in your area who can also diagnose driving problems and help the driver learn safer practices.

Increasing safety with new technology

Technology can help make a car (and its driver and occupants) safer. Seatbelts, air bags, and anti-lock brakes are common now, as are GPS systems that give directions and alerts about approaching exits and turns. But there's more.

The Hartford and the MIT AgeLab, which has been a leader in driver safety for older people, convened a group of experts to review the past decade of research and innovations in driver safety. Following are the top ten technologies they recommend:

✓ **Smart headlights:** Adjust the range and intensity of light based on how far away the traffic is and reduce glare

✓ **Emergency-response system:** Offers quick assistance in case of a medical emergency or collision

✓ **Reverse monitoring system:** Warns drivers of objects to the rear of the vehicle to help drivers judge distances and back up safely

✓ **Blind-spot warning system:** Alerts you to oncoming traffic by a flashing light in your side view mirror and a beep or steering wheel vibration

✓ **Lane-departure warning:** Helps drivers avoid wandering into another lane

✓ **Vehicle-stability control system:** Helps keep the car in the intended line of travel, especially when the driver underestimates the angle of a curve or encounters severe weather

✓ **Assistive parking system:** Enables vehicles to park on their own or indicates distances to objects, making parking easier and reducing stress

✓ **Voice-activated system:** Allows drivers to access features by voice command so that they can keep their eyes focused on the road

✔ **Crash-mitigation system:** Detects when the car may be in danger of a collision

✔ **Drowsy driver alerts:** Monitor the degree to which a driver may be inattentive and alert them to pay attention

Some of these devices may be standard in a new car (probably an expensive model) or could be installed by a car dealer. Generally, each manufacturer prices these technologies as part of an equipment package. For example, smart headlights might be part of an "all-weather" package because of their capacity to compensate for poor weather conditions as well as bends in the road. Such a package can range from $500 to $2,000 or more.

The more advanced systems are usually available first on the more expensive cars such as Lincoln and Lexus. Manufacturers are unlikely to market these devices as appropriate for older adults because they want to appeal to a younger, hipper market. Consumers have to know about them and ask for them to be included. If your parent objects that these adjustments are for "old people," point out that they are future-oriented and sophisticated, not stodgy at all.

Systems such as OnStar for General Motors vehicles are helpful in emergencies; they call for help, giving your location. Other systems are available for different manufacturers. They are paid for on a subscription bases.

It is also essential to make sure that regular maintenance on the car is performed. If you don't think it's being done, work with your parent to set up a schedule with a mechanic you trust to go over the car at regular intervals, even if it's not being driven a lot.

A car that drives itself

What would Karl Benz, the inventor of the original *Motorwagen,* or Henry Ford, whose assembly line for his Model T changed American life, think about a car that doesn't even need a driver? Such a car is only a few years away, according to Google cofounder Sergey Brin. This futuristic design builds on the types of sensors and adaptive technology already available. Proponents say that huge numbers of people who are older or have disabilities will regain their mobility and independence. Young people will not have to pay such high rates of insurance. Accidents will decrease. These driverless cars should also save fuel and ease congestion. Because they can sense when cars ahead of them are braking, as humans are unable to do, they can drive much closer to each other. But will people be able to overcome their ingrained fear of riding in a vehicle that doesn't have a human at its controls? Time will tell, but remember that when the first automobiles were introduced, the common cry was, "Get a horse!"

Making adaptations for disabilities

If you or your parent has a disability that makes driving an ordinary car difficult or impossible, you need a specially adapted vehicle. It may be a station wagon with a wheelchair lift, a car with special steering or braking equipment, or any number of other adaptations. The National Highway Traffic Safety Administration (NHTSA) has guidelines on adapting motor vehicles for older adults and alternative guidelines for people with disabilities, which you can find at www.nhtsa.gov/search?q=adapting+motor+vehicles&x=0&y=0.

A driver-rehabilitation specialist and a mobility-equipment dealer can help design the best features for you. The National Mobility Equipment Dealers Association can refer you to a dealer in your area at www.nmeda.org. A new vehicle modified with adaptive equipment can cost anywhere from $20,000 to $80,000.

Financial assistance may be available from your state government, nonprofit organizations, and some motor vehicle manufacturers. Some states waive the sales tax if you have a doctor's prescription, and the cost may be tax-deductible.

In considering a new vehicle or adaptations to the one you or your parent already own, the NHTSA suggests that you consider the following issues:

- ✔ Does the vehicle have the cargo capacity (in pounds) to accommodate the equipment you require?
- ✔ Is there adequate parking space at home for loading and unloading the vehicle?
- ✔ Is there adequate parking space to maneuver if the driver uses a walker?
- ✔ What additional options would be necessary to operate the vehicle safely?

When looking for a new vehicle, the NHSTA recommends looking for features that take into account the physical and visual challenge of aging:

- ✔ High or extra-wide doors
- ✔ Adjustable foot pedals
- ✔ Large interior door handles
- ✔ Oversized knobs with clearly visible labels
- ✔ Support handles to assist with entry and exit
- ✔ Large or adjustable-size print for dashboard gauges

✔ Seat adjusters that can move the seat in all directions; the driver's line of sight should be 3 inches above the adjusted steering wheel

✔ Dashboard-mounted ignition rather than steering column-mounted ignition

If a third party — an insurance company, state agency, nonprofit organization, or VA — is paying for a new vehicle, adaptive devices, or other modifications, find out if there are any limitations on what may be covered. Get a written statement on what a funding agency will pay before you or your parent agree to buy or make the changes.

A driver's license may need to be modified to note any restrictions. And the insurance company should be notified of the adjustments.

Knowing When It's Time to Give Up the Keys

When all the gentle conversations and vehicle adaptations have failed to make your parent a safe driver, then you need to take action. It is time to take away the keys and maybe even the car.

Don't react based on a single conversation or a single incident (unless your parent caused a major accident). If you have driven with your parent and noted safety lapses, mention them. Keep the emphasis on protecting others. Concern for others may be a stronger motivation than concern for oneself. Older people typically don't want to be a burden on their families, but they may not realize that an accident would create a major financial and possibly legal burden.

You may be able to enlist the support of a doctor to limit or forgo driving altogether, particularly if your parent has some medical or cognitive condition, such as Parkinson's or Alzheimer's disease, that affects driving. Your relative may be more willing to accept intervention if you identify the disease as the problem, rather than the driver's skill. A person with dementia may get lost even in familiar places, in addition to the lapses in judgment that are often symptoms of this condition. Presenting a united front with a doctor improves your chances of success.

If all else fails, you may have to consider disabling the car, failing to renew the driver's license or having it revoked, canceling the insurance, or taking away the keys. Even these measures may not be enough, as some very determined older people will find ways around them, such as calling a mechanic to fix the car or driving without a license or insurance. Taking the car away is a final step, but even then, a person may borrow a car from a neighbor or friend. Of course, if there is more than one driver in the household, none of these options may be feasible. Vigilance to prevent driving may be the only answer.

In your conversations, be sure to acknowledge how difficult this transition is. Being able to suggest alternatives to driving may help — perhaps not immediately, but in the long run — to change a decades-old driver into a more or less willing passenger. See the next sections for solutions on moving from driver to passenger.

Finding Alternatives to Driving

Housing and transportation are two basic needs of older adults, and they are often connected. Many older adults live in neighborhoods that are not near public transportation, particularly in rural areas. Housing in areas close to public transportation may be unaffordable for older people on fixed incomes. It's not surprising that so many older people don't want to give up their driving, which often results in the loss of independence. Depending on where you or your parent lives, there may be a few or many alternatives for getting around.

The National Center on Senior Transportation (`www.seniortransportation.net`) groups transportation options into four categories in addition to bicycles and walking:

- ✔ Public transit (buses, light rail transit, trains/subways)
- ✔ Paratransit (reservations-required vans or cars for people who cannot drive or who have disabilities)
- ✔ Private transit (taxis, car services)
- ✔ Specialized transit (programs organized by hospitals, senior centers, religious or volunteer organizations to serve particular populations)

The next two sections discuss the public and private options available to older people.

Public transportation options

Most public transportation routes are designed for getting to and from work at times workers are most likely to use the services, not where or when older people may want to go. And public options may not be well set up for people with limited mobility. Even in New York City, in the extensive subway system, not all stations are equipped with elevators, so a person who has difficulty with stairs may be able to get down to the tracks to get on a subway train but find that there is no elevator service at the destination station. Buses are now more likely to have lifts or ramps for wheelchairs or walkers and specially designated seats for passengers who are older or have a disability. Still, this adaptation is not universal. And buses have designated routes and stops, which may or may not be convenient.

The Americans with Disabilities Act (ADA) requires transportation agencies that provide fixed-route services (bus or train) to also provide paratransit services to people with disabilities who live within three-quarters of a mile from the fixed routes. These restrictions mean that not all older people will qualify for public paratransit services. Other differences include:

- **Destination:** Some services only link to specific services, such as going to the doctor or shopping; others are more flexible and go where the passenger wants to go within the service range.

- **Assistance:** The limitations that make it difficult for older people to drive may also limit their ability to use public transportation or paratransit. Some services provide mechanical assistance (buses that have wheelchair lifts or ramps and special seating; paratransit drivers who assist passengers getting on and off).

- **Information:** Even if the service is available, if you have difficulty finding out the routes and how to make arrangements to use it, the benefits can be lost.

- **Socialization:** While bus and van drivers should focus on the road, the way they greet passengers and help them on and off makes a difference. On a familiar route, passengers should feel free to chat, share their experiences, comment on the journey, and generally make the trip enjoyable. Some may prefer not to join in, and that should be respected as well.

The Beverly Foundation, no longer in operation, created a list of five characteristics of senior-friendly transportation:

- **Availability:** Service available when needed during days, evenings, and weekends

- **Acceptability:** Clean, safe, and courteous

- **Accessibility:** Van comes to the door, bus stop is close by, vehicle is easy to enter

- **Adaptability:** Adjustments for special needs such as wheelchairs or walkers

- **Affordability:** Fees are low enough for people on restricted budgets, options for discounts

You can use these standards to evaluate the options available to your parent. Check with the local government office that runs the public transportation system to obtain a map of the system, which may or may not have up-to-date information on accessibility features. You can annotate the map with information on, for example, which subway stops have elevators and which bus routes go to shopping areas.

 Area Agencies on Aging and Aging and Disability Resource Centers may offer fare assistance programs for eligible riders who can purchase vouchers at a discounted rate. The vouchers can be used to pay for services from participating transportation providers, including public transportation, taxi companies, or others.

Private options

Where public transportation is not available or appropriate, some private services can fill the gap. Following are some of the more popular options:

- ✔ **Supplemental transportation programs (STPs):** STPs are nontraditional transportation services for older adults who don't drive and others who need assistance. Most STPs provide door-to-door rides, and some arrange for a driver to stay with passengers until they are ready to go home. Some STPs are organized by religious institutions or other community groups. The Beverly Foundation has a map of STPs in America at `http://beverlyfoundation.org/map-of-stps-in-america`.

- ✔ **Volunteer programs:** Programs organized by faith-based organizations or private agencies often have a network of volunteers who provide transportation for shopping, doctor's appointments, and recreation. They may offer one-way, round-trip, or multistop rides, usually at no cost or on a donation basis.

- ✔ **Taxis:** Taxicabs are common alternatives to driving. Some cities restrict licensed cabs to picking up passengers on the street; others have some way to call from home or the doctor's office. Some taxi companies have wheelchair-accessible vehicles. Older people may balk at the expense, but you can point out that maintaining a car is much more expensive than an occasional taxi ride.

- ✔ **Car services:** This option is like a more upscale taxi. The cars are generally more comfortable, although more expensive than taxis. Some are wheelchair-accessible. If you set up an account with a credit card, you or your parent can be billed at the end of the month, which gives you a record of expenses. The newest variety of car service, available only in some cities, is a service that is accessed using a phone app. The app identifies your location and sends the nearest driver to pick you up.

✔ **Hiring a driver:** Some people may have the option of hiring their own driver when needed (as in the movie *Driving Miss Daisy*). It need not be a full-time position. If you hire a driver, make sure the person's driver's license and insurance are valid and up-to-date.

✔ **Family and friends:** Probably most older people get rides from family, friends, and neighbors. One person may offer to take the older person shopping or to religious services. Another may volunteer to go to the doctor and wait until the visit is finished. These are the traditional ways people who don't drive have been helped over the years, and they still work. However, you need to be aware of whether these volunteer drivers are themselves of an age or condition in which their driving capacity may be at risk.

✔ **Transportation provided by independent or assisted-living or other residence- or community-based organizations:** These options have become increasingly important and desirable for older individuals and are often used to get to and from doctors' offices, entertainment sites such as movie theaters, and so on.

The Hartford's "Getting There" Worksheet is a systematic way of reviewing local options. It includes sections on family and friends, local programs that may offer rides, demand-responsive services or paratransit, private program services, taxis and car services, and mass transit. It provides a separate worksheet to determine costs. Measured against the cost of owning and operating a car, these costs may actually be much less. You can find the worksheets at `http://hartfordauto.thehartford.com/UI/Downloads/FamConHtd.pdf`.

For example, the section on family and friends, the top alternative to driving for older adults, asks these questions:

✔ Are people available to provide rides at the times required?

✔ To what extent are family or friends able or willing to provide rides?

✔ Do people provide the rides willingly or do they resent having to adjust their schedule?

✔ Can the older person trade something for a ride (making dinner, taking the driver to lunch, paying for gas)?

You and your parent can answer these questions yourself. But to get the information for the public or other private options, you have to do some research. To find out what is available in your community, check with the local Area Agency on Aging, the state Aging and Disability Resource Center, senior centers, healthcare providers, and others who may know about options. Giving up the keys should lead to new ways of getting around, not the end of living fully in the community.

Part III

Legal and Financial Planning for Long-Term Care

A Quick Guide to the Parts of Medicare

✓ **Part A:** Medicare Part A covers inpatient care in a hospital, rehabilitation services in a skilled nursing facility or rehabilitation hospital, hospice care, home healthcare (under certain conditions), and inpatient care in a religious nonmedical healthcare institution.

✓ **Part B:** Medicare Part B is an optional component that helps cover medically necessary services like doctor's visits, outpatient care, durable medical equipment, and many preventive services like flu shots. You have to pay a monthly premium to be enrolled in these Medicare services. But Part B is heavily subsidized, so unless you have very good private insurance, it almost always makes sense to choose this option.

✓ **Part C:** Medicare Part C offers an alternative to original Medicare called the *Medicare Advantage program,* a collection of health plans (such as Health Maintenance Organizations and Preferred Provider Organizations) that combine Parts A and B services (usually with Part D prescription drug coverage) in their benefit packages. The plans are offered by private companies with Medicare approval. They must cover all the services in original Medicare but may also offer extra coverage, such as vision, dental, hearing, and health and wellness programs.

✓ **Part D:** Medicare Part D covers prescription drugs. You pay a monthly premium, which changes every year. If you receive Social Security benefits, your Medicare premium is deducted from the check.

In the digital age, when you draw up a will, you have to think not just about tangible property but also virtual information and assets. This free article located at www.dummies.com/extras/planninglongtermcare gives some tips on this developing area.

In this part...

☛ Take a look at the differences in what Medicare and Medicaid cover in terms of medical and nonmedical care. Also consider whether you may be eligible for both programs or have private healthcare and long-term care insurance that can play a part.

☛ Look at the pros and cons of long-term care insurance in today's market. I also review reverse mortgages, disability insurance, annuities, and life settlements.

☛ Keep control of your finances by drawing up a will and perhaps a trust.

Chapter 10

Unraveling the Rules of Medicare and Medicaid

. . . .

In This Chapter

▶ Complementing a long-term care plan with Medicare benefits

▶ Examining Medicaid eligibility and long-term care services and supports

▶ Understanding options if you're eligible for both programs

. . . .

"**M**edicare does not cover long-term care!" Maybe you've come across this warning dozens of times, or maybe this is the first time you've read it. What most people mean by this warning is that Medicare doesn't cover a long stay in a nursing home (although it does cover a short stay for rehabilitation therapy) and does not provide 24-hour personal care at home or in an assisted-living facility. Although Medicare's limitations are real enough, Medicare does cover many of the healthcare services you or your parent or other relative need to live safely at home and in the community.

Medicaid, a federal-state program for low-income individuals, does cover long-term care in nursing homes and many home- and community-based services, but its eligibility and other rules vary by state and set stringent limits on income and assets. Some people — policymakers call them by the awkward term *duals* — are eligible for both Medicare and Medicaid and can coordinate benefits from both programs.

Understanding the framework of these public programs is the first step to figuring out how these programs may or may not apply to you or your parent and how they may relate to other kinds of healthcare or long-term care insurance. Dive into this chapter to discover how these programs work.

As you start to navigate public healthcare programs, keep in mind that your State Health Insurance Assistance Program (SHIP) is a valuable resource. The SHIP advisors can guide you through the maze of Medicare, Medicaid, and other insurance plans. You may find that you are eligible for more than you realized. Find your state SHIP at www.medicare.gov/contacts/organization-search-criteria.aspx.

The Distinction between Medicare and Medicaid

Sometimes long-term care is described as separate from medical care or is seen only as nursing home or personal care at home. My definition of long-term care begins with what an individual needs, not who pays or who provides the service. From that perspective, an individual needs both medical care and nonmedical services. Medicare pays for the medical care needed by someone who has a chronic condition or a disability but does not pay for the nonmedical services that person needs. Medicaid, however, pays for both for eligible people.

Here is an essential but still often misunderstood distinction between Medicare and Medicaid:

- **Medicare:** A federal health insurance program for people aged 65 and older and younger people with certain conditions and disabilities. Over 50 million Americans are enrolled in Medicare.

- **Medicaid:** A federal-state program that pays for healthcare and long-term care for low-income people. Over 70 million Americans, including more than one in three children, receive healthcare through Medicaid over the course of a year, and over 55 million are enrolled at any point in time.

For more comprehensive information on Medicare, see AARP's *Medicare For Dummies* by Patricia Barry (published by Wiley).

Taking a Look at Medicare Basics

Medicare is the main source of payment for medical care for retired or not-employed older adults. If you or your parent live in your own home, assisted living, a multigenerational home, or some other non-nursing-home setting, you need access to medical care for primary care, preventive care, management of chronic conditions, hospital care, post-hospital rehabilitation services and home healthcare, and emergencies, as well as prescription drugs and, for some conditions, durable medical equipment. Medicare generally pays for this necessary medical care.

In addition to Medicare eligibility parameters, the following sections also cover Medicare's two options: original Medicare and Medicare Advantage plans. I also discuss Medicare's role in providing necessary medical care services.

The Affordable Care Act (ACA, also commonly called Obamacare) does not affect Medicare eligibility. If you or your parent are enrolled in Medicare, you don't have to do anything. The ACA did make a few changes to Medicare: Some preventive measures such as mammograms and colonoscopies are now free, and a timetable has been set for closing the so-called doughnut hole in Part D for prescription drugs (discussed in the later section "Prescription drug coverage").

Are you eligible for Medicare?

If you or your parent is 65 or older, you are probably already enrolled in Medicare. Enrollment is automatic when you start collecting some form of Social Security benefits. If you are 65 or older and not yet collecting Social Security benefits, you have to enroll online, over the phone, or in person through the Social Security Administration.

However, not everyone over 65 is automatically eligible for Medicare. You have to be a U.S. citizen or a legal resident of the United States for over five years. Residents of Puerto Rico are eligible. If you (or a spouse) have worked at least a total of ten years (40 credits) and contributed to Social Security under the Federal Insurance Contributions Act (FICA) through your employers, you are eligible.

Earning 40 work credits only means that you don't have to pay monthly premiums for Part A services. Anybody who is a citizen or legal resident for at least five years can get Part B and Part D services by paying premiums for them like everybody else.

The U.S. Supreme Court ruling in June 2013 that struck down Section 3 of the Defense of Marriage Act has implications for Medicare eligibility. The Act had defined a *spouse* as a "person of the opposite sex," so the Court's decision opens Medicare eligibility and benefits to same-sex couples. The Department of Health and Human Services has begun to issue specific policy changes, including same-sex married couples' rights under Medicare Advantage plans to reside in the same nursing home, regardless of whether that state recognizes same-sex marriages. For more information, see Chapter 17 on LGBT issues in this book and the National Resource Center on LGBT Aging at www.lgbtagingcenter.org/resources/pdfs/Post-DOMA_Medicare.pdf.

If you are uncertain whether you or your parent qualifies for Medicare, contact Social Security at 800-772-1213 or go to www.medicare.gov/MedicareEligiblity. The Medicare Rights Center has a useful fact sheet, "Medicare Q and A" on eligibility and the timing of enrollment at www.medicarerights.org/PartB-Enrollment-Toolkit/Part-1-QA-General.pdf.

What's included in original Medicare

Original Medicare includes Parts A, B, and D benefits. (Part C applies only to Medicare Advantage and is just another way of packaging Parts A, B, and D benefits.)

Additional Medicare eligibility

Medicare also covers younger people with end-stage kidney disease or amyotrophic lateral sclerosis (ALS), as well as people with other disabilities who have received Social Security Disability Insurance (SSDI) benefits for a total of 24 months from the Social Security Administration or the U.S. Railroad Retirement Board. The months you wait for your application to be approved are counted in meeting this 24-month requirement. If you or your spouse's work history does not reach the required threshold but you meet the citizenship or residency requirements, you can still enroll in Medicare Part A (hospital coverage) and pay a monthly premium, as well as in optional Part B (outpatient coverage), for which everyone pays a monthly premium. It is a good idea to do this because if you enroll later, you risk paying permanent late penalties. But if you are covered by a group health-insurance plan provided by an employer for whom you or your spouse still works, you can delay enrolling in Part B without a penalty until your employment ends.

✔ **Part A:** Medicare Part A covers inpatient care in a hospital, rehabilitation services in a skilled nursing facility or rehabilitation hospital, hospice care, home healthcare (under certain conditions), and inpatient care in a religious nonmedical healthcare institution (a place for Christian Scientists who need assistance but have religious objections to conventional medicine). Medicare Part A does not require additional premiums for eligible beneficiaries; if you do not have enough working quarters to qualify, you can enroll and pay a monthly premium. There is a deductible (amount you have to pay before Medicare starts paying) if you are hospitalized; in 2014 this is set at $1,216 for each benefit period of 60 days.

Hospital stays these days are generally very short, and patients who require further care are frequently transferred to a rehabilitation program in a skilled nursing facility. If this happens to you or your parent, it does not mean that you have been placed permanently in a nursing home. Although the Medicare benefit period ends at 100 days, you may be discharged much earlier, perhaps within two to three weeks. You don't have to pay any fees for the first 20 days of each benefit period. For days 21 through 100, you pay a coinsurance amount per day of $152, and if you stay past day 100, you pay all costs for each day, unless you have additional insurance that covers these costs.

To be eligible for Medicare coverage of a rehabilitation program in a skilled nursing facility, you must have been hospitalized as an inpatient for three days prior to the transfer. Some hospitals have been classifying patients as being in *observation status,* that is, not formally admitted to the hospital, even though they may be in a bed on a hospital unit getting the same treatment as an officially admitted patient. This has financial implications; their stay is not covered under Medicare Part A, which has a one-time deductible for the stay, but under Part B, which bills for every service separately as if the hospital were an outpatient setting. Moreover, days spent in observation do not count as inpatient days toward the three-day nursing facility requirement, so the patient is responsible for the entire cost of the rehab stay. This policy is being contested and may change, but for now it is worth asking at every hospital stay whether the patient is admitted or under observation.

✔ **Part B:** Medicare Part B is an optional component that helps cover medically necessary services like doctor's visits, outpatient care, durable medical equipment, and many preventive services like flu shots. You have to pay a monthly premium to be enrolled to obtain coverage for these Medicare services. But Part B is heavily subsidized, so unless you have very good private insurance, it almost always makes sense to choose this option.

✔ **Part D:** Medicare Part D, which covers prescription drugs, is also optional but strongly advised. You pay a monthly premium, which changes every year. If you receive Social Security benefits, your Medicare premium for both Parts B and D are deducted from the check.

Medicare doesn't pay for everything. Even if it does cover a service, you generally have to pay the following fees:

✔ A deductible (a certain amount of actual medical costs you incur before insurance starts to pay)

✔ Coinsurance (your share of these costs after the deductible has been reached, typically 20 percent)

✔ Copayments (the fixed amount you pay, for example, at a doctor visit)

Many people purchase Medicare Supplemental Insurance (Medigap) to help pay for these additional expenses. These policies are offered by private insurance companies and have to meet federal and state requirements. Medicare has information on how to find Medigap policies in your state at www.medicare.gov/supplement-other-insurance/medigap/whats-medigap.html. You can also compare Medigap policies at www.medicare.gov/supplement-other-insurance/compare-medigap/compare-medigap.html.

Current Medigap policies don't include prescription drug coverage, but if you have a policy purchased before 2006, it may still cover drugs. If you or your parent has an old policy labeled H, I, or J, you can still use it, but it's drug coverage part is not nearly as good as Medicare Part D. These policies have become more expensive as fewer and fewer people use them. On the other hand, if you switch to Part D now, you have to pay late penalties in addition to the plan's premiums.

What you get with Medicare Advantage plans

Medicare Part C offers an alternative to original Medicare called the *Medicare Advantage program,* a collection of health plans (such as Health Maintenance Organizations and Preferred Provider Organizations) that combine Parts A and B services (usually with Part D prescription drug coverage) in their benefit packages. The plans are offered by private companies with Medicare approval. They must cover all the services in original Medicare but may also offer extra coverage, such as vision, dental, hearing, and health and wellness programs. Medicare Advantage plans set their own fee schedules, and this is important information when you are choosing a plan.

In original Medicare — a fee-for-service arrangement — you go to a doctor who participates in the program and pay a copay, and the doctor bills Medicare for the visit and any tests or procedures that were performed. Medicare Advantage plans receive a set amount every month for each person enrolled in the plan, whether they use many services or just a few. The plan can charge different copays and have different rules about whether you need a referral to see a specialist, for example, or whether you can only go to doctors or hospitals that belong to the plan. There are several different kinds of Medicare Advantage plans, and their rules, costs, and benefits differ and can change each year. You can change plans once every year and at other times in certain circumstances.

If you enroll in a Medicare Advantage plan, you can't buy a Medigap policy. This kind of insurance can be used only with original Medicare and can't be used for any expenses under a Medicare Advantage plan. However, if you drop your Medigap policy to join a Medicare Advantage plan and then decide to go back to original Medicare, you may not be able to get the Medigap policy reinstated.

For more information about Medicare Advantage pans, go to the Medicare plan Finder at www.medicare.gov/find-a-plan.

Prescription drug coverage

Medicare Part D covers prescription drugs, which is often an expensive part of medical care. Following are the two main ways to get prescription drug coverage:

- ✔ Part D plans, which add drug coverage to original Medicare
- ✔ Medicare Advantage plans, which include Part D prescription drug coverage (MA-PDs).

If you are choosing among Part D plans, you need to consider a few variables:

✔ Are the drugs you take on the plan's formulary (list of drugs)?

✔ Is the pharmacy you generally use in the plan's network?

✔ Does the plan require you to use generic rather than brand name drugs, or to give certain drugs a trial before it will approve more expensive ones?

✔ Do you have to pay a deductible or copayment for drugs?

✔ Are financial-assistance plans available?

Most Medicare Part D plans have a so-called *doughnut hole,* a gap in coverage that begins after you and your drug plan have spent a certain amount for covered drugs. In 2014 that amount is $2,850. After you're in the doughnut hole, in 2014 you pay 47.5 percent of the plan's costs for covered brand-name drugs and 79 percent of the plan's costs for covered generic drugs. What you've paid from the beginning of the year — deductibles, co-insurance, and copays (but not the drug plan premiums) — counts toward getting out of the coverage gap, as do any discounts for brand-name drugs that you get in the gap. After you reach $4,550, catastrophic coverage takes over and pays 95 percent of Part D drug costs. To estimate how much you will have to spend in the doughnut hole, go to AARP's calculator at `http://doughnuthole.aarp.org/`. Also see `www.medicare.gov/part-d/costs/coverage-gap/part-d-coverage-gap.html`. Under the Affordable Care Act, the doughnut hole will shrink every year until it disappears in 2020.

Even with Medicare Part D, prescription drugs can be very expensive. Financial assistance may be available from Medicare, your state, pharmaceutical companies, or charities. Here are some resources for financial assistance:

✔ **Extra Help:** Medicare's Extra Help program provides low-cost Part D coverage for people with incomes and assets under a certain level. Income limits are higher if you have dependents living with you or if you live in Alaska or Hawaii. Assets include money in savings or checking accounts, stocks, bonds, and other investments, but not your home, car, or household items. If you qualify and join a Medicare drug plan, you get help paying for your monthly premium, yearly deductible, coinsurance, and copayments. If you have Medicaid and live in a nursing home, this drug coverage is free. To apply for Extra Help, go to `www.socialsecurity.gov/i1020` or call `800-772-1213`.

✔ **State Pharmacy Assistance Programs:** Many states have State Pharmacy Assistance Programs (SPAPs) that help some people pay for prescription drugs based on financial need, age, or medical conditions. To find out what is available in your state, contact your State Health Insurance Assistance Program (SHIP). Find your state SHIP at `www.medicare.gov/contacts/organization-search-criteria.aspx`.

✔ **Pharmaceutical assistance programs:** Many major pharmaceutical companies offer assistance for people who are taking their drugs but cannot pay the full price. There is a list of pharmaceutical assistance (or patient assistance) programs at www.medicare.gov/pap/index.asp. Even if the drug company is not on the list, try calling the company to see what help you can get. The formal request must be made by a doctor.

✔ **Charity programs:** Charity programs include organizations that help people with low incomes pay for prescription drugs. These organizations often serve people with a particular disease, such as cancer or neurological conditions. The Medicare Rights Center lists some of these charities at www.medicarerights.org/pdf/copay_charities.pdf.

Private insurance you may have (such as retiree benefits) in addition to Medicare may help with prescription drug coverage. Check with your plan to see how it coordinates benefits. Medigap supplemental insurance, however, does not cover drug expenses.

The Medicare Rights Center has a comprehensive guide to financial assistance for prescription drugs with information by state. You can access the guide at www.medicareinteractive.org/page2.php?topic=counselor&page =scriptslide_id=1351.

Durable medical equipment coverage

Medicare Part B covers durable medical equipment (DME), which includes devices like canes (except white canes for blind people), walkers, wheelchairs, hospital beds, commodes, and other aids that a person with a disability or a chronically ill person needs at home. (*Home* can be a house, an assisted-living facility, or wherever the person lives.) A walker, for example, that you need only to take a walk down the street would not be covered.

DME can be used over and over, distinguishing these items from disposable supplies like adult diapers, bandages, and sterile gloves that can only be used once. Disposable items like these are not covered by Medicare. However, nonreusable diabetic supplies like test strips and lancets are covered, as are oxygen supplies.

In July 2013 Medicare started a National Mail-Order Program for diabetic testing supplies. You need to use a Medicare national mail-order contract supplier if you want to have these items delivered at home. You can still purchase them at your regular pharmacy or other supplier. The costs are the same and include a 20 percent coinsurance payment.

Phone or mail offers to supply DME at extremely low costs are likely to be scams. Make sure that you're alert to these phony offers and buy only from suppliers that Medicare has approved.

DME is one of the most confusing parts of Medicare, and the rules keep changing. However, here are some points to remember:

- ✔ Medicare only covers DME ordered by a physician.

- ✔ The equipment has to be ordered from companies that have an agreement with original Medicare or with a Medicare Advantage plan.

- ✔ Some areas of the country are included in Medicare's Competitive Bidding Program, which is designed to prevent overcharging to Medicare. It applies only to original Medicare and may mean that you have to change suppliers for certain items. For more information, go to www.medicare.gov/what-medicare-covers/part-b/durable-medical-equipment-bidding.html.

- ✔ If you are in original Medicare, you are responsible for a 20 percent coinsurance payment of the Medicare-approved amount (which may not be the full price).

- ✔ Some items can be rented instead of purchased. There are special rules for renting oxygen equipment.

- ✔ Medicare only pays for the basic model. If you or your parent needs a customized wheelchair or a special bed, you have to pay the extra charge.

- ✔ Medicare covers repairs and maintenance to keep equipment in good working order, but the rules are different depending on whether you own or rent the equipment. Delays in getting DME repaired are unfortunately common.

- ✔ If your claim for DME that a doctor has ordered is denied by Medicare's contractor in your region (a private insurance company that reviews Medicare claims), you have the right to appeal that decision.

Home healthcare services

Help at home is probably the most often-needed service for an older adult, and it's the area where Medicare coverage is weakest and private costs are highest. Medicare does pay for some home healthcare services, however, under these conditions:

- ✔ A doctor confirms in writing that he or she has examined the person within 30 days and that the patient needs skilled nursing care, such as care provided by a registered nurse or physical therapist. Without this signed paper, the home healthcare agency cannot "open the case" (begin treating the person). The doctor can be a hospitalist (employed by the hospital) or a community-based doctor. The visit has to be face-to-face, not a phone conversation or a report from a nurse.

✔ If there is a documented need for skilled care, the person may also receive some home-care aide services, although usually for a few hours a day or a few days a week.

✔ The person is homebound (meaning that leaving the house is hard).

✔ The person needs only short-term or part- time skilled services.

✔ The services are provided by a Medicare-approved home health agency (HHA). The HHA may have its own home health aides or contract with licensed agencies to provide these workers, but Medicare will not pay for services provided only by licensed agencies or companion agencies. (See Chapter 14 for a description of the various types of home care agencies.)

I cover more home-care issues in Chapter 14. You can also find more information from Medicare at www.medicare.gov/homehealthcompare/search.html and www.medicare.gov/Pubs/pdf/10969.pdf.

Getting Medicaid Ground Rules

Medicaid, a publicly funded healthcare program for low-income families and individuals, is a shared responsibility of the federal and state governments. While eligibility for Medicare is generally based on the applicant's age, eligibility for Medicaid is generally based on the applicant's income and assets. Medicaid pays for more than 60 percent of people living in nursing homes. Only a quarter of people enrolled in Medicaid are older adults or people with disabilities, but they account for nearly two-thirds of all Medicaid spending because they need more and often expensive healthcare.

The federal government sets basic rules about what must be included in state Medicaid plans and shares the costs. The federal government matches state Medicaid funding on at least a 50 percent basis, but the match may be higher in states with low per-capita income. States set their own eligibility requirements and have considerable flexibility in designing their benefit packages.

Medicaid is changing as the ACA is implemented in the more than 20 states that have agreed to expand this program with additional federal funding. (The number of states in this category is not final.) In general, these changes do not affect people applying for long-term care services and supports in their homes or communities or in nursing homes. At a minimum, if you or your parent are already on Medicaid, make sure you read any notices you get about changes in coverage.

TIP

States call their Medicaid programs by different names: Medi-Cal in California, TennCare in Tennessee, and MassHealth in Massachusetts, for example. Some states seem to go out of their way to avoid using Medicaid in their program name. For the name and program offices in your state, go to www.medicaid. gov/Medicaid-CHIP-Program-Information/By-State/By-State. html and follow the link to your state's website.

Are you eligible for Medicaid?

To receive federal funding, state Medicaid programs are required to cover certain populations, such as children in low-income families and pregnant women. Older adults with low incomes and persons with disabilities who receive cash assistance through the Supplemental Security Income program (SSI) are eligible in the states that use SSI criteria. (Eleven states continue to use more restrictive 1972 welfare eligibility standards.) Eligibility requirements differ considerably from state to state. Some people who are not now eligible for Medicaid may become eligible as the ACA is implemented in those states that have opted to accept the Medicaid expansion program. This website gives you some basic information on eligibility requirements in your state: www.healthcare.gov/do-i-qualify-for-medicaid.

Unlike Medicare, where there are clear federal eligibility standards, Medicaid varies by state. However, there are certain basic approaches:

- ✔ According to federal rules, Medicaid must cover certain populations (such as children in low-income families, pregnant women, and people with disabilities receiving SSI).

- ✔ States set their own, typically stringent, levels for income, often some percentage of the federal poverty level.

- ✔ States limit the amount of assets a person can retain to be eligible for Medicaid; this is usually a small amount.

Medicaid is intended as a safety net, and states take that goal seriously.

In addition to income and asset limits, 34 state Medicaid programs have *medically needy* programs that assist people who have high medical expenses but whose income exceeds the maximum threshold for Medicaid eligibility. Older people living in nursing homes and children and adults with disabilities compose nearly half of the 2.8 million people enrolled in these programs.

Eligible participants are allowed to subtract their healthcare expenses from their income. States vary in their rules for eligibility and the way they determine the number of months a person has to pay these expenses privately before Medicaid kicks in. Some of these people may become eligible for Medicaid directly through ACA. See the report from the Kaiser Commission on Medicaid and the Uninsured for state-by-state information at `http://kff.org/medicaid/issue-brief/the-medicaid-medically-needy-program-spending-and`.

Starting in October 2013, all states were required to have a new Health Insurance Marketplace or exchange. These are websites where various health plans can offer their policies to prospective consumers. The Marketplace offers information about a range of selected private health plans as well as Medicaid. People with certain income levels can receive subsidies, and the goal is to benefit everyone because of the large risk pool. For more information about your state, go to `www.healthcare.gov` or see the state profiles at the Kaiser Family Foundation website, `http://kff.org/state-health-exchange-profiles`.

There have been well-publicized difficulties in the health exchange startup. You may want to ask a family member or friend to help you access the information you need. The ACA also offers funding to local nonprofit organizations, or "navigators," that may assist individuals with enrollment in the exchange. To find navigators in your area, go to: `https://localhelp.healthcare.gov`.

As of January 2014, the federal government established new methods of calculating eligibility for health insurance and subsidies under the ACA, including Medicaid. Access to health insurance was expanded to new groups, and the income eligibility level was increased to 138 percent of the Federal Poverty Level (FPL), which varies by the number of people in the household. There is also a new method of calculating income based on IRS tax records, called MAGI (modified adjusted gross income). People who do not fit these new categories are called non-MAGI applicants. The goal is to have a standard and streamlined process of application and choice of health insurance. Many states have established navigator assistance sites to help people figure out whether they fit into the MAGI or non-MAGI groups, so check your state Medicaid office for assistance.

In the past several years, Medicaid programs have been under pressure to control costs, and one way they have done this is to tighten the eligibility requirements. In some places the entry process is very time-consuming and difficult. On the other hand, some states are streamlining the process by making it easier to enroll online or without a face-to-face interview.

Becoming eligible for Medicaid is one challenge; what happens after death can be another. The 1993 federal estate recovery rules require state Medicaid programs to recover from the estate of an individual over the age of 55 certain benefits paid on behalf of a Medicaid enrollee. They might be payments to a nursing home, home- and community-based services, or hospital and prescription drug services. There are limits, however. States cannot recover money from the estate of a Medicaid enrollee who is survived by a spouse, child under the age of 21, or a disabled child of any age. States vary in how aggressively they pursue estate recovery. It is important to understand the provisions of your state's estate-recovery program. Although the amount recovered for the state is usually very small, it can present hardships for the surviving family members. For more information, see AARP's report on varying estate recovery practices at `http://assets.aarp.org/rgcenter/il/inb137_medicaid.pdf`.

Estate-recovery laws are different from filial responsibility laws, which exist in 30 states and generally require adult children to provide support to their indigent parents, with some exceptions. These laws have seldom been enforced, but in 2012 a Pennsylvania court upheld a decision requiring a son to pay a nursing home $92,000 for his mother's care while she applied for Medicaid. She left the county before Medicaid determined that she was not eligible. In cases like this, the nursing homes are the party seeking payment, not the government recovering its expenses. Some states are moving to repeal these laws. Here's a link to a blog on state laws by a law professor: `http://lawprofessors.typepad.com/elder_law/2013/08/filial-support-laws-news-from-montana-new-hampshire.html`.

How Medicare and Medicaid were born

In the early days of the Republic, John Adams and Thomas Jefferson, who had very different ideas about the role of government, supported legislation that created a federal hospital for merchant mariners, whose contribution to the economy of a growing nation was essential. The mariners paid a tax taken directly from their wages. These hospitals spread across the country, but no other groups were included. In the early 1900s, President Theodore Roosevelt proposed some form of healthcare plan under his Progressive platform. Again, no interest. Even President Franklin Delano Roosevelt's New Deal, which created the Social Security Act, did not include healthcare.

In the late 1940s, President Harry S Truman championed the idea of a national healthcare plan. Over the next 20 years, there was a fierce debate about this idea. The American Medical Association, among others, was adamantly opposed, fearing such a plan would limit physician income. Some politicians were opposed on the grounds that government had no role in healthcare, and some states did not want to pay for healthcare for poor people. Then along came President Lyndon B. Johnson, who forged a compromise as part of his "Great Society." In amendments to the Social Security Act, Medicare would only cover older people who would otherwise have to rely on their children for support.

Medicaid was created under a different amendment. Poor people, who were already receiving cash assistance, would be covered, and the federal government would share the costs with the states. Johnson signed Medicare into law on July 30, 1965, and gave the first two Medicare cards to Harry Truman and his wife, Bess. Many people, including Republican President Richard Nixon, assumed that it was only a matter of time before the U.S. adopted a comprehensive national healthcare plan. On that basis, in 1972 he signed into law a Medicare provision that included people with end-stage renal disease, regardless of age.

What services Medicaid offers

Federal rules require states to provide a basic set of services to Medicaid recipients, including hospital stays, doctor visits, preventive care, laboratory and X-ray services, transportation to medical care, home health services, and nursing-facility care. States have the option of adding, among other things, physical and other kinds of therapy, personal care, hospice, and case management. Prescription drug coverage is optional, as are dental and vision services. Many Medicaid services are designed for children and pregnant women.

Unlike Medicare, Medicaid covers long-term care in nursing homes and in the community through home- and community-based waivers (permission from the federal government to spend money that would have gone to nursing homes on community-based services instead) and other approaches.

States can determine the criteria for nursing home care and home-and community-based services, so a person eligible in one state may not be eligible in a neighboring state. Usually some level of functional limitations is required, like being unable to take care of personal basic needs like bathing, dressing, going to the toilet. Many nursing home residents have cognitive problems like dementia, which limits their ability to function independently.

How Medicaid works with home- and community-based programs

Because nursing-home care is so expensive, states have moved toward caring for these individuals in the community. Someone with functional limitations can receive care at home that may include personal care, homemaking services, case management, transportation, and other long-term services and supports. Even with these services, which may be limited by funding or workforce shortages, family members often provide some or most of the care.

Most states have a variety of Medicaid services that operate under different waiver programs from the federal government (for example, waivers for programs that include a package of services targeted for people with specific disabilities, such as traumatic brain injury or HIV/AIDS). A waiver means that the federal government allows a state to use some of its Medicaid funding for specific services that keep people in the community. However, it can be confusing to sort out which services a person may be eligible for and whether there are waiting lists and other barriers such as limits on the duration and types of services.

Some states use Medicaid waivers to allow recipients to enroll in assisted-living facilities. There may be restrictions, however — for example, requiring the recipient to pay for room and board with their own resources, or covering only certain services — and not all assisted-living facilities accept Medicaid.

In January 2014 the Centers for Medicare & Medicaid Services issued a rule that strengthened community-living options for people on Medicaid by affirming that states can include assisted living facilities as part of their home- and community-based services. The rule provides a transition period for states to ensure that standards are met. Most assisted-living facilities aren't set up to provide extensive medical services. You can check for your state's program at `www.payingforseniorcare.com/medicaid-waivers/assisted-living.html`.

The availability and quality of these services varies considerably by location. Some states have robust home- and community-based programs and strong leadership; others do not. Variations also result from the state's population and income characteristics, the types of providers in the state, and the state's spending priorities. Many states have waiting lists for waiver programs.

Aging and Disability Resource Centers (ADRCs) can help with referrals to appropriate programs. Operated by the U.S. Administration for Community Living, they are intended to be one-stop shopping for referrals to long-term care services. For the ADRC in your area, contact Eldercare Locator at 1-800-677-1186 or go to `www.eldercare.gov/Eldercare.NET/Public/Index.aspx`.

Medicaid-managed long-term care

Many states are now setting up managed long-term care programs to provide better coordination of services, more efficient program administration, and better monitoring of quality, and (it is hoped) reduced costs. These programs are run by private companies under contract to the state that typically receive a per-member, per-month fee for care. In some states, some groups of people who have been receiving long-term services and supports are being moved into managed long-term care programs, and newly eligible individuals will start out in this kind of plan. Some states offer a choice of managed care plans, while others do not.

These programs are evolving, and their characteristics vary by the length of time the program has been in operation, the population included, the types of services provided, program oversight, and the number of plans allowed within a state. Proponents claim that managed long-term care programs provide better integration of physical and behavioral health. Critics worry that managed long-term care plans will avoid enrolling the sickest and most vulnerable people or will fail to provide the extensive and costly care they need. Vigilant monitoring is needed to ensure that plans meet their obligations to all clients.

Depending on the competition among plans within an area, people eligible for Medicaid long-term care services can choose from several plans. Here are some questions to ask whether you are the person choosing a plan or a family member:

✔ Will someone come to the home to assess the person's needs?

✔ Will the person and family be able to participate in the development of the care plan and raise concerns ?

✔ If a family member is involved in care, will that person's needs for training and support be evaluated?

✔ Will the same aide who has been caring for the person be allowed to stay on?

✔ Is there a number to call when problems arise?

✔ How are complaints or grievances resolved?

✔ How does the person change plans?

To keep informed about Medicaid managed-care plans in your community, contact the state's Medicaid office, the state's long-term care ombudsman (who investigates complaints), or a legal-aid organization that advocates for low-income people. Some states have set up special ombudsmen for Medicaid managed long-term care. You can find the ombudsman office in your state on the map at www.ltcombudsman.org/ombudsman.

Coordinating Benefits

About 10 million people qualify for both Medicare and Medicaid. Although they are a diverse group, many are heavy users of acute medical care (hospitalization) as well as long-term services and supports. Depending on income level and assets, a dually eligible person may get the full range of Medicaid services and assistance with Medicare premiums, deductibles, and cost-sharing (full dual) or just financial assistance in paying Medicare premiums and fees (partial dual).

With some combinations of payers, squabbles can occur about who pays for what and who pays first — the arcane world of *CoB,* or *coordination of benefits.* If the payers are Medicare and Medicaid, however, the rules are clear. Medicare is the primary payer for covered services. To simplify the process, ACA created a new office in the Centers for Medicare and Medicaid (CMS) to coordinate benefits for people who are dually eligible: www.cms.gov/Medicare-Medicaid-Coordination/Medicare-and-Medicaid-Coordination/Medicare-Medicaid-Coordination-Office/index.html. Although you aren't likely to interact directly with this office, it is a good resource.

People who have Medicare and are eligible for the full Medicaid benefit package are automatically qualified for Medicare's Extra Help program of financial assistance for prescription drugs.

PACE programs

Another program worth investigating is the Program of All-Inclusive Care for the Elderly (PACE). Although supported by both Medicare and Medicaid, participants do not have to be dually eligible for both programs. In fact, however, according to the National PACE Association, more than 90% of participants are dually eligible.

PACE programs have been in operation since the 1970s. The first program was created in San Francisco's Chinatown. The original program, called On Lok (Cantonese for "peaceful, happy abode"), served families whose elderly relatives had immigrated from China, Italy, and the Philippines. In 1990, the first programs received Medicare and Medicaid waivers to support their efforts. As of January 2014, 99 PACE nonprofit programs are operating in 31 states. For a listing, go to www.npaonline.org/website/download. asp?id=1741&title=PACE_in_the_States.

PACE programs serve individuals who are 55 or older (and eligible for Medicare based on disability, ALS, or end-stage renal disease), are certified by their state to be eligible for nursing-home care, are able to live safely in the community at the time of enrollment, and live in a PACE service area. Because the PACE programs offer comprehensive services, a PACE participant may not be enrolled in any other Medicare Advantage plan, Medicare Prescription Drug, Medicaid prepayment plan, or optional benefit, such as a 1915c Home and Community Based services waiver. It is important to note that PACE participants are also not eligible for the Medicare hospice benefit.

PACE provides these comprehensive services primarily in an adult daycare center: primary care, hospital care, medical specialty services, prescription drugs, home care, physical and occupational therapy, recreation therapy, nutritional counseling, transportation, and social-work counseling. Adult daycare includes nursing care; physical, occupational, and recreational therapies; meals; social work; and personal care. Hospital and nursing-home care are provided when necessary. All prescription drugs are provided.

People who have Medicare but not Medicaid can pay a monthly premium for the long-term care portion of the PACE benefit. There is no deductible or copayment for any drugs or services that the PACE healthcare team approves.

Why aren't there more PACE programs? The business model is difficult to sustain as aging clients need more extensive services. Participation of a multidisciplinary team is essential but may be difficult to organize in some locations. And in some locations, there may not be a sufficient population of eligible older adults to support the program over time. Some policymakers have suggested lowering or removing the entry age to allow for a larger pool of clients.

Coordination with other health insurance

As if figuring out Medicare and Medicaid weren't complicated enough, some people also have other kinds of insurance such as retirement insurance, government employee insurance (Federal Employee Health Benefits Program or FEHB), COBRA (continuing insurance after employment ends), or TRICARE (insurance for military personnel and their families).

If you are not employed, Medicare is your basic health care coverage after you reach the age of 65. But if you retire before then, the most common type of insurance that figures into long-term care planning, has been retirement healthcare insurance. However, this kind of insurance may be phased out like pension plans, with individuals left to figure out their own health-insurance strategies before Medicare begins. The healthcare insurance exchanges created under the Affordable Care Act offer another possibility and by law cannot require medical underwriting, which can be used to refuse coverage to people with pre-existing conditions.

Be sure to check with your employer or union to find out what coverage is available. Employers aren't required to provide retiree coverage and can change benefits or premiums at will.

Also find out who else might be covered under the retirement plan (a spouse or dependent child, for example) and what happens to the plan when you are eligible for Medicare. Your employer's benefits administrator can explain the process.

Chapter 11

Paying for Care: Long-Term Care Insurance and Other Options

- -

In This Chapter

▶ Considering the pros and cons of long-term care insurance

▶ Getting help from a disability or life-insurance policy

▶ Letting your house bring in income with a reverse mortgage

▶ Using regular income from an annuity

- -

*I*f you have read this far (and even if you haven't), you know that no form of insurance or healthcare coverage is free. The costs may be direct (as in Medicare premiums, coinsurance, or copays) or indirect (as in using up your own assets before you qualify for Medicaid). Planning to cover the costs of insurance is important but challenging. The marketplace is changing, and options that seemed adequate 10 or 20 years ago are now not so attractive.

In this chapter, I review the main options and offer some suggestions for questions to ask yourself, your parent, or the agent who is selling the product. These are decisions that you should discuss with professionals, especially a financial adviser who doesn't stand to gain by your choices or an elder-law attorney. Insurance is a necessary component for aging; the aim of this chapter is to help break it down so you can find what works for you. In addition to long-term care insurance, other options to provide financial help include disability insurance, life settlements, reverse mortgages, and annuities. I delve into these topics as well.

Reviewing the Ups and Downs of Long-Term Care Insurance

Long-term care insurance is a product that seemed to fill a big gap in paying for long-term care. Yet only about 7 to 9 million Americans have purchased these policies, and this coverage pays for only about 12 percent of the nation's long-term care costs. But for those who are receiving benefits, it is clearly an important asset.

To make a decision about whether long-term care insurance is right for you, you have a number of points to consider. First, here is my quick definition of long-term care insurance: a policy you purchase when you're healthy and at an age when you can afford the premiums, with the expectation that when you reach the stage of life when you need assistance at home or in a nursing home, the benefits will be available to help pay for the types of care you need. This is the promise, and indeed it is fulfilled for some people, so it's a good idea to consider long-term care insurance to see if it fits your situation (as best you can predict it).

Medicare and private insurance don't cover all older persons' needs, and long-term care insurance was created to help fill that gap. As a start, here are the most significant items that Medicare Parts A and B and private insurance do not cover:

- **Nursing-home care** (except for short-term rehabilitation stays). In 2013, the median annual rate for a private nursing home room was $83,950, according to the Genworth Cost of Care Survey.

- **Assisted-living facilities.** The median cost is $41,400 year, but costs vary depending on location and services provided.

- **Adult daycare.** Non-24-hour care has a median daily rate of $65.

- **Home healthcare aides** (except in limited, short-term circumstances). The private pay median rate charged by a licensed home healthcare agency is $19 an hour.

- **Customized durable medical equipment.** This cost can range from a few hundred dollars to many thousands.

- **Disposable supplies** (with a few exceptions).

- **Deductibles, coinsurance, and copayments.**

- **Some prescription drug costs.** Medicare Part D covers these costs but with a doughnut hole that requires you to pay until you reach the designated cap (see Chapter 10).

- **Home or vehicle modifications.**

- **Special foods.**

Not what was expected

When long-term care insurance came on the market in the 1980s and 1990s, insurance companies miscalculated on several fronts: They did not expect people to live as long as they do now or to draw on the benefits for as long a period. Nor did they anticipate the increasing costs of long-term care. On the other hand, they expected more people to stop paying premiums, thus creating a pool of funds that would not need to be paid out as benefits. Basically, they set the premiums too low, hoping to attract a large market. Low interest rates also affected profits. As a result, long-term care insurance has not been as profitable as anticipated, and many companies have left the market. Still, long-term care insurance policies are still in force and new ones are being sold.

Depending on the policy, long-term care insurance will help fill some but not all these gaps. For example, nursing-home care and home healthcare aides are generally included, but home and vehicle modifications are not.

Of course, these costs vary across the country, but wherever you live, they add up quickly and are not going to get cheaper. If you need these items or services for years, they can overwhelm a family budget. A recent study of out-of-pocket spending in the last five years of life found an average of $38,688 for individuals and $54,412 for couples in which one spouse dies. Spending on healthcare exceeded baseline total household assets for a quarter of the subjects and surpassed non-housing assets for 43 percent. Alzheimer's disease was the most costly — $66,155 — while gastrointestinal disease cost $31,069.

In calculating your need for additional coverage for the costs of long-term care, consider all your assets: savings, IRAs, pensions, 401(k) plans, Social Security income, and other resources. If you are still working, make sure you're contributing the maximum amounts allowable. You may find that you have more financial resources to draw on than you realized.

You need to consider the following three general questions in determining if long-term care insurance is right for you:

- ✔ Should I buy long-term care insurance?
- ✔ Should I continue to pay the increased premiums on my existing policy?
- ✔ How can I ensure that the benefits I expect to receive are delivered?

The next three sections serve to help in answering each of these questions. I also include a section on hybrid policies, which are gaining momentum in the market.

Buying long-term care insurance

The decision to buy long-term care insurance is largely one for people to make before they reach retirement age. It's usually prohibitively expensive for an older person or unavailable because of the person's health status. Long-term care insurance is *medically underwritten,* meaning that people with preexisting conditions that are likely to get worse are priced out of the market or may not be offered coverage. Most people who buy long-term care insurance are in their 50s and 60s, although some companies sell policies to people in their 70s.

The decision to buy long-term care insurance depends on many factors, such as your (or your parent's) age, health status, other savings or assets that can be used to pay for long-term care, and other financial responsibilities such as tuition for college-age children. To these factual considerations, I would add an emotional one: your tolerance for risk and uncertainty.

If you will feel more secure with a long-term care insurance policy and you can afford the premiums, then your task is to investigate the options and choose a company that you trust. Thirty-one states now have long-term care group insurance options that don't require medical underwriting. Purchasing the policy as part of a group may — but is not guaranteed to — offer some protection against steep premium increases, which have become common, even among large group policies. You may be eligible for some limited federal tax credits for qualified long-term care insurance policies, and some states have tax credits too.

 Some employers offer group long-term care insurance to their employees. You should certainly consider this possibility if you have a medical condition that would make you ineligible for coverage as an individual. If you are in good health, you should compare the cost of the employer-based option with what you would pay as an individual. You might find that individual coverage is cheaper. Remember too that your employer may not continue the offer or could change insurance carriers, which would have financial implications for you. See the SCAN Foundation's policy brief on employer-based long-term care insurance at `www.thescanfoundation.org/sites/default/files/ TSF_CLASS_TA_No_14_Employer_LTCi_Participation_FINAL.pdf`.

 Current or former federal employees, active and retired members of the uniformed services, and their qualified relatives can apply for coverage under the Federal Long-Term Care Insurance Program. You can apply at any time during the year. There are exclusions for certain medical conditions or combinations of conditions described in the application at `www.ltcfeds.com/ epAssets/documents/full_underwriting_app.pdf`. You can get more information at `www.ltcfeds.com/eligibility/index.html` or by calling 1-800-582-1337.

When you look into long-term care insurance, make sure you ask insurers the following questions:

- ✔ **Are there coverage exclusions for some conditions, such as mental-health problems or substance abuse?**

- ✔ **Are there waiting periods for some preexisting conditions?** Long-term care insurance policies usually define a *preexisting condition* as one for which you received medical advice or treatment within a defined period, for example, within the past six months or a year. The policy may include a provision that it will not pay for costs related to that condition for a specific period such as six months or longer after the policy goes into effect. Some companies look further back in time than others.

- ✔ **How long is the elimination or waiting period before benefits start?** This is different from the waiting period for preexisting conditions. The waiting period in this instance is like a deductible. You have to pay a certain amount of your own money after you are eligible for a benefit before the policy kicks in. Some people decide to pay for the first 30, 60, or 90 days of their care, so their policies don't begin paying benefits until the waiting period has expired. Some companies sell policies with a specific dollar amount as the policy deductible instead of a waiting period. Some companies count only the days you receive paid care against the waiting period; others count every day from the first day you become eligible for and receive care. Some companies require you to meet this waiting period once in your lifetime; others require you to meet it each time you qualify for benefits and need long-term care assistance.

- ✔ **What does the policy pay for?** Does it cover services provided at a range of facilities, including assisted living, adult daycare, and nursing homes? Do these facilities have to be licensed?

- ✔ **Does the policy have restrictions on who can provide the services?** Does the home healthcare aide have to be licensed or supervised by a home health agency, or can you hire a family member, friend, or neighbor? Are there restrictions on the services the home healthcare aide can provide, such as administering medications?

- ✔ **How is eligibility for services defined?** Usually there is some threshold of activities of daily living (ADLs), which include bathing, dressing, and going to the toilet. A good policy should include the need for supervision due to cognitive problems, such as wandering or memory loss, as a trigger for paying for services.

- ✔ **How much does the policy pay?** It may be a fixed amount per day, per month, or a percentage of the costs.

- ✔ **Who decides what is covered and what is not?** You may disagree with the company about whether a service is needed.

- ✔ **How long will coverage last?** If you choose a shorter period, say three years instead of ten, the premiums will be less.

✔ **What is the payment schedule?** Some policies pay a daily or monthly amount. Others have what has often been called a *pool of money,* and if you don't use your full benefit in one month, it will roll over and extend the life of your policy.

After you gather all this information, you can evaluate whether a policy provides the coverage you may need in the future. Then ask yourself one important question: Can you afford the premiums? Remember that if you purchase a policy in your 50s or 60s, you are likely to pay premiums for 20 to 30 years or long before you need the benefits. And you should expect your premiums to increase over time. One suggestion is that if the premiums amount to more than 7 percent of your income, you probably can't afford them. But like all rules of thumb, this depends a lot on your situation and values.

Premiums are more affordable if purchased in your 50s or 60s when you are eligible for coverage. Remember that once you're diagnosed with a medical condition considered serious by an insurer, you will likely be unable to purchase long-term care insurance.

Long-term care insurance does not replace Medicare. It is intended to cover the services that Medicare does not.

Continuing to pay rising premiums

Many people approaching retirement are now finding that the long-term care insurance policy they counted on is on shaky ground. Five of the ten largest sellers of long-term care insurance, including giants like MetLife and Prudential, have sharply reduced or discontinued sales. As the insurance market is shrinking, premiums are rising — from modest increases to a stunning 77 percent. Women, who on average live longer than men, are likely to be charged higher premiums when they apply for individual policies. The policies now in force are likely to be honored, but they may be transferred to another company. And because the businesses are ceasing to write new policies and therefore adding many fewer payers into the system, premiums are likely to accelerate as more policyholders die.

As part of its Model Law on Long-Term Care Insurance, the National Association of Insurance Commissioners mandates that insurers offer a nonforfeiture benefit if the policyholder stops paying premiums. Some states have mandated a nonforfeiture benefit provision for all LTC policies, but others require insurers to offer at least one of a list of options, including a shortened benefit period or giving up an inflation-protection clause. This means that if you agree to shorten the benefit period or give up part of an inflation-protection provision, your premiums won't be raised quite so much.

How you decide to handle this situation, should it arise, depends on how much you have already contributed to the policy and what sacrifices you would have to make to keep it active. You can also appeal the increases to the company and make a hardship case for keeping the premiums affordable. Some states may have options for assistance in these cases, such as a shortened benefit period.

Getting your claims paid for

Even if you have an active policy, premiums all paid, and you believe you have been paying for eligible care during the waiting period stated in the policy, you're not in the clear.

You still have to submit claims and documentation that the services you are receiving are indeed covered by the policy. Companies can deny claims for many different reasons. The paperwork to justify what seem to be clear-cut needs and services can be daunting.

These are the primary reasons for claims denials:

- ✔ **Deductibles:** During the waiting period of 30, 60, 90, or 100 days, the costs of care can run to thousands of dollars. The company may calculate the waiting period so that it lasts much longer if the person is only receiving home care a few days a week.

- ✔ **Ineligibility:** The company may decide that the person's functional problem doesn't qualify for assistance.

- ✔ **Unlicensed caregivers:** Some plans require the policyholder to hire a licensed caregiver and won't pay for anyone else. Other policies, called cash plans, have fewer restrictions. California does not allow companies to require licensed caregivers.

- ✔ **Assisted living:** Some plans, written before assisted living became popular, pay only for nursing-home care. In some cases a 24-hour nurse on site is required for assisted living to be approved, but many assisted-living facilities do not provide this level of nursing care.

- ✔ **Inadequate documentation:** Keeping track of care provided by a home care worker is essential for payment but may not be within the worker's training or capacity. Without proper documentation of each service, the company may deny the claim.

For more information about long-term care insurance and what to look for in policies, see the guide produced by the Wisconsin Office of the Commissioner of Insurance at `http://oci.wi.gov/pub_list/pi-047.pdf`. Although specific to that state, the advice is generally useful. The National Association of Insurance Commissioners has a Shopper's Guide to Long-term Care Insurance. Call it for information at 866-470-6242 or order at `https://eapps.naic.org/forms/ipsd/Consumer_info.jsp`.

Seeking out hybrid policies

In the past few years a new product has come on the market to meet the needs of people who want some protection against the costs of long-term care but do not want to get locked into a long-term care insurance policy. The new policies are called *hybrid* or *linked* policies because they combine a life-insurance policy with long-term care benefits.

This is how it works: You purchase a life-insurance policy for, say, $200,000, and pay for it with a single premium — maybe $50,000 to $75,000. This money goes into an account for long-term care benefits if and when you need them. The death benefit, minus any money spent on your long-term care, goes to your beneficiary.

This option may be a good one for you if

✔ You have a reason to buy life insurance in the first place; someone, a spouse or dependent child, for example, relies on you for financial support.

✔ You have a sufficient amount of money put away to pay for the premium without creating any hardship for you or your family.

✔ Your health status is good and you are considered insurable (even common medications will be taken into consideration).

So far these policies are not widely available. They are niche products, and if you fit into the niche, they may well be something to investigate.

Utilizing Disability Insurance

Most people don't consider disability insurance as part of long-term care if they think about it at all. Disability insurance pays for a portion of lost income if you become disabled and unable to work because of an accident or illness. Most disability insurance is provided by employers, not purchased by individuals. If you become disabled, and have this type of insurance, you don't lose all your income, so you do not have to use up savings or other assets to pay for care that isn't covered by health insurance. Usually you have a 90-day waiting period for benefits to begin, and they last for about three years, when most people are able to go back to work. But some disability claims last much longer. Although disability insurance does not pay for long-term care directly, it is an income source at a time when a person is not receiving salary. Consider it an additional resource, not a substitute for basic coverage.

You can use the money to pay bills, for home care, or for anything else. There are no requirements for submitting claims as there are in long-term care insurance.

The decision to buy disability insurance or to add to an employer's coverage is a personal one, influenced largely by your assessment of the risk of an event that is low probability but high impact. The Council for Disability Awareness, an insurance-supported organization, has a calculator called "What's My Disability Quotient?" You can figure out your own risk at www.whatsmypdq.org. Again, your tolerance for risk may have little to do with the probabilities of an accident or illness.

Selling Your Policy: Life Settlements

Life settlements — which essentially means selling existing life-insurance policies at a steep discount — are being marketed as a way to get cash for long-term care. The appeal for older adults is easy to understand, especially if keeping up the premiums on the policy is a financial strain.

The practice recalls the so-called *viatical settlements* that arose at the height of the HIV/AIDS epidemic in the 1980s and 1990, when many young men were dying quickly and did not have either money to pay for their care or families for whom they were responsible financially. Investors bought up policies in the expectation that the policyholders would die quickly, and many unethical practices followed. But unlike the viatical-settlements industry, the life-settlement industry focuses on individuals with a longer life expectancy or needs for long-term care.

Some states are authorizing older residents to use their existing life-insurance policies to pay for long-term care. This practice gives the residents money to pay for care and helps the state avoid costly Medicaid bills. In Texas, for example, people applying for Medicaid can now sell their life-insurance policies to a third party at a discount — more than the cash value of the policy but significantly less than its death benefit. For example, an 87-year-old female with a $65,000 policy would qualify for a monthly benefit of $1,115 for 15 months and a funeral benefit of $3,250, for a total of $16,725. The money goes into a special account for the policyholder's long-term care, and the person is still be eligible for Medicaid when that money runs out. Similar bills have been introduced in other state legislatures.

Caution is always a good first step when considering any insurance arrangement. Here are some things to consider:

- Conversion of a life insurance policy into a long-term care benefit is not a long-term care insurance policy.

- The financial institution that buys your policy gets the death benefit. In exchange for money now, the beneficiary named in the policy gets nothing. If your spouse or a dependent child will need financial support in the future, a life settlement removes that option.

- Older people with serious health conditions who are unlikely to live long are a prime target for unscrupulous brokers. Be wary of hard sell pitches.

- Life settlements have high transaction costs. Commissions paid by life-settlement companies to brokers and other consultants can be as high as 40 percent.

- The lump sum you receive is likely to be taxable. Depending on state law, it may also make a person ineligible for Medicaid.

- If you change your mind and want to purchase another life-insurance policy, you may be unable to find one that will accept you, and the premium will certainly be higher.

- One less-costly alternative is a 1035 exchange, so called because it stands for Section 1035 of the Internal Revenue Code. This provision allows you to exchange an insurance policy you own for a new one insuring the same person without paying tax on the investment gains on your original contract.

For more information on life settlements and 1035 exchanges, see "Seniors Beware: What You Should Know About Life Settlements" at www.finra.org/investors/ protectyourself/investoralerts/annuitiesandinsurance/p018469, produced by the Financial Industry Regulatory Authority, an independent regulatory organization empowered by the federal government to protect investors.

Check your state's insurance laws regarding life settlements for information that must be provided. For an example, see New York State's comprehensive list of items: http://law.onecle.com/new-york/insurance/ ISC07811_7811.html.

Beware of STOLIs (stranger-originated life insurance). STOLI transactions usually involve an older person being approached by a life-insurance agent or another party to obtain new life insurance, with the policy being controlled from the start and paid for by a third party. Some older individuals are offered compensation for his or her participation as the insured. The person could be considered a participant in a fraud on the insurance company.

State laws generally prohibit someone from initiating or facilitating the issuance of an insurance policy for the intended benefit of a person who, at the time when the policy is issued, has no insurable interest in the life of the person being insured. Someone with an insurable interest is a family member or someone who has a substantial economic interest in the continued well-being of the person (a business partner, for example).

Considering a Reverse Mortgage

Many older adults are house-rich and cash-poor. The equity built up over years of reducing a mortgage is a tempting resource. Reverse mortgages, also known as *home-equity conversion mortgages* (HECMs), are designed to take advantage of this asset without requiring the home to be sold.

Reverse mortgages are different from home equity loans, which you may have used to remodel a kitchen or make other improvements. In a home equity loan, a bank loans you a certain amount of money, which you repay, with interest, in monthly installments. In a reverse mortgage, you receive a line of credit, a lump sum, or monthly payments, which are not repaid until you sell the home, move permanently into a nursing home, or die.

On the positive side, except for a single-purpose reverse mortgage, for which a lender might require you to use the proceeds to pay property taxes or undertake home repairs, you can use the money for medical or other bills. And the proceeds are generally tax-free (consult your financial adviser).

As you may expect, you need to meet certain qualifications and be prepared for some financial requirements. Here's are the basics you need to know:

- ✔ You or your parent must be 62 years old or older to qualify.

- ✔ The homeowner is responsible for taxes, insurance, utilities, maintenance, and all the other responsibilities.

- ✔ You may have to pay a large origination fee and closing costs as in a standard mortgage.

- ✔ Your total debt increases as the funds are paid out.

- ✔ Reverse mortgages are not now available for co-op apartments.

- ✔ A reverse mortgage is best suited to a home in which the existing mortgage has been paid off or is small enough to be paid off with the proceeds of the reverse mortgage.

The Federal Trade Commission explains three types of reverse mortgages:

- ✔ **Single-purpose reverse mortgages** are offered by some state and local government agencies and nonprofit organizations. These are the least expensive option, and the proceeds can only be used for the specified purpose (not long-term care). This option might be required for paying for home modifications or repairs or property taxes. Most low- or moderate-income homeowners can qualify.

- ✔ **Federally insured reverse mortgages,** known as home-equity conversion mortgages (HECMs), are backed by the Federal Housing Administration (FHA), an arm of the U.S. Department of Housing and Urban Development (HUD). Before applying for an HECM (pronounced *heck*-um), you must meet with a counselor from an independent government-approved housing counseling agency, who explains the loan's costs and financial implications. You can choose from among several payment options. These loans are widely available, have no income or medical requirements, and can be used for any purpose. You can find out more at `http://portal.hud.gov/hudportal/ HUD?src=/program_offices/housing/sfh/hecm/rmtopten`.

The requirements to qualify for a federally insured reverse mortgage were tightened in September 2013. Because many reverse-mortgage borrowers did not have enough money to pay insurance and property taxes during the downturn in the housing market and the economy (which is probably one of the reasons they wanted a reverse mortgage in the first place), the FHA now requires prospective borrowers to undergo a financial assessment to ensure that they have the capacity and willingness to meet their financial obligations. Based on the results of the financial assessment, the borrower is required to set aside enough money from the loan to pay for property taxes and insurance. There are also limits to the initial mortgage insurance payments and limits on the amount of the loan that can be taken out in the first year.

- ✔ **Proprietary reverse mortgages** are private loans backed by the companies that develop them. These mortgages are likely to be more expensive and have high upfront costs. They may, however, offer more money than HECMs for expensive homes with high appraisal value.

In October 2013 the U.S. District Court for the District of Columbia ruled that the Department of Housing and Urban Development (HUD) violated federal law by failing to protect the surviving spouses of holders of reverse mortgages from foreclosure. The spouses were not named on the mortgages but, the court ruled that they were "homeowners" protected by the HECM. The lenders had demanded that the surviving spouses pay off the loan. The case was brought by AARP Foundation Litigation on behalf of two spouses. Even with the court ruling, it may be prudent for both spouses to sign an application for a reverse mortgage, even though it may mean a smaller loan if one spouse is much younger than the other. HUD has not yet indicated what its new policies will be.

The National Council on Aging has a booklet on reverse mortgages, billed as the "official reverse mortgage consumer booklet approved by the Department of Housing at Urban Development; go to `www.ncoa.org/news-ncoa-publications/publications/ncoa_reverse_mortgage_booklet_073109.pdf`. You can also check out AARP's booklet "Reverse Mortgage Loans: Borrowing Against Your Home," at `www.ahttp://assets.aarp.org/www.aarp.org_/articles/money/financial_pdfs/hmm_hires_nocrops.pdf`.

Once again, scammers see a vulnerable target in older people who have equity in their homes but may be having financial difficulties. Fannie Mae, the federal agency that guarantees mortgages, reports an increase in two types of fraud. A *turn-around mortgage* promises to stop foreclosure. *Equity theft schemes* sell the homeowner a new residence, give them a property deed, and then request the person to obtain a reverse mortgage. The criminals then take off with the proceeds. As always, the best prevention is to deal only with trusted and well-known lenders. The U.S. Department of Housing and Urban Development (HUD) has a list of lenders approved by the Federal Housing Administration available at `www.hud.gov/ll/code/llslcrit.cfm.` For advice on avoiding mortgage fraud, see `www.fanniemae.com/content/tool/mortgage-fraud-prevention-consumers.pdf`.

Receiving Money through Annuities

Annuities are investments that guarantee a steady income as long as the annuitant (the person holding the annuity) lives. Several different types of annuities are available. For example, *immediate annuities* pay a monthly sum in exchange for a one-time (or more than one-time) premium. *Deferred annuities* are more like investment products and have the possibility of being converted into payments at a later, unspecified date.

The main advantage of annuities is that you can receive a series of guaranteed payouts. No additional annual contribution is required once you "annuitize" or start receiving payments.

The main disadvantages — other than the stipulation that you have a bundle of cash just sitting around with which to purchase the annuity — are the commissions that you pay the broker (as much as 10 percent), high annual fees for managing your money, and the high surrender charges (some as high as 20 percent) if you take out your money within the first several years. In addition, there is no FDIC insurance with an annuity as there is in a bank account.

Meeting the guaranteed returns has proved costly for some companies in the current economic environment. As a result, these companies are trying to persuade holders of variable annuities (in which contracts allow changes in investments) to take buyouts or move their investments into ones with lower returns. It is important to review all communications about an annuity, because some of these changes to the contract or rider may not be immediately apparent.

If you have a deferred annuity, when you do take out your money (preferably after the age of 59½ to avoid taxes), you have several payout options:

- ✔ **Income for a guaranteed period; say 5 or 20 years.** If you die before the end of the period, your beneficiary receives the remainder of the payments for the guaranteed period.

- ✔ **Lifetime payments, with no survivor benefits.**

- ✔ **Income for life with a guaranteed period-certain benefits.** You receive a guaranteed payout for life that includes a certain benefit period. If you die during that period, your beneficiary continues to receive the payout for the remainder of the period.

- ✔ **Joint and survivor annuity.** Your beneficiary continues to receive payouts for the rest of his or her life. In certain situations, a married person must choose this option unless the spouse agrees in writing to a different withdrawal method.

Some financial advisers believe that annuities should be considered only after you have reached the limit on other investments with tax advantages like 401(k) plans or IRAs. At that point the tax-free growth rate may be attractive, especially to people in high income-tax brackets.

Some options for more flexible annuities, such as taking part of a pension as an annuity, may make this option more affordable and attractive to employees. An AARP "In Brief" discusses these features at http://assets.aarp. org/rgcenter/ppi/econ-sec/fs189-annuities.pdf.

The appeal of a guaranteed retirement income is understandable and powerful, but it is also important to know all the costs and risks. For all major financial decisions, consult a knowledgeable advisor and investigate all the details.

Chapter 12

Financial Matters: Money Management, Wills, and Trusts

*I*n many families, money is a taboo topic. Talking about bank accounts or wills happens only when a crisis occurs. All too often, when a person dies, he doesn't even leave a will to guide the heirs. "Why make a will," some people reason, "when it will be expensive and complicated? My family will know what I want." And predictably, conflict and confusion ensue.

Wills are only one of the legal and financial instruments that should be discussed, created, and periodically reviewed as part of a long-term care plan. Managing money is a huge issue when dealing with elder care. Knowing how to deal with an older person's funds is essential for handling home care or assisted-living expenses. This chapter reviews general reasons for the primary legal documents and suggests some points to consider. However, it doesn't substitute for the advice of an experienced attorney, and you shouldn't rely solely on the information presented in this chapter in assessing your own situation.

Managing Money

Giving up control of money matters is often difficult for an older person, just as it is hard to give up driving. Many older people view losing any control over their finances as the beginning of the end of their independence.

However, because financial matters are so vital to aging comfortably and can be so difficult to manage, passing part of the control over to a trusted person not only makes sense but is imperative in certain situations.

Right now, before a crisis, talk to your parent about the options for managing money should illness occur. Two basic options allow for shared control: a joint bank account or a financial power of attorney. The two options can be combined. I delve into the logistics of each option in the following sections.

Opening joint bank accounts

When you or your parent is no longer able to follow a budget or keep track of money coming in and out, it may be in everyone's best interest to have a shared bank account with a trusted family member responsible for managing it. But many older people have had their own bank account(s) for decades, possibly a joint account shared with a spouse, and giving up some or all control to a child or other relative can be hard. If you are thinking of opening a new joint bank account, with a parent as co-owner, here are some points to consider:

- ✔ In most joint bank accounts, with a right of survivorship, there is no mine and yours. Two people have access to the account in its entirety, no matter which person earned or deposited the money. One person can withdraw the entire amount for any purpose without notifying the other owner.

- ✔ Most joint accounts are set up so that the entire account passes to the second person if one person on the joint account dies. But in certain states this presumption can be challenged. The joint amount of money in the account is not included in the person's estate to be divided among the heirs. If the amount in the account is substantial, other family members may object. Even if the amount is small, other heirs may see this uneven distribution of assets as unfair. There may be income and inheritance tax implications as well.

- ✔ An alternative but little-used option for a bank account is a *multiparty account without a right of survivorship,* sometimes called a *convenience account.* In this type of account the cosigner has the authority to make deposits and withdrawals, but in the event that the primary person dies, the remainder of the account goes into the estate and does not pass to the co-signator. Although banking laws permit these accounts, many banks do not encourage their use, possibly because they require extra training of staff and monitoring. Still, if this seems a good option, talk to a banker about it.

Adding another person to a bank account could have implications for future Medicaid eligibility. The account could be considered a transfer of assets at less than fair market value. If this transfer happens within five years of an application to Medicaid, the person is penalized according to Medicaid look-back rules.

Obviously, setting up a joint bank account should be done only with someone you trust completely. Even so, it may be prudent to keep only the minimum amount necessary to pay bills in the account and avoid bank fees that might apply to a minimum balance. A large amount of cash sitting in a bank account can turn out to be an attractive nuisance, applying to this situation a term describing something on a property that a child may find both dangerous and appealing. If the joint owner of the account takes out money for personal use, even with all the best intentions of repaying the money, there's always the possibility that he or she won't be able to fulfill that promise. The annals of elder abuse are filled with stories of relatives, household help, and new "friends" who have taken advantage of a trusting older adult to enrich themselves or to pay themselves for taking care of an older person when that was never part of the agreement. Best not to put temptation into the picture.

A key concept in all these situations when someone has access to another's money is *fiduciary duty,* which occurs when one person depends on another to act in his or her best interest. The responsible person has a duty of loyalty to act only for the elderly person's benefit and to act with good faith in furthering his or her interests. Furthermore, he or she has a duty to disclose all relevant information. Anyone taking on the responsibility of a joint bank account should be reminded about these ethical and legal requirements.

Is cash sitting in an old bank account?

Some people open a variety of bank accounts and then forget about them. In an earlier era, banks offered toasters and other items to entice new customers, and thrifty people took advantage of the offers. Sometimes a spouse opened an account to keep some money hidden. Make sure you look for any bank accounts that may fit this profile. Check drawers and folders for evidence of these accounts. If the accounts are unused for a period of time, usually three to five years, the bank or financial institution is required to send a letter to the account holder (which probably goes into the pile of junk mail) before the money is turned over to the state. Newspapers periodically publish lists of unclaimed bank accounts. One estimate is that more than $33 billion in unclaimed funds are in the United States For a map with contact information of state offices handling unclaimed funds, go to www.unclaimed.org.

Consider drawing up an agreement that states the sources of money to be deposited such as (Social Security, pension, family contributions), how it will be spent (such as rent or mortgage, household expenses, doctor bills, household help), and what should happen to the balance if the co-signator dies. This document would not be legally binding but would make clear to both parties (and to the rest of the family) how the joint account will be used. The agreement may need to be changed if circumstances change.

Granting financial powers of attorney

If you need to step in to help take care of an older person's finances, an alternative to holding a joint bank account is receiving financial power of attorney. Two types of power attorney are available: conventional and durable.

Conventional power of attorney

Conventional power of attorney is granted by a document, signed by one person, giving another person permission to take care of different kinds of financial affairs, like signing checks, agreeing to pay a contractor for home repairs, handling bank accounts, and taking care of other tasks. The power of attorney may be limited to specific tasks, such as paying monthly bills, or it may be general and all encompassing (allowing everything including selling property and assets like stocks, filing taxes, or managing a retirement account).

Depending on state laws, some powers cannot be assigned to another person. Those include the power to make, amend, or revoke a will; change insurance beneficiaries or vote.

The person signing the document is known as the *principal,* and the person who is designated to act in the principal's name is called the *agent* or *attorney-in-fact.* Typically, a power of attorney goes into effect right away, but the principal can set it to expire on a certain date, and the principal can revoke the power of attorney at any time. Furthermore, conventional power of attorney ends if the principal becomes legally incapacitated, which means he or she is unable to understand and make decisions.

If you are the agent, be sure you sign a check, for example, as John Brown (your name), attorney-in-fact for Mary Brown (your mother) to avoid personal liability.

Durable power of attorney

Because a conventional power of attorney ends when the principal (the person who signed away some powers) becomes legally incompetent, many people choose what is known as a *durable power of attorney,* which continues even if the person becomes incapacitated. Therefore, durable power of attorney lets the agent remain in control of certain financial and legal matters even if the principal is no longer able to understand the decision to be made or its implications. For example, a person with advanced dementia would be considered incapacitated, as would a someone in a coma. All states recognize some form of durable power of attorney, but the specifics vary.

Another version of durable power of attorney is called a *springing durable power of attorney.* It sets conditions under which the durable power of attorney goes into effect; for example, when a doctor certifies that the person has become incapacitated. The springing durable power of attorney may be more acceptable to an older person and avoids the lengthy, costly, and emotionally difficult process of guardianship, an alternative that I discuss in the last section of this chapter. However, the document must be very clear about what counts as the springing event so that the principal, agent, and other third parties who need to rely on the power of attorney can easily determine when the principal intended the agent to take over. Without clarity, a court may have to decide. This would negate one of the benefits of having a power of attorney, which is that financial and legal matters can be handled without going to court.

Even if you have a durable power of attorney in a form approved by your state, your bank or other financial institution may require its own form. Even the Social Security Administration requires its own version of a power of attorney. Be sure to ask your bank whether it honors the standard form or requires its own.

Just as in joint bank accounts, as the agent in a durable power of attorney, you are required to act in the person's best interests, maintain accurate records, and avoid any conflict of interest. Most people are not well versed in the fiduciary responsibilities that accompany being named an agent in a durable power of attorney. The same temptations that can occur in a joint bank account are present with a durable power of attorney, and here the stakes may be even higher. Therefore all financial actions taken on behalf of the person who is incapacitated must be transparent, and all family members involved in the care of the older person be apprised of significant outlays. There may be disagreements, but better to have them resolved early rather than cascade into serious trouble.

A durable power of attorney for financial affairs does not include making healthcare decisions. That requires a separate document, which can be called by different names but is usually termed a *healthcare proxy* or a *durable power of attorney for healthcare.* They're discussed in Chapter 16.

Where There's a Will...

If you have any money, property, family heirlooms, or just personal treasures, or if you have children or other dependents who will need a new guardian after your death, you need a will. (In some cases a trust is an appropriate way to distribute property instead, and I discuss that type of document later in this chapter.) A will ensures, as much as possible, that your wishes are followed. One way to convince a resistant older person of the importance of creating a will is to make one yourself or to remind the person that you went through the process, and though it wasn't easy, it was a relief to have completed it.

Many people believe that if you die without a will, your family will automatically divide up your property. Not exactly. A person who dies without a will is legally *intestate*. In that case, state law operating through a probate court determines how the property will be divided, often leading to outcomes that the person would never have wanted. Blood relatives will likely be favored over domestic partners. Children will be treated equally, even if one of them has been estranged from the parent for years. Stepchildren may not be included, even though they are well loved. Such unwanted outcomes can be avoided through the creation of a valid will.

Many people underestimate the value of their possessions, not just in monetary terms but also in sentimental value to family members. An older person may say, "That old painting? Who would want that?" The answer may be, "A lot of your children or grandchildren who remember it hanging on your wall when they came to visit." Or the opposite may happen. Your parent may say to more than one person, "When I'm gone, that painting is going to be yours. It's worth a lot of money."

"Who Gets Grandma's Yellow Pie Plate?" an online resource, has advice about distributing items that are laden with family history and thus have great potential for conflict. For example, a widowed father who remarries should consider his biological children's wishes about their mother's belongings. The website has many cautionary stories. Check it out at `www.extension.umn.edu/family/financial-security/who-gets-grandmas-pie-plate/`.

Instructions about burial or cremation and funeral or memorial service plans should not be put in a will. A will is generally read several days or weeks after death, when it is too late to honor the person's wishes. If you or your parent has specific directions, they should be put in a separate document to be opened at death. It is best to alert family members about this document to avoid conflicts. The USAA Educational Foundation has a useful brochure, "A Guide for Your Survivors," with advice on preparing instructions for funeral or memorial services, available at `www.usaaedfoundation.org/life/life_579_a_guide_for_your_survivors`.

Preparing a will is very important and will be a valued document when an older person passes. Take a look at the following sections to find out how to get started and what types of wills are available.

As early as possible, consult an attorney who can guide you through the process of taking inventory of your assets, determining what kind of will best suits your situation, choosing the executor, what provisions to include, and how to finalize the will.

Taking inventory of your assets

In considering a will (and for estate planning in general), start by making a list of assets to be distributed, including

- ✔ Liquid assets (things that can quickly be turned into cash), such as bank accounts (checking and saving), certificates of deposit, and money market funds

- ✔ Fixed assets, including bonds

- ✔ Certificates of deposit that are payable to a named person on death

- ✔ Retirement accounts, such as 401(k) plans, IRAs, Keogh accounts, and pensions, if they have designated beneficiaries

- ✔ Transfer-on-death stock accounts, payable to a named beneficiary

- ✔ Valuable personal items such as jewelry, antiques, artwork (items with only sentimental value can be kept in a separate list)

Community property is the law in nine states (Arizona, California, Idaho, Louisiana, Nevada, New Mexico, Texas, Washington, and Wisconsin). This means that property acquired during a marriage is shared equally by a married couple regardless of who earned the money. Only the share owned by one person can be distributed in a will. This may call for some Solomonic decisions, but it can be addressed in a will by a spouse giving his or her half of the community property to the surviving spouse.

Considering types of wills

According to the American Bar Association, there are several types of wills:

- ✔ For an uncomplicated estate, a *simple will* provides for the outright distribution of assets.

- ✔ A *pour over will* assigns some assets to a trust that has already been established.

✔ A *holographic will* is handwritten but not witnessed. About half the states recognize this kind of will, but it's not a preferred option.

✔ An *oral will* is spoken but not written down. Very few states recognize this kind of will, and then only in cases of final illness. Again, it's not a good option.

Choosing the executor

Choosing the executor (the person responsible for making sure that the instructions in the will are followed) is an important step. Being named as an executor is not an honorary title; it involves a considerable amount of time-consuming work. The executor has to create an accurate accounting of assets to be distributed, find all debts that need to be paid, and resolve tax questions. Consultants such as accountants and attorneys may need to be hired. Unhappy relatives may need to be placated. The ideal executor is a person adept at understanding finances who is detail-oriented and even-tempered.

If this job description fits someone in the family, then that person would be a good choice. If not, then look outside the family for a trusted friend or professional. A professional will expect to be paid, and fees may be a flat amount or a percentage of the estate.

Do-it-yourself wills: Cheaper but riskier

In recent years, many books, software, websites, and services offer templates for writing a will without consulting an attorney. The appeal is obvious: You still have to pay for the basic materials, but the cost is much less than an attorney would charge. However, do-it-yourself wills do not take into account the specific circumstances that need to be addressed and may not have as precise wording as a lawyer-written will. Unless someone is watching out for details, the will may not be signed and witnessed in a way that makes it valid in your state. A court may conclude that an invalid will is no will at all and determine how to distribute the estate. If you decide to take the DIY route, make sure that you have thoroughly considered all the worst-case scenarios so that you can account for them in the will. Also have someone else check the document for proofreading errors ($100.00 when you meant $10,000) or failure to include a person's name where you are asked to [Insert Name Here].

The person named as executor should be willing to take on that job, because if the person declines, a court will name another executor and it may be someone you or your parent would not choose. You should name an alternate in the will in case your first choice to be executor cannot serve.

Taking the final steps

Making decisions about the will is only the first step, according to the American Bar Association. There are still several things to do:

1. **Execute the will.** This step means having witnesses present as you sign the will. All states require at least two witnesses as proof that the will is valid; that is, that the person signing the will knew what he or she was doing. Their signatures must be notarized. The witnesses should be people who are not named in the will to receive any gifts (even of modest value). The person named as the executor should not be a witness. Usually the witnesses are employees in an attorney's office, who do this every day.

2. **Decide where to keep the will.** You should have only one signed original that you keep in a safe place. The attorney who drafts the will may or may not take the responsibility of storing it for you. Unsigned copies may be distributed to any family members who need to know about its contents. They should know where the original is stored.

    Putting the original will in a safe deposit box is not a good idea, because some banks restrict access to safe deposit boxes until there is a court order that it can be opened.

3. **Revisit the will at regular intervals.** Creating a will is important for all adults. But people who create a will at one stage of their lives (for example, when they have young children) may forget about the will as the children grow up and have children of their own. Almost everything has changed in their lives. But the same will exists. Any major life-changing event — divorce, death of a family member named in the will, remarriage, birth or adoption of a new child, sale of a business, moving to a new state, onset of a life-threatening illness — is a reason to review a will and make appropriate changes. In the case of moving to a new state, you need to make sure that the new location will honor your will executed in another state, or you may need to draw up a new will. Your priorities may be the same or they may be different. In either event, the will should be up-to-date.

Settling the Estate with Probate

Probate is a word that is often preceded in advice columns by *avoiding*. What exactly is probate and why do so many people want you to avoid it?

Probate is the process of settling an estate. It is also the name of the state court that handles wills and estates, among other responsibilities. The probate court determines the validity of the will, reviews the executor's inventory of assets and list of creditors, and determines what debts should be paid and what taxes are owed. After all these obligations are taken care of, the remainder of the estate is distributed according to the terms of the will. Failing to write a will is not a good way to avoid probate, because a court will be involved in settling your estate anyway.

Why are people so eager to avoid probate? For one thing, it can be costly. It involves court fees, attorney fees, and other fees, which can add up. Some costs are set; others may depend on a percentage of the value of the estate.

Secondly, it can take time. Heirs eager to get their share of the estate may be frustrated by the slow but steady process of probate. Time has to be allowed for creditors to be notified and to come forward, ownership of assets to be determined, and all the other details that have to be resolved and can complicate settling an estate. It can take 9 to 12 months to close a larger or complicated estate.

Many states have streamlined the probate process, allowing spouses and minor children to get the money they need to live on without waiting for the entire estate to be settled. Other states have a simple probate process for smaller estates that can be closed in weeks. They have also reduced some of the costs.

 Probate addresses only certain assets in an estate. Joint bank accounts, pay-on-death accounts, life-insurance policies, retirement accounts, other assets with a named beneficiary, and property in trusts do not normally pass through probate.

There are different kinds of probate, depending on state law:

- **Small-estate:** The simplest form of probate that can be used (but not in every state), for estates ranging in value from $1,000 to $10,000, depending on state law.

- **Unsupervised or independent:** A reasonably simple and cheap form of probate used when the estate is more than the value of a "small estate" but doesn't require a lot of court supervision. It can be requested when all the beneficiaries agree (and consent, if the will requires consent).

- **Supervised:** Typically applied to large estates and wills with complicated provisions, with the court playing a major role in approving every action. Supervised probate is used if the is contested, someone named in the will requests it, or the court is concerned about the executor's abilities.

If the will involves property in more than one state, the probate court in each state will be involved, adding to the costs.

One of the best ways to avoid the costs and delays of probate is to have a good estate plan in place. If the will is up-to-date and properly prepared, all the provisions are made in clear simple language, and the beneficiaries are advised about what they can expect (and won't be getting), the chances are that the will can be probated at minimum cost and with minimum delays. Of course, the more money that is involved and the more people who will stand to gain from the will, the more likely it is that there will be complications. Even so, planning can reduce some of the potential problems.

Reviewing the Rules on Estate Taxes

"In this world nothing can be said to be certain, except death and taxes." So said Benjamin Franklin in 1789. And in the administration of estates after a person's death, the two are inextricably linked. To add to the complexity, the Internal Revenue Service itself says, "The laws on Estate and Gift Taxes are considered to be some of the most complicated in the Internal Revenue Code." Among its many publications is a guide to estate taxes, available at www.irs.gov/pub/irs-pdf/p950.pdf.

Part of the executor's responsibilities in overseeing the provisions of the will is to ensure that all taxes have been paid, including income taxes and estate taxes.

After a period of considerable uncertainty about the status of federal estate taxes, the situation seems stable — for now. In January 2013, with the passage of the American Taxpayer Relief Act, the amount an individual can exclude from estate taxes, including gifts given during one's lifetime, is $5.25 million, an amount that is scheduled to increase slightly in 2014. A married couple's exclusion is $10.5 million. According to the Tax Policy Center, a nonprofit arm of the Urban Institute and the Brookings Institutions, just 3,800 estates are expected to be big enough to owe any federal taxes in 2013. The amounts an individual can give as a gift tax-free each year also increases from $13,000 in 2013 to $14,000 in 2014.

States have their own estate or inheritance taxes, so be sure to investigate the rules in your state. State taxes are lower than federal taxes but still can affect the distribution of assets — and the tax man gets paid before the family.

Consulting with a very experienced tax attorney or accountant is advisable. There may be some ways to reduce a tax bill, but unless your own or your parent's estate is worth many millions of dollars, taxes should not be your primary concern.

Establishing a Trust

A *trust* sets aside certain assets or an amount of money for another person. It allows money to be disbursed over time rather than as a lump sum both before and after the grantor's death. A trust is a good option to consider for people with beneficiaries who aren't able to manage money well. These beneficiaries may have developmental disabilities, be minors, or just be unreliable with money. Sometimes trusts are used to transfer property, such as a vacation home, that is not easy to divide evenly among several beneficiaries. They are also often used by people with substantial assets because they can help reduce estate taxes. Probably the most common reason people set up trusts is that they want to control the disposition of the property more readily than they can in a will.

You can set up a trust so that the beneficiary receives the proceeds of the trust after your death or upon reaching a certain age. For instance, you can set up a *testamentary trust* in which you put some assets with conditions on their use, such as for a grandchild's education or when the child reaches the age of 25.

If you choose to prepare a trust, you still need to have a will. The will provides a safety net if for some reason some of the trust property cannot be transferred.

A trust can hold money, real estate, stocks and bonds — anything of monetary value. The trustee is a person or institution that you select to manage the trust property. The trustee has a fiduciary duty (that term again!) to use the property as the grantor has indicated. The property stays in the same place, but legal ownership is transferred to the trust.

If, after reviewing information about wills and probate, you realize that your estate or your parent's will probably qualify for a simplified probate process, will not have a big tax bite taken out after death, and will not involve complicated financial arrangements, then setting up a trust will probably not get you much but will be costly and cumbersome. Even so, many people are attracted to the idea of a living trust (maybe it's the word *living,* which moves planning out of the realm of death).

A living trust is often touted both as a way to retain control of assets and to avoid probate. This is how a living trust works: You set up a trust that you both own and control as both the trustee and the beneficiary while you are alive and not disabled. You also name the successor trustee who will manage the trust after your disability or death and successor beneficiaries who will get the assets in the trust after your death. You can name someone else as trustee if you choose, and you can revoke that decision later.

Read on for a list of advantages and disadvantages with living trusts and information on other kinds of trusts.

Pros and cons of living trusts

Living trusts have the following advantages:

- ✔ If you become disabled and you have named someone as a successor trustee, the trust provides a way to manage the assets placed in the trust.
- ✔ A trust is a private document and does not become public as does a will.
- ✔ A trust is easy to change.
- ✔ Assets in the trust do not go to probate.

There are, however, some potential problems.

- ✔ You have to remember to transfer legal title to the assets you want to be held by the trust.
- ✔ Just like a will, you have to remember to update the living trust in case of a life-changing event. The person named as beneficiary may now be an ex-spouse.
- ✔ Having a trust can affect your eligibility for Medicaid or other benefits.
- ✔ Because the management of a living trust is outside a court's jurisdiction, there is no oversight, which means no probate court costs but also no supervision in case of disagreements. You could go to all the trouble of creating a living trust and still have your estate wind up in court.

Be wary of salespeople who pitch kits that promise to include everything you need for a living trust — at a cost of several thousand dollars. They take the money and run, or give you a document that does not fit your circumstances and may not even be valid in your state. Several states have filed consumer fraud actions against these con men. If you or a parent is really a good candidate for a living trust, you need competent legal advice from an experienced lawyer in your community. The "free lunch" session on how to avoid probate with a living will kit is going to cost you.

Special-needs trusts

There are many different kinds of trusts — such as charitable trusts to give money to favorite organizations, generation-skipping trusts, spendthrift trusts, and others — but one additional type deserves particular attention because it applies to a lot of people. A *special-needs trust* is an instrument that allows a parent or other person to set aside money for the care and needs of a person with disabilities. This money does not count in the determination of the person's eligibility for Medicaid or other government benefits, an important consideration. It can be spent on items and services that improve the person's quality of life. The trustee may be a parent or other relative who manages the trust in the disabled person's best interests.

Special needs trusts are valuable protections for disabled persons and help assure that they get appropriate care. Legislation has been proposed that would permit individuals to set up their own special needs trusts so they do not have to rely on family or courts. Fore more information, see `www.naela.org/Public/Advocacy_Public_Policy/Public_Policy/SNT_Fairness_Act.aspx`.

Looking into Guardianship

While many people see the value of living trusts, online wills, and other financial instruments, guardianship has few advocates because it is a costly and often demeaning process for the person, whose frailty and inabilities to manage have to be presented in court. Court-appointed guardianship (or conservatorship) does have a role in protecting the property and decision making for older adults who are unable to make decisions themselves and do not have natural advocates such as a trusted family member with authority to make decisions. Generally, guardianship is used as a last resort when the person has failed to plan for their disability and now needs the help of someone else to make important decisions about their care and finances. This sometimes necessary court process can be costly and unpleasant. Having a stranger appointed as guardian introduces another element into an already difficult situation.

Even if the court-appointed guardian is a family member, the responsibilities of being a guardian are more onerous than simply being a caring child or nephew. You will be required to report periodically to the court about how you are spending the money and how you are caring for the incapacitated person. You have a fiduciary duty to properly manage the resources for the benefit of the family member.

Following are the two kinds of guardianship:

- **Guardianship of the estate:** Having authority to manage money and other assets; this is called *conservatorship* in some states
- **Guardianship of the person:** Having the responsibility to make health-care and other decisions that affect the well-being of the person

Guardianship situations usually arise when a person is mentally ill, has an intellectual disability, advanced dementia, or otherwise lacks *capacity*. Courts determine capacity in different ways, depending on state law, but it generally involves a legal finding that a person cannot make certain kinds of decisions. Capacity is specific to the task or decision. Someone may have capacity to make healthcare decisions but not to manage money.

If there is conflict among siblings, for example, over whether a parent's assets should be used to hire home care workers, or to place the parent in a nursing home, one sibling may file a guardianship petition to be able to make the decision. The court may appoint one person or co-guardians.

If no family member or friend seems to be an appropriate guardian, or the family situation appears irrevocably torn, the court may appoint a person outside the family to take on this role. It could be a private professional guardian, public guardian, volunteer, or attorney.

Although the guardian is required to act in the person's best interests or expressed interests, sometimes courts do not fully investigate the background of the guardians they appoint, and their shortcomings are realized only after they have committed fraud or abused or neglected their wards.

Money matters and legal issues are complicated. Don't make any decisions without consulting an experienced attorney.

Part IV
Managing Your Health for the Long Term

Eight Questions to Ask When Choosing a Home-Care Agency

- ✔ What types of services do you provide? (If you need special kinds of care, such as ventilator assistance or wound care, be sure to ask about them. Some agencies contract these services to specialized agencies.)

- ✔ Do your aides have special training to deal with medical conditions like dementia, paralysis, or stroke?

- ✔ What kind of supervision do your aides receive? Does a nurse review the case regularly and ask for their observations about the person's care?

- ✔ Do you screen aides before you hire them? Do you do a background check, and what does it include? Is the criminal background check for your state only, or is it nationwide?

- ✔ How much do you charge per hour?

- ✔ Can your agency arrange for medical equipment when needed?

- ✔ How do you handle complaints?

- ✔ Do you provide 24-hour access in case of emergencies?

When taking many medications, you need a system to sort out what to take, when to take them, and where to find answers to questions. Go to www.dummies.com/extras/planninglongtermcare for a free article that gives some tips about managing the mini-pharmacy in your home.

In this part...

✔ See why and how to find a doctor who is familiar with the problems of aging, whether it's a geriatrician, internal-medicine doctor, or family-practice doctor.

✔ Cut through the confusion surrounding home care with a discussion of the many varieties of services, who provides them, and who pays. I also offer some tips on working with home health aides, who are the mainstay of formal home care.

✔ Choose a good, person-centered nursing home if placement in one is your best or only choice.

✔ Delve into advance-care planning. I review the various forms of advance directives and describe two options for advanced illness: palliative care and hospice.

Chapter 13

Choosing Good Geriatric Care

In This Chapter

▶ Understanding the special medical needs of older adults

▶ Finding the right doctors

▶ Managing medications

*A*ging is a normal process, not a disease. But older people are more likely to have conditions that affect their ability to manage day-to-day life on their own and that require frequent checkups, often with several different doctors. They take many medications and over-the-counter preparations. They may also experience episodes of acute illness requiring a hospital stay.

The term *geriatric care* covers a wide spectrum of necessary services, but, most often, it refers to managing the medical side of aging — from doctors to hospitals to medications. Who is in charge of managing the medical side of long-term care for you or your parent or other relative? That answer used to be fairly simple: "The doctor who has treated my family for years." In today's complex and constantly evolving healthcare system, the answer is all too often: "I guess it's the primary care provider from the health plan or maybe it's her cardiologist." An honest answer might be: "Nobody seems to be in charge."

This chapter outlines some steps to take to ensure good geriatric medical care, and it also gives some cautions. The information is intended to provide general information and does not substitute for advice from a qualified physician or other healthcare professional.

Checking on the Special Medical Needs of Older Adults

The good news is that Americans are living longer, and many older adults are in good or excellent health. However, with increased longevity comes the likelihood of medical conditions that require ongoing attention.

Many factors contribute to length of life, but in general women live longer than men. If you are a man who celebrated your 65th birthday in 2003, you can expect to live to the age of 81.8; a woman of the same age can expect to live to 84.8. Of course, these ages are averages, and everyone knows 90- and 100-year-old men who are doing fine and women who have died at much younger ages.

Increased longevity, has increased the burden of chronic disease. In earlier days people died from acute (rapid onset) conditions like pneumonia, bacterial infections, or accidents. Although these causes of death still exist, the more common conditions are chronic; that is, they last a long time and can be treated but typically cannot be cured.

Identifying common chronic conditions

It is rare for someone to reach advanced old age without some chronic condition. Here are some of the most common conditions:

- **Heart disease:** According to the U.S. Centers for Disease Control and Prevention, heart disease is the leading cause of death (27.7 percent) for both men and women over the age of 65 and for all races and ethnicities.

- **Cancer:** Cancer is the second most common cause of death, a position it has held since 1938. Various forms of cancer account for almost a quarter of deaths in men and 19 percent of deaths in women. Although deaths from breast and colorectal cancer among women have decreased, the rising mortality from lung cancer has kept the overall rates stable.

- **Hypertension:** Hypertension (high blood pressure) is the most prevalent condition among older adults, affecting 71 percent of people over 65. Untreated or poorly controlled hypertension can lead to strokes.

- **Dyslipidemia:** Too much LDL (low-density lipoprotein) or " bad" cholesterol, a condition known as *dyslipidemia,* affects 45 percent of older adults and is associated with blood clots and heart disease.

- **Arthritis:** Arthritis is the third most prevalent condition among older adults, affecting 60 percent of women and 42 percent of men. It is a leading cause of disability.

- **Diabetes:** One in five older adults has diabetes, and men are less likely to be aware of their condition than women. Poorly controlled diabetes can cause serious complications, including amputations and vision problems.

✔ **Alzheimer's disease:** Alzheimer's disease is the fifth leading cause of death for people over the age of 65. This statistic may be an under-estimate because the immediate cause of death may be recorded as some other condition. More than 5 million people have this disease or another dementia. It is probably the most feared chronic disease, more so than cancer.

✔ **Lung disease:** Lung conditions, such as chronic obstructive pulmonary disease (COPD), emphysema, or chronic bronchitis, affect 14 percent of older women and 11 percent of older men. Not surprisingly, COPD is three times higher among current smokers compared with those who have never smoked.

✔ **Osteoporosis:** Osteoporosis (thinning of bones) is more common among older women (26 percent) than men (4 percent). Osteoporosis increases the risk of fractures after a fall.

✔ **Vision problems:** Cataracts are the most common vision problem among older adults, affecting 41 percent. People with diabetes are more likely to have cataracts and glaucoma than non-diabetics.

✔ **Incontinence:** Over a third of older adults experience urinary inconti-nence, and the prevalence is higher among women (47 percent) than men (18 percent).

✔ **Mental health problems:** Mental health problems — depression, anxiety, obsessive compulsive disorder (OCD, which manifests in hoarding), and others — add to the burden of physical conditions.

Dealing with multiple ailments

Approximately one in four Americans has at least two chronic conditions, but the burden of chronic disease is even higher in older adults. Among Medicare fee-for-service beneficiaries, over two-thirds have two or more chronic conditions. About one in seven have six or more, and this group accounts for almost half of total Medicare spending. Older adults with several chronic conditions are known in medical jargon as *multimorbid.*

Chronic conditions are not only difficult to manage on their own; they fre-quently lead to loss of function. A person with two arthritic knees or hips has a hard time just getting around without pain, and immobility leads to other problems. Strokes can affect speech and movement. Heart disease and COPD may limit activity. And of course memory and behavior problems associated with Alzheimer's disease and other dementias that worsen over time create difficult situations in which the older person's personality, judgment, and ability to communicate undergo major changes.

Preventive measures, such as those to reduce the risk of falls, can help. These are discussed in Chapter 5. And the benefits of good nutrition, exercise, social activity, and moderation in alcohol use are well known, if not always followed. Genetics, we are learning, plays a part as well.

Whatever the combination of factors that apply to a specific person, it is essential to have good medical care — that is, care that takes into account the way aging affects the body and, the difference in medication absorption and side effects between older adults and the younger populations on which most drugs were tested. When looking for a doctor to manage your or your parent's care, as important as technical competence is the professional's ability to focus on the whole person, not just body parts and disease. I give more guidance on finding a good doctor in the following section.

Finding the Right Specialist to Manage Care

Geriatricians and gerontologists are both specialists in aging. What is the difference?

- *Geriatrics* is a medical subspecialty. *Geriatricians* are physicians, primarily internal medicine doctors, who have taken additional training that focuses on the diseases of aging and their treatments. They have been certified by the American Board of Internal Medicine to practice geriatric medicine.

- *Gerontology* is a multidisciplinary study of the mental, physical, environmental, and social aspects of aging. *Gerontologists* do research, teach aging in universities, participate in organizational planning and policy, and contribute to the broad knowledge about the impact of aging on individuals and society.

Perhaps the simplest distinction is this: While both geriatricians and gerontologists are called *doctor,* a geriatrician is an M.D. or a D.O. (doctor of osteopathy) and a gerontologist is usually a Ph.D. An M.D. can prescribe medications; a gerontologist can't. Geriatricians see patients individually, while gerontologists generally do not, although they may work in settings like nursing homes or government agencies to advise on practice and policies.

Within geriatric medicine, there are even more specialists: geriatric psychiatrists, cardiologists, pulmonologists, and others. Some nurses and social workers also become specialists in this field.

Considering the need for a geriatrician

Is it essential for an older adult to be treated by a geriatrician? No. many internists (internal medicine doctors) and family physicians provide excellent primary care for older adults. Although they may not have advanced training, they have the benefit of experience. Among their patients are undoubtedly many older adults, and experienced doctors have learned that older adults need more time during office visits and react differently to medications than their younger patients.

The American Geriatric Society recommends that a geriatrician should be consulted in the following circumstances:

- ✔ An older person's condition causes considerable impairment and frailty. These patients tend to be over the age of 75 and coping with a number of diseases and disabilities, including cognitive (mental) problems.
- ✔ Family members and friends are feeling considerable stress and strain as caregivers.

Many older people want to stick with a doctor they have known for years. (But the doctor, of course, is aging too, which may be something to consider.) If you or your parent or other relative have a good relationship with a doctor and the care needed is not highly specialized, then you have no reason to make a change.

However, be sure to be particularly observant about symptoms that may indicate a change in your or your relative's condition, or a medication side effect that may be related to a person's age. If your regular doctor doesn't take questions or observations about memory or behavior changes seriously, this may be a sign that it's time for a change. Family members and sometimes older persons themselves are often the best reporters of changes that may indicate something serious. Maybe it's a side effect of a medication (even one that has been taken for a long time) or even a urinary tract infection. Maybe it's a sign of depression. Maybe it's a sign of early dementia. Geriatricians are able to do comprehensive evaluations of these worrisome but often nonspecific reports and can recommend further testing if necessary.

If your regular doctor refers you to a specialist, ask specifically about that person's experience and qualifications for treating older adults.

Finding a geriatrician

If, for whatever reason, you are looking for a new doctor, I recommend finding a qualified geriatrician. But it's not as easy as it sounds, because there's a shortage of geriatricians (see the nearby sidebar "The shortage of geriatric specialists"). Some established geriatricians are not taking new patients, or they may require a long wait for an initial visit. Many geriatricians see patients only part of their time because they are involved in training programs.

Here are some suggestions for finding a geriatrician:

- ✔ **Check online:** Members of the American Geriatrics Society (geriatricians, geriatric nurse practitioners, and geriatric physician assistants) who wish to participate in its referral program are listed at `www.healthinaging.org/find-a-geriatrics-healthcare-professional`. The Society does not endorse individual providers, but all the physicians listed are either Board Certified in Geriatric Medicine (internists) or have a Certificate of Added Qualifications in Geriatric Medicine (family physicians).

  Some commercial websites also offer to help you find a geriatrician. These lists can be useful but they are not comprehensive, and the doctors have probably paid to be listed.

- ✔ **Contact a hospital:** Contact a hospital or academic medical center in your area. Its "Find a Physician" lists provide names and qualifications.

- ✔ **Use Medicare resources:** If you or your parent is a member of a Medicare Advantage plan, look at the list of providers in the plan to find geriatricians.

- ✔ **Ask around:** Use the old-fashioned method of asking friends and family. Ask specific questions about how efficiently the office is run, whether the doctor has good communication skills with older adults, whether he or she has emergency back-up if needed, and any other questions that may apply to you or your parent. Is the office easily accessible, even for a wheelchair? Are the staff pleasant and responsive to older people? If you have to be admitted to a hospital, which one will it be? Does the doctor make hospital and home visits?

The shortage of geriatric specialists

According to the American Geriatric Society, currently about 7,500 certified geriatricians are working in the United States. Given projections about the increase in the 65-and-older population, approximately 17,000 geriatricians are needed to take care of 12 million people (30 percent of the population over 65). In addition, there are only 1,600 geriatric psychiatrists, and less than 1 percent of registered nurses, pharmacists, and physician assistants and 2.6 percent of advanced practice nurses are certified in geriatrics. The situation is no better in other professionals that routinely see older adults; about 3 percent of psychologists devote the majority of their practice to older adults, and 4 percent of social workers specialize in geriatrics. The future does not look promising, as very few medical school graduates are pursuing advanced training in geriatrics. The lack of interest may be because geriatrics is not a high-income specialty, work schedules are less predictable than in other specialties, and working with older people may not be considered as stimulating or challenging as other fields. Yet older adults account for a disproportionate share of all health care services, from 26 percent of all physician office visits and 35 percent of all hospital stays to 90 percent of all nursing home care.

Navigating Hospitals

Nobody likes having to go to the hospital, but it is a necessary factor in the long-term equation. Often times, elder people utilize the hospital as a go-to solution for illness remedies when other options are available. When a hospital stay truly is necessary, there are certain points to keep in mind to help the experience go more smoothly. The next sections discuss these areas.

Where to go for emergencies and non-emergencies

Emergency departments (EDs) are often the first stage of a hospital stay. Most people still call them *ERs* for emergency room, but the formal term is ED. Whatever the title, they are usually busy, chaotic, and difficult environments for anyone, but particularly for an older person. Yet all too often they are the default solution for a problem instead of a well-considered decision.

Emergency departments

EDs are meant for real emergencies — difficulty breathing, choking, loss of consciousness, severe pain — not for problems that can be treated at home or at an urgent care center and followed up with a doctor visit in the next day or two. Of course, no one wants to make a mistake by discounting the seriousness of a medical complaint, but calling the doctor's office or a nurse hotline to get a professional opinion about the urgency of the complaint can help you avoid unnecessary trips to the ED.

If the person answering the phone at the doctor's office doesn't ask questions or offer any suggestions but just says, "Take your mother to the emergency room," it is likely a bad sign about the care being provided.

Some hospitals have created special EDs for older adults who are not sick enough to be admitted to the hospital but are not ready to go home. These special units are quieter, staffed by nurses and others used to working with older adults, and more comfortable than the typical ED. Patients can stay in these settings while tests are run, medications are given, they're observed for side effects, and until someone can provide a safe ride home. Ask whether your local hospital has this kind of special ED.

Urgent care centers

An alternative to an ED visit is an urgent care center. Urgent care centers are appropriate for situations that are not clearly emergencies but that require immediate attention; for example, a twisted ankle, rash, or bad cold. Staff (often ED-trained doctors) can evaluate the problem, take X-rays, and prescribe medications. If they feel that an ED visit is required, they can call an ambulance. If you do go to an urgent care center, make sure to inform the regular doctor about what happened and what was recommended.

Urgent care centers can be a very convenient and useful option. The number of urgent care centers in many parts of the country have been increasing. They are often less expensive than an ED and may be located nearer to you. The waiting time is also usually shorter than in an ED, and these centers take most insurance plans.

Being admitted to the hospital

A hospital stay, especially a long one or one that involves being in an intensive care unit (ICU), is certainly upsetting for everyone, and infection is an ever-present risk. Older people in particular tend to become disoriented by the noise, lights, constant questioning, and different people coming in and out of the room. Long waits in cold corridors for X-rays and other tests add to the misery.

Patients may not get enough to eat, especially if doctors order them to fast before procedures. Getting a full night's sleep is next to impossible. Patients often take painkillers or other medications that can leave them confused, or even delirious, especially in the unfamiliar surroundings of a hospital. Extended bed rest can weaken patients' muscles and bones. Even with kind and caring staff explaining what is happening (not always the case), a hospital stay is almost guaranteed to be unpleasant at best and debilitating at worst.

Some hospitals have special units for older people called Acute Care for Elders (ACE) units. They are staffed by a specially trained interdisciplinary team, which can include geriatricians, advanced practice nurses, social workers, pharmacists, and physical therapists. The team assesses patients daily, and nurses are given an increased level of independence and accountability. These units have been shown to shorten length of stay and result in lower cost while maintaining patients' functional abilities. If hospitalization is necessary, ask if your hospital has an ACE.

If you or your parent have been given a bed on a regular hospital floor, make sure that you have formally been admitted as an inpatient. If the doctor or nurse isn't sure, ask the admitting office. The hospital may claim that you were under *observation*, even though you received the same services as everyone else. Because you have not been formally admitted, Medicare will not consider this stay as a Part A (hospital) benefit, for which you pay only an inpatient deductible, but as a Part B (outpatient) benefit. Your portion of the bill may be higher and will include costs for lab tests, X-rays, medications, and other things that would be typically covered under Part A. And if you go to a rehab program in a nursing facility after this stay, you will have to pay privately since you will technically not have had the required three-day inpatient hospital stay. Legislation has been proposed to change Medicare rules on observation stays, but the outcome is pending. For now, make sure you ask whether you are admitted or on observation. There is no way to appeal the hospital's decision to place you on observation, but you can register a complaint with the hospital administration and with Medicare. The Center for Medicare Advocacy has advice on filing a complaint at www.medicareadvocacy.org.

Your primary doctor, whether a geriatrician or not, may or may not visit you in the hospital. Increasingly hospital care is managed by specialists called *hospitalists*. These doctors are trained in critical care medicine and are skilled at handling medical crises that happen to seriously ill patients. They generally work in teams so that someone from the team is available at all hours of the day and night and on weekends. This also means that you or your parent may not see the same person every day. Hospitalists are employed by the hospital or belong to a group practice that is under contract to the hospital. They do not generally see patients after discharge, although some groups do have physicians who work both in the hospital and in the community. For more information, see the United Hospital Fund's Next Step in Care guide to hospitalists at www.nextstepincare.org/Caregiver_Home/Hospitalist.

Planning for a hospital stay

Hospitalization for an elective (planned) surgery for an older adult is in theory easier than an admission through the ED because you have time to get ready. But there's a lot to think about, no matter what the reason for the surgery.

All surgery has risks, and you want to be sure that the potential benefits are worth the risks. Someone's age alone should not be a reason to decide against surgery, but a very frail person in poor health and perhaps with moderate or advanced dementia is probably not a good candidate for surgery. Be sure to ask about and consider alternatives.

The surgeon is generally a specialist recommended by the geriatrician or the primary care physician. An orthopedic surgeon replaces hips and knees, a cardiac surgeon replaces valves and inserts pacemakers and stents, and a renal surgeon takes care of kidney problems. They are expert in their specific area, but you need someone to look after the whole person, and that is the geriatrician or primary care doctor.

It is important that these doctors talk to each other, not just in the initial referral but also as the surgery is approaching and definitely afterward. The time spent in the hospital may be very short, which is a good thing, but it also means that the recovery time needed at home is longer, and care must be taken to avoid complications. Older people react differently to anesthesia, may experience more pain, and take longer to recover than younger people undergoing similar surgery.

Many hospitals will inform a primary care doctor when one of his patients is admitted, but this doesn't always happen. If you are the patient, ask a family member to call your regular doctor's office to give that information and the name and contact information of the hospital doctor in charge of your care. And ask the hospital doctor — probably a hospitalist — to contact your regular doctor to discuss your diagnosis and treatment. This is especially important as you get ready to be discharged because you will need follow-up at home. Both hospital and primary care doctors are busy and may need some reminders about making sure they both know the specifics of your care.

Because so many older adults are undergoing surgery, the American Geriatrics Society and the American College of Surgeons worked together to create a series of guidelines for surgical teams. These "best practice" guidelines are intended for surgeons, but they are also useful for the person undergoing surgery and family members. Here are some of the key points:

✔ Talk to the surgeon about what to expect from the surgery:

• What are the treatment goals? Will the surgery fix the problem or will there still be limitations?

- What kind of anesthesia will be used? Are there common side effects?

- How long will the surgery last? How long will the person be in the recovery room?

- How will pain be treated? (Don't be misled by the common response, "There won't be much pain, just a little discomfort.")

- Will there be physical limitations such as being able to climb stairs, get in and out of bed, and use the toilet? Even a generally successful surgery like hip replacement is always followed by a period of restrictions on mobility. Can the person follow instructions so that the surgery is not undone by a fall or other accident?

✔ Ask where you or your parent will go after surgery. You may expect and want to go home, but the surgeon may recommend a short stay of a few weeks in a rehabilitation program, probably in a nursing home rehab unit. There you can recover more fully and get therapy to restore and improve function. Even that new hip takes time to get used to, especially if you have been in pain and not walking properly for some time before the surgery.

✔ Ask about costs. Medicare or other insurance will cover some or all of the surgeon's fees (but there will be a copayment) and the hospital fee. But the anesthesiologist will submit a separate bill. Review Medicare's policies at `www.medicare.gov` if you are in Original (fee-for-service Medicare), and if you are a member of a Medicare Advantage plan, ask the plan for details about costs. For Medicaid and other insurances, ask the case manager.

✔ You or your relative may be eligible for some skilled nursing visits and possibly physical therapy at home after discharge from the hospital or rehab program. Ask about those services as well, because it will take some time to get used to being at home, and everyone can benefit from some extra help.

✔ Make sure the surgeon is aware of any special problems, like depression or alcohol use that may affect responses to surgery or recovery. For a comprehensive list of the guidelines, go to `www.nextstepincare.org/Caregiver_Home/Elective_Surgery`.

Polypharmacy: Too Many Drugs?

People take a lot of medications and vitamins, dietary supplements, herbal preparations, and other drug-store items that don't require a doctor's prescription. People mistakingly think that if it's advertised on TV, it must be good for you. If it's new, it must be better. If it's sold without a prescription, it must be safe. If it's "natural," it must be better than something created from chemicals. If it's been around for years, like aspirin, it can't hurt you. For all of these beliefs, the reality is: Not exactly. Taking aspirin, for example, is sometimes used jokingly, as in "Take two aspirin and call me in the morning." But overdoses of aspirin can kill, and even nonlethal doses can cause stomach bleeding and other problems.

With all these drug-promoting ideas in the culture, it might seem as though everyone follows the directions from the doctor, pharmacy, or package label very carefully. Not at all. People get into trouble when they take too many of the wrong medications or skip some that they should be taking and generally adopt a casual attitude about these powerful concoctions. According to the U.S. Centers for Disease Control and Prevention, more than 700,000 ED visits every year are related to adverse drug events. And a growing epidemic of addiction to prescription medications is taking a toll on all ages across the United States.

Older people are particular likely to be subject to *polypharmacy,* the taking of a lot of drugs. They see many doctors, who prescribe many drugs without consulting the doctors who prescribed similar or other drugs. People often don't tell doctors about everything they are taking and not taking. When the doctor asks, "Are you taking your medicines?" the answer is likely to be "Yes," when the reality is "Not so much." And the doctor may not ask if you're taking any other medications." Even if the question is asked, people may answer with what they consider a truthful "No," because they don't realize that all the over-the-counter items are in fact medications, not harmless concoctions.

It's certainly not patients' fault if they are confused. Medicines come in brand names (the advertised versions) and generic preparations, which are cheaper but have harder names to remember. Hospitals have their own formularies (list of drugs they use), which may not be the same as the drugs used at home.

Using caution with certain drugs

Recognizing that certain drugs are potentially risky for older adults, the American Geriatric Society periodically updates a list called the Beers Criteria for Potentially Inappropriate Medication Use in Older Adults. This list contains 34 medications and types of medications that are "potentially inappropriate" for older people and can be replaced with safer or more effective medications or non-drug remedies. Some drugs are listed to be used only with caution. The 2012 Beers List is available at www.americangeriatrics. org/files/documents/beers/2012BeersCriteria_JAGS.pdf.

The Beers List and other similar lists are not the final word on whether a particular drug is right for you or your parent. The drugs on the list have been approved by the Federal Drug Administration, so they are marketed legally. But if you are taking one of these drugs or your doctor prescribes a new one, you need to review the choices and any alternatives. One of the drugs that the list says to avoid or use only with caution may in fact be the best choice for your specific condition. But unless you ask, you won't know why the doctor has recommended this drug instead of another one that seems to be less risky.

Healthinaging.org, an educational arm of the American Geriatric Society, has prepared a list, viewable at `www.healthinaging.org/files/documents/tipsheets/meds_to_avoid.pdf`, of ten medications older adults should avoid or use with caution. For example, long-lasting nonsteroidal anti-inflammatory drugs (NSAIDS) used to reduce pain and inflammation can increase the risk of indigestion, ulcers, and bleeding, as well as increasing blood pressure, and make heart failure worse. Shorter-acting NSAIDs like ibuprofen are better choices. Other medications on the list are certain diabetes drugs, and medications use for anxiety and insomnia.

Getting medications right

You can do many things to make sure that you're taking the right medications at the right time in the right dose:

- ✔ Keep an updated list of all your medications, prescription and OTC, and show it to every doctor at every appointment. Review the list at least once a year and certainly after a hospital stay.

- ✔ Whenever a new drug is prescribed, ask why you should be taking it, what side effects to look out for, whether it interacts with any of the other drugs you are taking, and what to do if you miss a dose.

- ✔ Read the label on the bottle. If the type is too small or the language too dense, ask the pharmacist for an easy-to-read version.

- ✔ Follow the directions, and if you don't understand them, ask the doctor or the pharmacist. Sometimes medical professionals think that directions are clear ("Take this on an empty stomach") when they are not. Take the drug for as long as you've been told — not for a longer or shorter time.

- ✔ Report any changes in your medical condition, which may be related to a new drug. If the reactions are serious, such as an extensive rash, difficulty breathing, or swelling in your throat, they count as emergencies. Call 911 or go the nearest ED.

- ✔ Throw out any unused medications. Don't give them to anyone else, and don't take medications that were not prescribed for you.

Insurance may cover certain drugs and not others. Even with insurance coverage, drugs can be expensive. If you have financial problems and need help paying for prescriptions, see the resources listed in Chapter 10.

Other risks and questions

Given the well-known and serious risks of polypharmacy in older adults, it is not surprising that among the American Geriatric Society's "Five Things Physicians and Patients Should Question," medications accounted for four of the five items. This list is part of the "Choosing Wisely" Initiative of the American Board of Internal Medicine Foundation, in which various medical for specialties came up with their own list of common but questionable practices in their field.

Four of the five recommendations concerned medications, and the first is a common medical procedure:

- **Don't recommend percutaneous (tube) feeding tubes in patients with advanced dementia; instead, offer oral assisted feeding.** Tube feeding is associated with agitation, increased use of physical and chemical restraints and worsening pressure ulcers. Careful hand-feeding for people with severe dementia is at least as good as tube feeding in terms of the outcomes of death, aspiration pneumonia, functional status, and comfort.

  Tube feeding is a procedure that has emotional and ethical as well as medical implications; the AGS recommendation focuses on the medical risks and benefits. It is particularly important for nursing home practice where tube feeding is sometimes a method of convenience, not a medical or ethical choice.

- **Don't use antipsychotics as first choice to treat behavioral and psychological symptoms of dementia.** These drugs provide limited benefit and can cause serious harm, including stroke and premature death. Identifying and addressing causes of behavior change can make drug treatment unnecessary.

- **Avoid using medications to achieve hemoglobin A1c >7.5% in most adults age 65 and older; moderate control is generally better.** The A1C test, which has other names, is a common blood test used to diagnose type 1 and type 2 diabetes and then to gauge how well you're managing your diabetes. The A1C test result reflects your average blood sugar level for the past two to three months. Specifically, the A1C test measures what percentage of your hemoglobin — a protein in red blood cells that carries oxygen — is coated with sugar (glycated). Some studies have shown that efforts to reduce the A1c levels to less than 7 percent have resulted in higher mortality.

- **Don't use benzodiazepines or other sedative-hypnotics in older adults as first choice for insomnia, agitation, or delirium.** Large-scale studies have consistently shown rates of motor vehicle accidents, falls, and hip fractures leading to hospitalization and death can more than double in older adults taking these drugs. Their use should be limited to alcohol withdrawal or severe anxiety disorder unresponsive to other therapies.

- **Don't use antimicrobials to treat bacteriuria (the presence of bacteria in the urine) in older adults unless specific urinary tract symptoms are present.** Urinary tract infection is diagnosed with specific clinical symptoms.

Chapter 14

Demystifying Home Care

. . . .

In This Chapter

▶ Understanding the many types of home care

▶ Choosing a home care agency or finding your own workers

▶ Working with home-care aides

▶ Learning about doctor home visits

. . . .

*H*aving the right kind of help at home can make a significant difference in an older person's quality of life and ability to remain in familiar surroundings. But the right kind of help is different for each person and is often hard to find. And for a person who values independence, accepting that help is difficult, even when the need is clear.

Studies show that families provide an estimated 80 to 90 percent of care at home. But when family care is not available or sufficient, you have the options of different types of services, different agencies that provide them, and different health and long-term care insurance coverage. You may pay privately for workers you hire on your own. Some public programs allow family members or friends to be paid to provide care. This chapter gives you basic information to get started on your search.

Examining the Many Varieties of Home Care

Home care sounds simple, doesn't it? Many people think of home care as having an all-purpose assistant/homemaker/aide who spends the whole day (and maybe stays overnight) helping with personal care, doing household chores, and reminding you or your parent to take your medications — basically, doing whatever needs to be done. This description can be accurate, but only for some people, and even then mostly for those who can pay out of pocket.

Home care services can range from relatively straightforward tasks like helping someone get dressed and preparing meals to a level of care that involves operating and monitoring complex medical equipment and doing wound care and giving injections or infusions. Where you or your parent fit on this spectrum of need determines what kinds of services you may be eligible for and who will provide them, not to mention who will pay.

Home care services can be provided by:

✔ Physicians

✔ Registered nurses

✔ Licensed practical nurses

✔ Physical, occupational, respiratory, and speech therapists

✔ Social workers

✔ Home health aides or personal-care attendants

✔ Equipment vendors who supply durable medical equipment

Each of these people can play an important role in home care, but often you or a family member has to coordinate the different visits and services. This in itself can be a major responsibility involving a significant and ongoing commitment of time.

This chapter first looks at home healthcare services provided by professionals through agencies, which are sometimes covered by insurance. I then turn to the option of hiring a home care worker independently. The final section looks at physician home visits.

The AARP Caregiving Resource Center has a lot of information about home care and access to experts who can answer your questions. Go to www.aarp. org/home-family/caregiving or use the call-in number (877-333-5885), which has extended hours of 7 a.m. to 11 p.m. ET Monday through Friday and 9 a.m. to 5 p.m. Saturdays. You can also use the Long-Term Care Calculator (at www.aarp.org/relationships/caregiving-resource-center/LTCC) to estimate costs in your area.

Services from a Home Care Agency

Policymakers and researchers often distinguish between formal and informal services. In policy-speak, *formal* services are services provided through an agency and paid for by insurance or privately; *informal* services are those provided by unpaid family members or friends. (No data are available on the numbers of people who do not use an agency but who instead hire and pay home care workers directly. Even though these workers are paid, they would probably be considered informal help since they are not supervised by a home healthcare agency or public entity.)

For Medicare and most private insurance, the threshold for eligibility for formal home care services is the need for skilled care. *Skilled care* is defined not by what it is but by who provides it. In other words, skilled care is provided by a nurse or a physical therapist or other professional. Some examples of skilled nursing care are IV injections, tube feedings, and wound care. Physical therapists work with you to improve mobility, balance, and strength.

The opposite of skilled care is not unskilled care. Home care aides provide care that is sometimes called "unskilled," but that is an erroneous label. Home care aides do personal care like bathing and dressing, help people move from bed to chair, and generally help them do they things they used to be able to do but no longer can on their own. Care provided by home care aides, especially if the person has dementia or cognitive deficits, is immobilized, or is uncooperative or verbally abusive, requires a high level of skill, not to mention patience and tolerance. The language of home care policies and practice, however, recognizes only what professionals do as *skilled.* And even when you or a family member learn to do the same tasks as a nurse, the task is no longer called skilled care.

Different kinds of home care agencies

The definition of services is mirrored in the different types of home care agencies.

- ✔ **Medicare-certified home health agencies (HHAs):** These are agencies approved by the Center for Medicare & Medicaid Services (CMS) and licensed by the state to provide skilled services, primarily nurse visits, but also physical therapy or social-work visits, among others. Medicare will only pay for services provided through an HHA. If there is a skilled need, HHAs may also provide aide services through their own aides or through another agency, usually a licensed agency, with which they have a contract. Medicare does not pay for aide services at home unless there is a skilled need.

  You can compare HHAs in your area at www.medicare.gov/homehealthcompare/search.aspx. This site can give you some general information, but it can't tell you about important aspects of care such as how reliable and friendly an agency's workers are.

- ✔ **Licensed home care agency:** Most but not all states license home care agencies to provide nursing services and aides who do personal care. Some are contracted through Medicaid to provide long-term personal care. The Genworth 2013 Cost of Care Survey reported a national median hourly rate through licensed agencies of homemaker or companion services to be $18 and the personal care services to be $19. Obviously, rates vary by geographic area.

✔ **Non-medical or companion agency:** These rapidly growing agencies are not usually licensed by state health departments or regulated by the federal government, and their services are not covered under health insurance because they are deemed nonmedical. Companion services include reading and conversation, assisting with clothing selection, organizing the mail, and picking up prescriptions from the pharmacy. Workers have varying levels of experience and training. Frequently companion agencies are locally run businesses that are franchises of large, brand-name companies. The rates for these services can range from $15 to $25 an hour.

Companion agencies may list medication management among the non-medical tasks within their range of expertise. However, if you or your family member are taking many medications of different sorts or they have to be taken in specific doses or at specific times, a companion may not have the necessary training to help with this task if it involves anything more than reminding the person to take the pills that have already been set up in a pill box.

✔ **Employment or registry agencies:** These agencies provide names of nurses and aides available to provide home care. You contact and pay them directly. Your state may also maintain a registry through the Department of Health. PHI National has a map showing which states have this service at `http://phinational.org/policy/resources/phi-matching-services-project`. Some states limit access to publicly funded (Medicaid) clients; others are more flexible.

Medicare only pays for home healthcare services provided by a certified HHA, and both Medicare Advantage plans and private insurance may require you to use only an HHA within their network. If you pay privately and want to use an agency, you can decide which one to use.

Choosing a home care agency

Many people do not investigate home care agencies until they have a crisis. Often the crisis involves a hospitalization. The hospital discharge plan may include a referral to home care, and you may get a list of agencies that accept your insurance. In such a situation, you don't have a lot of time to investigate the options. But even so, you should ask questions about the agency before you sign an agreement. Be especially careful to find out how the agency screens, trains, and supervises home care workers. If you are not in crisis mode, you have more time and should do a thorough search.

A hospital discharge planner may not refer you to home care services. If you think you or your parent needs these services, ask the discharge planner to make a referral. A referral can also be made by a doctor in the community.

Although there are federal guidelines for training home health aides, each state has its own system of education and certifications. For a state-by-state list of required training hours, see `http://phinational.org/policy/states`. Most states require the federal minimum of 75 hours of training and 16 hours of clinical experience. Some states exceed these requirements. Most states have no training requirements for personal care attendants.

Here are some questions to ask the agency, whether you're paying privately or expect insurance to cover the services:

- What types of services do you provide? (Be sure to ask about special kinds of care, such as ventilator assistance or wound care. Some agencies contract these services to specialized agencies.)

- Do you provide back-up help if the assigned worker is not available?

- Do your aides have special training to deal with medical conditions like dementia, paralysis, or stroke?

- What kind of supervision do your aides receive? Does a nurse review the case regularly and ask for their observations about the person's care?

- Do you screen aides before you hire them? Do you do a background check and what does it include? Is the criminal background check for your state only, or is it nationwide?

- How much do you charge per hour?

- Can your agency arrange for medical equipment when needed?

- How do you handle complaints?

- Do you provide 24-hour access in case of emergencies?

If your family member does not speak English, has cognitive problems, or follows certain religious or cultural routines, you should inform the agency.

Paying for Home Care

Medicare has been the single largest payer of home healthcare services, although Medicaid is catching up. Medicare home healthcare services are largely home health visits, whereas Medicaid's are mostly in the category of personal care visits. Because Medicaid home care varies by state, I start this discussion with Medicare. For people who are eligible for both programs (the *duals*), Medicare is the first payer.

Looking at Medicare's rules for eligibility for home healthcare services

Medicare's eligibility rules are fairly stringent:

✔ You or your parent must be under a doctor's care, and the doctor must have established a plan of care that is reviewed regularly. The doctor must have examined you within the previous 30 days. In Medicare terminology, this is called a "face-to-face" visit.

✔ The doctor must certify that you need one or more of the following skilled services:

- Intermittent (part-time) skilled nursing care (fewer than eight hours a day over a period of 21 days or fewer than seven days a week)

- Physical therapy

- Speech language-pathology services

- Continued occupational therapy (although OT, which involves therapy to restore function for everyday tasks, is not a skilled service that makes you eligible for home care on its own.)

These therapy services must be specific, safe, and effective for your condition and be performed only by qualified therapists, and the amount, frequency, and duration of the services must be reasonable.

✔ The doctor must certify that you are homebound, which means that:

- It is not recommended that you leave the home because of your condition.

- You need help (such as using a wheelchair, walker, special transportation) or someone else's assistance.

- Leaving home requires a considerable and taxing effort.

- You can leave home only for medical treatment or short, occasional absences for nonmedical reasons. You can even go to adult day care, but the home care services will be provided in your home.

✔ Medical social services to help with social and emotional concerns related to illness are covered. However, many home care agencies have limited social work staff.

✔ Some medical supplies, like wound dressings, are covered when they are ordered as part of your care. Durable medical equipment is covered separately.

✔ Finally, as already noted, these services must be provided by a Medicare-certified Home Health Agency (HHA).

If you qualify for Medicare home healthcare services, you may also be eligible for some home health aide services. This bears repeating: Medicare does not cover aide services unless you are also getting skilled care services. Aides provide personal care and some tasks like making lunch and taking care of the individual's laundry (not the family's lunch or laundry).

For more details, see Medicare's guide to home care at `http://www.medicare.gov/publications/pubs/pdf/10969.pdf` or call Medicare at 1-800-633-4227. You can also call the Medicare Rights Center, which has trained volunteers to answer questions by phone (800-333-4114). If you or your relative belongs to a Medicare Advantage plan (a private company that contracts with Medicare to provide benefits), check with the plan.

Duration of home healthcare services under Medicare

You probably want to know how long Medicare will continue to pay for home healthcare, but that question is not easy to answer. Under Medicare, home health agencies receive payment based on a 60-day episode of care. Some cases require the full 60 days of expensive care; other cases are closed in a shorter period and require mostly routine care. Under this prospective payment system, agencies have an incentive to close cases rather than keep them open.

If your doctor refers you or your parent for home healthcare services, a nurse from the agency will come to the home to do an evaluation. An agency does not have to accept the case if it can't offer the needed services, the home is not safe, or for other reasons. The agency, however, cannot discriminate on the basis of race, religion, or other personal characteristics.

Based on the evaluation, the nurse determines where you or your parent fit into one of 153 home health resource groups (HHRGs). (If fewer than five home care visits are expected to be necessary, the case is not included in these categories.) Where you fit in this complicated scheme plays a part in how long the episode of care lasts. The HHRGs range from groups of relatively uncomplicated cases to those involving people who have severe medical conditions or functional limitations and need extensive therapy. If an episode of care involves an unusually large number or costly mix of visits, the HHA may be eligible for an *outlier payment* — an extra fee based on the more-intensive-than-average services.

On average, Medicare home healthcare clients have two episodes of care per year (not necessarily consecutive and not necessarily lasting 60 days). Each episode of care involves an average of 17 visits, 80 percent of them by a nurse or therapist. Home health aide visits account for only about 15 percent of visits.

What does this mean in practice? As an example, the nurse who does the evaluation may recommend a schedule of services, including a nurse visit two to three times a week, a physical therapist twice a week, and a home health aide for four visits a week of two to three hours each. This schedule will be reviewed and may be changed weekly. If the number of visits starts to decline, or the physical therapy visits stop, ask the agency how much longer the service will continue.

Some home healthcare services can go on for a longer period, for example, for treating chronic obstructive pulmonary disease (COPD) or continuing occupational therapy. A doctor can recertify a person for home care services, although the continuing need for skilled services will have to be documented.

Appealing Medicare decisions on home care

Home health agencies are required to give you advance notice (a Home Health Advance Beneficiary Notice, or HHABN) in the following situations:

- When you will be receiving medical services and supplies that Medicare doesn't pay for; you will have to agree to pay for these services on your own.

- When you're required to make a 20 percent copayment of the Medicare-approved amount for medical equipment, such as wheelchairs, walkers, and oxygen equipment. The Medicare-approved amount may not be the same as the supplier's bill.

- When the HHA reduces or stops providing you with some services or supplies because the doctor has changed the orders.

- When the home health agency plans to give you a home health service or supplies that Medicare probably won't pay for. (The determination that Medicare won't pay is made by a contractor, not Medicare itself. These are insurance companies under contract to Medicare to review claims.)

Starting in 2014, claims for continuing rehabilitation services cannot be denied by an assertion that the patient is not improving. The Medicare standard is whether a skilled service such as physical therapy is needed to prevent or delay deterioration, not whether the person is going to get better. Go to the Center for Medicare Advocacy's website for more information on the lawsuit, *Jimmo* v. *Sebelius*, that led to a federal court ruling on this question: www.medicareadvocacy.org/.

The home health agency is supposed to give you a written document called a Notice of Medicare Provider Non-Coverage at least two days before all covered services end. The notice should tell you the date all your covered services will end and how to ask for a fast appeal through the regional quality improvement organization (QIO). The QIO will generally give you an answer within two days. If the QIO decides coverage should end, you have to pay for any services you received while the appeal was being considered. You can find the QIO in your state at www.qualitynet.org/dcs/ContentServer? pagename=QnetPublic%2FPage%2FQnetTier2&cid=1144767874793.

Not all home health agencies provide the required notices in a written form or even in advance. The nurse or aide may simply tell you one day, "This is my last visit." If this happens, you can complain to the QIO. But try to keep on top of the situation by asking the nurse to give you an estimate of how long services will last. In general, think weeks, not months.

Understanding Medicaid home care

Medicaid provides long-term services and supports for low-income older adults and people with disabilities. Since the beginning of Medicaid in 1965, most of these services have been provided in institutional settings, but over the past decade a greater emphasis has been placed on "rebalancing" the system and keeping people in the least restrictive setting, which means the individual's home or in the community of the individual's choosing. To accomplish this, many states are providing more home- and community-based services so that people don't have to go into nursing homes or other facilities, which are generally costly and not the individual's preference.

Medicaid's rules vary by state, and each state sets its own financial threshold for eligibility, which are typically very low income and few or no assets. Federal regulations require all Medicaid programs to provide home health services. Optional services include personal care and even private duty nursing. States can choose which optional services they want to provide.

In addition, states can apply for a variety of waivers from the federal government that allow them to provide a much broader range of medical and nonmedical service. Benefits can include case managements, home care aide services, personal care, adult day health care, and respite care, as well as other services states were not permitted to offer, such as home modification assistance. The goal of all these programs is to keep people safe and cared-for at home. These waiver programs, plus state funds, come under the general heading of home- and community-based services (HCBS).

States facing severe budget shortages may decide to eliminate optional services or opt out of waiver programs altogether. Agencies may restrict access through their practices of establishing eligibility for Medicaid itself or for specific waiver services. Not all states have agreed to participate in the Affordable Care Act's expansion of Medicaid, which includes financial incentives to expand the Medicaid ranks to include people who were formerly uninsured. See Chapter 10 for more information.

Although the range of HCBS may seem impressive (and in some states actually is), many states have waiting lists. You also may have difficulty finding out about these programs and whether you're eligible for them, and, if so, whether there are any limits on the services. It is at best a patchwork quilt, without strong seams holding the pieces together.

Many states are changing the way they manage Medicaid by turning to Medicaid Managed Long-Term Care plans. Managed care organizations run these plans and are paid to coordinate services and supports. Although considerable potential exists for better integrated care and improved outcomes as well as higher utilization of community-based service options, these plans are still evolving. For more information, see the report by the National Senior Citizens Law Center at www.nsclc.org/wp-content/uploads/2012/09/Medicaid-LTSS-Guide-Final.pdf.

Whether a Medicaid enrollee receives services under the traditional Medicaid system or under a managed Medicaid plan, the person should be given adequate notice of a decision to reduce, deny, or terminate a Medicaid service, as well as an opportunity to appeal that decision. For further assistance with a Medicaid appeal, you can contact your local Legal Services Organization (http://lsc.gov/find-legal-aid) or the state's Protection and Advocacy (P&A) agency at http://www.ndrn.org/en/ndrn-member-agencies.html.

Other kinds of insurance

If you or your parent has long-term care insurance, the policy probably includes some home care services that you qualify for after certain eligibility thresholds have been reached. The criteria vary by policy but generally include some level of functional problems, such as needing assistance with at least two activities of daily living (ADLs). The policy may also include waiting periods during which you pay privately for care as well as restrictions on who can be hired. It is important to check the policy and ask your insurance agent to explain the process. (See Chapter 11 for more information.)

You may also be eligible for home care services from the Veterans Administration (see Chapter 17 for details), a retirement health insurance policy, or other resource. It may take some investigation to see how and if these policies work together. A family member or advisor may be able to help you.

Hiring home care workers on your own dime

After formal home care services end, or even before, many people turn to hiring home care workers themselves and paying them privately. The benefits include being in charge of the care, deciding how and when certain tasks are performed, and, in theory at least, having continuity of workers. People usually do better when they have the same aide or team over time. Some Medicaid programs permit qualified enrollees to hire and fire their own workers, with fiscal oversight.

Workers paid privately may charge less than an agency, but in some areas there is not much difference. The worker, of course, gets to keep more of the pay. A downside of hiring privately may be the lack of backup. If the regular worker is not available, you have to find a substitute on your own. You also have to juggle additional responsibilities for financial management and supervision. You can hire someone to manage the payroll and Social Security, but this adds to the cost. Yet this investment can make the difference between your family member's willingness to accept the help (not a foregone conclusion!) and your comfort with the quality of care being provided.

Starting January 1, 2015, if you hire home care workers directly, you will have to follow the new Department of Labor rules implementing the Fair Labor Standards Act. Most home care workers will have to be paid minimum wage and overtime. For more information, go to `www.dol.gov/whd/homecare`.

In interviewing potential aides, describe the aspects of care that are particularly important to you and ask how well the person can meet those needs. If you need night or weekend help, ask if the person will be available for those times.

You should get several recent references. Ask previous employers about the person's work habits, attitude, and reliability. Check with the state Department of Health's registry to see if any past complaints of abuse or neglect have been filed against the worker.

You may want to have a trial period before hiring a worker. Sometimes what looks like a good match turns out not to be one, and you'll be better off acknowledging that early on. Establishing a set of house rules that respect both your family member's privacy and your own as well as the home care worker's needs will help create a good working relationship.

Working with Home Care Aides

When you go to a doctor's office, outpatient clinic, or hospital, you enter someone else's space and give up some control. Your home, however, is your private space, and the strangers who come in and out to help are essentially your guests. Still, it's a different kind of relationship because the person comes to provide a service, not to chat. Bringing someone into your home or your relative's home can ease your responsibilities, but it should not add stress to your life.

Compared to nurses or physical therapists, aides typically will spend more time with you or your parent or other relative. To help make the arrangement more comfortable, plan to spend some time on the aide's first visit just getting to know each other and the physical space in which she (and it's almost always a woman) will be working.

The United Hospital Fund's guide, Working with Home Health Aides, offers some suggestions on establishing a good working relationship that can make your situation more comfortable. Here are some key points (and you can find the full guide at `www.nextstepincare.org/Caregiver_Home/Home_Health_Aides`:

✔ Be clear about what services you expect. Write these things down in a simple agreement. Clarify what the aide cannot do, whether because of regulations, competence, or willingness.

✔ Also include in writing the terms of employment: the hours and pay you have agreed on, whether or not meals and travel costs are included, and how much vacation time you offer.

✔ Have a backup plan in case the aide cannot arrive in time or has to cancel.

✔ Discuss how to handle emergencies. Leave a list of emergency phone numbers, including the doctor's office. Develop an emergency plan, and make sure the aide knows what it is.

✔ Talk about whether and when to call 911. If you or your parent has an in-home DNR (do not resuscitate), signed by a doctor, then the aide should not call 911 in an emergency. You should discuss with the aide what you mean by "emergency" and whom to call if it is not 911.

✔ Be clear that aides are not allowed to have visitors. You should also set limits on texting, phone calls, and other potential distractions from the job.

Respect and tolerance for individual and cultural differences is essential for both you and the aide. Ask the aide whether she prefers to be called by her first name or full name. And make sure she knows how you and your parent prefers to be addressed. Some older adults don't like to be called by their first name or "Sweetie" or other nicknames that are not meant to be offensive but may seem so.

Food and religious differences are areas in which conflict can arise. If you or your parent follows certain religious practices that are new to the aide, explain what they are and why they are important. Just as important are the aide's food preferences and religious practices. Aides should feel that they can observe their personal choices but they should not impose them on others.

Paying Family or Friends to Provide Care

After trying to navigate the maze of home care services and insurance require-ments, some people say, "Why can't I just get paid for taking care of my parent?" And in fact some options to do just that exist, but they are very limited. People generally do not know their options for getting services in their own homes, and unfortunately, there is no national clearinghouse to guide you through the maze of publicly funded programs. Particularly when people are quickly discharged from a hospital (and it is usually very quickly!), there is little time to do the leg-work needed to know about various options and how much they cost. It is pru-dent to find out about all the options in your community — ranging from care in the home to residential care — and then take the next best step.

As you look into having a friend or family member provide care versus hiring a professional, here are a few general points to remember if you consider taking on the job yourself:

> ✔ Wages will be low. Think rates for home care aides, not nurses.
>
> ✔ There are no benefits in the sense of paid vacations, health insurance, or pension.
>
> ✔ Where you live matters. State programs differ significantly.

The following sections provide some more information on who may pay for a friend or family member to provide routine, ongoing care.

State programs

Most states have programs that help pay for in-home care called variously *consumer-directed, participant-directed, cash and counseling,* or other titles. These programs differ by state in terms of funding, eligibility, option of paying family members, exclusion of certain categories like spouses or legal guardians, limits on the number of hours, wage scales, and more. Even within the same state, different programs may have different rules about whether family members can be paid. Waiting lists are common. As states cut their budgets, these programs may be further limited.

Most, but not all, programs require the person receiving care to be eligible for Medicaid. He or she also has to meet the requirements for the consumer-directed option. If you or your parent meets these requirements, a counselor will work out a monthly budget. Some states limit the budget to an amount that is not greater than the state would pay for home care agency services. With final approval, you or your parent can now hire and fire whomever you choose. Or you can use the money for other approved uses. States generally offer the services of a fiscal agent to manage the budget and file necessary reports.

For more background, go to the National Resource Center for Participant-Directed Services at `http://www.bc.edu/schools/gssw/nrcpds/` for specific information, follow up with your state's Medicaid or aging services department. It may take time to find the right person to help you.

Long-term care insurance

Some long-term care policies make payments to family members who are providing home care. However, they may exclude people who live in the same household. Ask the insurance agent to explain this benefit and its conditions.

Caregiver contracts

You or your parent may be willing to pay a family member directly through a caregiver contract. Consult an elder-care lawyer to make sure that the contract meets tax requirements, deals with inheritances, and is approved by all other interested parties (your siblings, for example). Be mindful of the emotional pitfalls in this arrangement. The pay should be reasonable and in line with what you would pay if you hired an aide.

Courts have not looked favorably on caregiver contracts that seemed to be ways to transfer assets — for example, by paying very high salaries — to become eligible for Medicaid or avoid estate taxes rather than pay for care. Avoid these situations be getting good legal advice.

Is There a Doctor in the House?

A doctor making a home visit? That may sound like a scene from a 1940s movie, but in fact the number of doctors who see patients in their own homes has recently increased. Usually doctors visit people who would have difficulty getting to an office or who are homebound for other reasons. Often doctors making home visits work in teams, so you get the added benefit of a nurse or physician's assistant and perhaps a social worker. Home-visit programs may be organized by a hospital, by a large physician practice in the community, or by a health plan. These organizations want to keep people out of the hospital, where care is more costly and debilitating for the person.

Medicare is conducting a three-year demonstration project called Independence at Home to test whether home-based care by teams of doctors, nurses, and other clinicians can reduce hospitalization and costs.

Insurance coverage varies, but some doctors' home visits can be covered under original (fee-for-service) Medicare. If you belong to a Medicare Advantage plan or have private insurance, check the plan. Physician visits are covered by Medicaid, but usually these visits are in a clinic or office. Some home-visit programs may accept Medicaid.

Here are some ways to identify a physician who makes home visits or a program in your area.

Some hospitals, academic medical centers, and health care systems have doctor visiting programs and doctors-in-training participate in home visits.

The American Academy of Home Care Physicians, founded in 1984, maintains a list by state and zip code of physicians, physician assistants, and nurse practitioners who make home visits. The Academy does not endorse any of these practitioners, so it's up to you to check out qualifications and fees. You can find the list at www.aahcp.org/associations/11307/files/ProviderLocator.cfm.

Also check your local hospital and medical center for physician home-visit programs. Beyond home visits, physicians participate in home care by referring people to home care agencies for services, certifying their need for skilled care, and approving a plan of care.

Chapter 15

Understanding the Role of Nursing Homes in Long-Term Care

. . . .

In This Chapter

▶ Understanding the difference between a nursing home short-stay rehabilitation program and a long-stay unit

▶ Selecting the right nursing home for a long stay

▶ Taking a look at new models of nursing homes

▶ Understanding residents' rights and responding to problems

. . . .

Don't skip this chapter because you have always said, "I will never put my mother in a nursing home!" or because you don't even want to think about this option for yourself. There is no denying that moving permanently to a nursing home is at the bottom of most people's wish list. And most people have other options for care at home and in the community. Short-term nursing home rehab programs are a frequent transition period from hospital to home. But for some people, particularly those with advanced dementia or complex medical needs for whom available family care and home- and community-based services are insufficient, a nursing home may be the most appropriate option for a long stay. If that choice becomes necessary, the decision should be based on good information and realistic expectations, not guilt or fear.

Just to be clear: A nursing home is a long-term care facility that offers 24-hour room and board and health care services, including nursing care, rehabilitation therapies, and a range of other treatments, and programs. People who live in nursing homes are referred to as residents, not patients. Nursing homes increasingly have two types of services: short-term rehabilitation programs and long-stay units.

In this chapter I discuss both types of nursing home care but the emphasis is on long-stay choices. I offer some steps for selecting a nursing home. I also describe some new models that stress "person-centeredness" and home-like settings. If you or your relative is in a continuing-care retirement community with a nursing home unit, you have already made an initial choice. (See Chapter 6 on assisted living for more information on continuing-care retirement communities and other options for people who need less medical care than nursing homes typically provide.) Finally, I provide some information about residents' rights that is important for follow-up once you or your parent has moved in.

Nursing Home Basics

By choosing a nursing home for a long stay, you are not abandoning your parent or other relative. You will need to remain involved at many levels to ensure that your parent receives the most appropriate care, is respected as an individual, and is able to maintain the highest level of function possible and enjoy a good quality of life. Starting with that premise, here are some basic facts about nursing homes today.

Defining nursing homes

Nursing homes are, in bureaucratic language, *skilled nursing facilities* (abbreviated as SNFs, and pronounced *sniffs*). Nursing homes, unlike assisted living or other community settings, offer skilled care by professionals such as nurses, doctors, and therapists. For instance, a nurse administers intravenous (IV) injections, and a physical therapist helps a person regain or maintain function, Nevertheless, the amount of time nurses spend with patients is limited. The facility may have a medical director onsite or a doctor may be on call.

The need for skilled care is not clear-cut for persons with dementia. Sometimes people with dementia, even advanced cases, do not have easily identified needs for skilled care (as the Centers for Medicare & Medicaid Services defines it). The facility gets a lower reimbursement rate from Medicaid for these individuals, assuming it will accept them in the first place.

The majority of nursing-home services are provided by aides (called certified nursing assistants or CNAs) who do personal care and assist with activities of daily living (ADLs), such as bathing and dressing. Federal law requires CNAs to have a minimum of 75 hours of training, although some states have increased the training requirement. These are the people with whom you or your parent will have the most contact. Getting to know them as individuals is important.

Nursing home residence on the decline

Although it may seem counterintuitive in an era in which the population is aging rapidly, the number of people living in nursing homes is actually declining. In 1995, 1.4 million Americans eligible for Medicaid (the prime payer of nursing home care) lived in nursing homes, but by 2010 that number had fallen to just over 1 million. Some of this decline can be attributed to states' efforts to provide more home- and community-based services as an alternative to more-expensive nursing homes. Some people who might have gone from home to nursing home are able to manage with help in an assisted-living facility. Another factor is probably nursing homes' own restructuring, as they focus more on sub-acute or post-hospital care and rehabilitation programs, paid for by Medicare at a higher rate than long-term care paid for by Medicaid.

Nursing homes vary by type of ownership:

- ✔ Voluntary homes are run by nonprofit organizations, which may be sponsored by religious, fraternal, or community organizations.

- ✔ Public or municipal homes are owned and operated by local governments.

- ✔ Proprietary homes are run by for-profit corporations, which may have only a few facilities or be national in scope. This sector now constitutes 69% of all nursing homes.

The type of ownership of a nursing home provides no guarantee of quality, which has to be assessed individually. There is some evidence to suggest that nonprofit nursing homes offer better quality care.

Some nursing homes are large, and some are very small. According to the CMS Nursing Home Data Compendium of 2012, however, the majority of nursing homes have between 50 and 200 residents. But again, size is not the key determinant of quality. Small homes may offer a more intimate environment, but large homes may have more specialized staff and more activities.

Moving from hospital to short-term rehab

More than 60 percent of nursing-home admissions come directly from hospitals, so it's not surprising that most people face the decision about entering a nursing home in a crisis or just after one. The crisis may be a stroke, a bad fall, or a worsening of a chronic condition. Going home from the hospital may be the preferred choice, but the family may not be able to provide the needed care, even with the home healthcare and rehabilitation therapy that Medicare and other insurance coverage provides (see Chapter 14). A short stay in a skilled nursing facility rehabilitation program is one option that can give the person and family time to adjust to the new requirements and be better prepared to manage at home.

Don't panic if the hospital nurse or social worker says, "We're sending you (or your parent) to a nursing home tomorrow." Although this information should not come at the last minute, it often does. What it usually means is that you are being referred to a rehabilitation program at a nursing home, not being sent to a nursing home permanently.

In these situations, you will be asked to make a quick decision about which nursing home rehab program to choose, and the choices may be limited. The discharge planner at the hospital may hand you a list of five nursing homes in the area and say, in effect, "You choose." The discharge planner will then see what is available right away. Your choices may be limited by the facilities' bed capacity, their ability to provide the kind and level of care needed, location, and other factors. Frequently the list includes only those nursing homes with which the discharge planner works on a daily basis; it may not include the full range available and appropriate.

If you are interested in nursing homes not on the list, you can ask that specific nursing homes be put on the list, but the hospital will not keep your parent until a bed in your preferred nursing home becomes available. You can try to push the hospital to delay discharge for a few days, and you can file a formal appeal to postpone it. (If you lose the appeal, however, you will have to pay the costs of the additional hospital days.)

The push to move patients quickly from hospitals to nursing homes is in hospitals' and nursing homes' economic interests. Hospitals want to ensure that they can discharge their patients quickly, and nursing homes want to maintain that source of new income. Medicare pays for the initial episode of nursing-home rehabilitation services if the person has been discharged after a minimum three-day hospital admission, but patients don't always get to stay for three days. Original Medicare pays for the first 20 days of each benefit period; you pay a coinsurance of $152 per day for days 21–100 (in 2014), and you pay all the costs for each day after day 100. You must be hospitalized for three days to start a new benefit period. If you have a Medicare Advantage plan or private insurance, check with the plan.

To be eligible for Medicare coverage for short-term rehabilitation services, you must have been formally admitted as an hospital inpatient for three days. If the hospital makes a referral to a rehab program for further treatment in a nursing home – for example, to improve your ability to walk after a fall – after an observation stay, no matter how long the stay lasted, Medicare will not pay.

Check to make sure your family member has actually been admitted to the hospital. You can also complain to the hospital if you are not given accurate or timely information.

There are steps you can take without the pressure of an imminent hospital discharge or a rapidly deteriorating situation at home. The first step is to look broadly at the options in your area. Then you can be more focused on specific nursing homes and how to evaluate them.

Sometimes a person admitted for a short-stay rehab program is unable to return home as hoped, and then another decision point is reached: to stay in the same nursing home as a long-stay resident or move to another facility. There may be interim steps to prepare for going home, for example, home modifications or hiring extra help. For advice on how to handle that transition, see the United Hospital Fund's Next Step in Care guide, "When Short-term Rehab Turns into Long-Term Stay," at `www.nextstepincare.org/ Caregiver_Home/When_Short_Term_Turns_into_Long_Term/`.

Comparing nursing homes for a long stay

Nursing Home Compare is an online tool that includes information on health inspections and complaints, staffing (hours of care provided by nurses and nursing assisstants per resident), and quality measures such as incidence of pressure sores. CMS maintains the database that compares more than 15,000 Medicare- and Medicaid-certified nursing homes that provide skilled services (`www.medicare.gov/nursinghomecompare/?AspxAutoDetectCookie Support=1`). You can search for a nursing home by name or look for nursing homes in your zip code. Medicare also has an extensive guide at `www.medicare.gov/pubs/pdf/02174.pdf`.

The online tool ranks nursing homes based on three ratings, two of which are self-reports by the nursing homes. Only state inspections are external evaluations. These three ratings (from a low of 1 to a high of 5 stars) are combined to calculate an overall rating. In addition, Nursing Home Compare reports penalties that have been imposed on the facility.

Nursing Home Compare is a valuable tool that allows you to eliminate some of the lowest-ranking nursing homes. However, it does not include many important factors such as the interactions between management and staff, and between staff and residents, how residents' individual needs and preferences are addressed, and the general atmosphere and style of the facility. These are factors you need to assess in your visits. Given two nursing homes with similar ratings, you need to take the next step of determining which one seems to best meet your needs or those of your parent. (See the following section for help choosing a nursing home.)

One thing to keep in mind is that Nursing Home Compare includes data from a limited period. More important, even the data coming from inspections in some states may tend to underreport deficiencies. And Medicare uses a grading curve, so exactly 10 percent of nursing homes in any one state are awarded the top ranking of five stars. This means that a lower-ranking nursing home might have just missed the cutoff on the ranking curve; on the other hand, it might mean that the curve limits the number of nursing homes that would fall into the lower categories.

In addition to Nursing Home Compare, many state departments of health have similar comparisons on their websites. Other sponsored websites offer to compare nursing homes, but they generally base their data on government websites and may include only facilities that pay to be on the list.

Visiting Nursing Homes for a Long Stay

A nursing-home visit is essential if you are deciding which facility is the best fit for you or your relative. Doctor and family recommendations are important, but nothing compares to what your own senses can tell you during a live visit.

The federal Centers for Medicare & Medicaid Services (CMS) sets minimum standards for nursing homes. States, however, are responsible for monitoring and ensuring that nursing homes provide the required level of care. Some states go beyond the federal requirement, but others are not so diligent.

Make sure you discuss the choices with your parent if at all possible. This may be difficult, but you can make a much better decision if you get as much information as possible about what's important to your parent: location, language spoken in the nursing home, meals, visits, activities, and so on. If your parent is unable to participate because of cognitive impairments or a medical condition, think of what you know she values as you visit various facilities.

Checking off important points

After you have narrowed the possibilities through Nursing Home Compare, your state's Department of Health, or another source, you can begin to focus on the most likely facilities. Medicare has a seven-page "Nursing Home Checklist" at www.medicare.gov/nursing/checklist.pdf. It is meant to be filled out at each nursing home visit and has room for your comments.

Comfort care for dementia patients

"Encouraging Comfort Care," the Greater Illinois Alzheimer's Association's guide for families of people with dementia living in care facilities, has a checklist with many useful suggestions. Unlike many other guides, this one approaches the need for hospice care, active dying, and what happens after death forthrightly. It also addresses medical decision-making around aggressive treatments and artificial nutrition and hydration, topics that are often avoided.

Particularly useful are six principles that should guide care for people with dementia. Staff members:

✔ Anticipate the needs of people with dementia.

✔ Know each person so well that basic needs never become major problems.

✔ Embrace the philosophy of "person-centered" care.

✔ Use a "soft" approach (using verbal and non-verbal cues to facilitate communication).

✔ Recognize and treat pain aggressively.

✔ Recognize you (the family member) as a true partner in care.

The guide is available at www.alzheimers-illinois.org/pti/comfort_care_guide.asp.

You can fill in basic information, such as whether the nursing home is Medicare- and Medicaid-certified and whether it has the level of care you need, including specialized services such as ventilator care or a special unit for persons with dementia.

Just because a nursing home has a dementia or "memory care" unit is not a guarantee that it provides good quality dementia care. Many residents with dementia may not even be on the special unit, and the staff may not have special training or expertise in providing person-centered care for people with dementia. If this is a priority, you need to investigate further.

A particularly important factor noted on the checklist is location. You want to be close enough so that you and family members and friends can visit often. Your continued involvement in your relative's life at the nursing home is critical to his happiness and well-being. Getting to know the staff, participating in activities, observing your relative in different situations — all these interactions are not just nice things to do but also indications to the staff that someone cares deeply about this person and will be actively engaged in monitoring their care. Don't underestimate the importance this may have in the quality of care your parent receives.

Don't rush through your nursing home visit, and make sure to visit more than once, preferably on a different time and day of the week. Evening and weekend visits are especially important, because staffing is likely to be lowest at these times. If you're using a checklist, remember that using your eyes, ears, and nose is more important than completing every item. You can learn a lot just by observing how people talk to each other, whether there are smiles and touching, or whether the atmosphere is chilly and controlled. Often the person who takes you on a tour of the facility is a salesperson who will not be part of your daily experience after you or your parent is admitted.

Here are some categories to review during a nursing home visit, with a few specific examples:

✔ **Resident appearance**:
- Are the residents clean and well-groomed?
- Are they appropriately dressed for the time of day and season?

✔ **Living spaces**:
- Is the nursing home clean, well-lit, and free of offensive odors? Note the use of sprays that cover up odors.
- Is the temperature comfor`?
- Is smoking allowed? If so, is it restricted to certain areas?
- Are all common areas, resident rooms, and doorways designed for wheelchair use?

✔ **Staff**:
- Does the staff appear to be polite and respectful to the residents?
- Does the staff wear name tags?
- Does the management run background checks for abuse and neglect before hiring staff? Are these state or national checks?
- Is there a full-time medical director on site? If not, how are physician services provided?
- Is there a licensed nurse on duty 24 hours a day and a registered nurse present at least 8 hours a day?
- How are physician services provided? Is there a medical director on site?
- Do families ever hire private duty nurses or CNAs to supplement care?

✔ **Residents' rooms**:
- Can residents have personal belongings and furniture in their rooms?
- Is there adequate storage space?
- What policies and procedures are in place to protect personal belongings and recover or compensate for their loss?
- Do residents have access to a personal phone, TV, and computer? Is there access to cable TV and the Internet? What are the costs?

🖊 **Menus and food**:

- Do residents get a choice of food at each meal?

- Can the nursing home provide for special dietary needs (low-fat, kosher, halal)?

- Are nutritious snacks available? How are they offered? Do residents have to request them?

- How many staff will be in the dining room during mealtimes to assist residents?

🖊 **Activities**:

- Ask to see a monthly activity calendar for three consecutive months, not including December (when holiday parties dominate).

- How are residents who are unable to leave their room able to take part in activities?

- How do staff encourage and facilitate residents' use of outdoor areas?

- Are trips to places outside the facility scheduled? What kind, how is transportation provided, and is there an additional cost?

- How are residents' views on the choice of activities solicited?

- If your family member enjoys certain activities like reading, knitting, or attending religious services, how does staff make these available?

- How does the facility provide opportunities to explore new activities, such as art, music, or writing?

🖊 **Care**:

- Does the nursing home ask about someone's personal routines as soon as he is admitted? For example, someone should note what time the resident gets up in the morning, what time he goes to bed, and when he prefers to take a shower or bath. In a person-centered approach, residents have more choices about their schedule, and quality of life is the focus.

- Is the same staff assigned to take care of the resident every day? Consistent assignment helps develop good relationships.

- Is there transportation for doctor appointments or other reasons? Will an aide accompany the person if you or another family member can't?

- Are there regularly scheduled care planning meetings with staff to discuss what is going well, what needs to be changed, and who will be responsible for carrying out the suggestions? If you cannot attend at the scheduled time, can the meeting be rescheduled or can you participate by conference call?

✔ **Safety**:

- Are exits clearly marked?

- Are there smoke detectors and sprinklers?

- Are handrails and grab bars appropriately placed?

- Do you understand the details of the required emergency evacuation plan? Make sure you get a copy. What are the plans for notifying you in case of an evacuation?

✔ **Resident or family council** — the 1987 Nursing Home Reform Law gives residents and family members the right to form independent councils to discuss issues related to care, safety, activities, or whatever else is appropriate:

- What is the name of the head of the family council and how can you contact him or her? The person leading the family council should not be a nursing home employee. Staff may attend resident or family council meetings but only at the request of the council.

- How does the nursing home inform family members of council meetings? Do notices appear in newsletters, bulletin boards, or in monthly billing?

- How often does it meet?

- What issues have been raised by the council?

- How have these issues been addressed?

Noting policy details

Medicare's nursing-home checklist and other similar checklists give you basic information about the nursing home. They may not tell you everything you want to know. Here are some important questions to ask:

✔ **What is the nursing home policy about transfer to an emergency department (ED)?** Is a family member consulted? In the past six months, how many residents were transferred to the emergency room and then returned to the nursing home for "care in place" — that is, providing the needed medical care at the nursing home?

Sometimes family members request transfer to an ED when they suspect something is wrong. And sometimes they're right because they notice small changes or big problems that staff may have ignored. However, transfer to an ED is not necessarily a good move. As a general rule, you want to avoid these transfers, which can be unnecessary and result in confusion, frustration, and even deterioration in the resident's condition.

Ongoing communication with staff will help you determine when a real emergency occurs, what can be handled at the nursing home, and when a physician needs to be called. But trust your own instinct as well. You may be seeing something new that staff have ignored. Improvements in this area have been demonstrated with the INTERACT training and interventions for reducing acute care transfers in nursing homes. More information is available at www.interact2.net. Although intended for staff training, these tools are being adapted to help family members recognize and report problems so that ED transfers can be avoided.

✔ **Does your family member have an advance directive that outlines the types of care he or she wants or does not want?** Does it include preferences about CPR (cardiopulmonary resuscitation)? Is this information known to all staff and easily available for ambulance and ED personnel? (See Chapter 16.)

✔ **What is the nursing home's policy or practice about feeding tubes?** Sometimes feeding tubes are recommended (with accompanying risks) because feeding by hand takes too long, not because it is medically necessary. This is a complex decision that should be discussed thoroughly and not seen as routine practice.

✔ **What kind of training do staff receive for specific situations?** Are they trained in dementia care? Do they receive sensitivity training about working with lesbian or gay residents or residents from different cultural or religious backgrounds?

Getting answers to these questions helps in streamlining your options and making the best choice possible.

Checking Out New Models of Nursing-Home Care

The stigma associated with nursing home scandals in the 1970s and 1980s, which led to the 1987 federal Nursing Home Reform Law, continues to some degree to this day. Many clearly substandard nursing homes still exist, and the industry has much room to improve. So diligence is still required, of course, but someone looking at nursing homes today is less likely to find the kind of warehousing and abuses that existed years ago.

Some efforts have been devoted not just to improving existing nursing homes but also to creating new models of care. The following sections highlight three examples.

Eden Alternative

The Eden Alternative was created in 1971 by Dr. William Thomas as an effort to de-institutionalize nursing home care. Eden Alternative does not own or operate Eden Homes; instead the organization works with facilities and individuals to create a caring community for elders (his preferred term for older adults). People live in small houses of 10 to 12 residents, and care partners — the people involved in daily activities — are given a major role. The emphasis is on placing the person as the center of the care and doing away with the hierarchy associated with the medical model of care. Medicaid funding may be available in some states. (Read more about the Eden Alternative philosophy and principles at `www.edenalt.org/our-10-principles`.) About 200 nursing homes in more than 30 states have joined the Eden Registry; they're listed at `www.edenalt.org/resources/eden-resources`. Facilities implement the Eden Alternative in different ways, so it is still important to visit and observe.

Green House Project

An offshoot of the Eden Alternative, the Green House Project was also founded by Dr. Thomas. The project, funded by the Robert Wood Johnson Foundation, has more than 100 homes in 32 states, with more in design. The basic idea is a new way to create senior housing by building or converting residential homes into settings that can provide high levels of care. Some of these homes are licensed as nursing homes and others as assisted-living communities. Green Houses take advantage of technology such as adaptive devices, computers, pagers, and ceiling lifts. They also try to live up to their name: In this case *green* means living in the natural world, with plants, gardens, and access to outdoor areas. For more information, go to `http://thegreenhouseproject.org/`. The site has an interactive map that shows the homes operating and in development by state.

Beatitudes

Comfort First, a program started at The Beatitudes Campus, a continuing-care retirement community in Phoenix, Arizona, works with people who have dementia by creating a personalized homelike environment, anticipating the resident's needs so that discomfort (and the behaviors that are often the resident's only way of expressing discomfort) is avoided. Personal comfort is promoted at all times. The program was started when Beatitudes partnered with Hospice of the Valley to create a model program in dementia care. The model is being tested in three New York City nursing homes, and training is available at the campus. For more information, see `www.comfortfirstcare.org`.

Culture change

All the efforts to improve nursing-home care come under the general heading of *culture change,* which means creating a person-centered environment. The Pioneer Network, a group of long-term care professionals, was formed in 1997 to move nursing-home practice from hospital-like management to a person-centered approach, which better integrates quality of life with quality of care.

The Pioneer Network has a consumer's guide to finding a nursing home involved in culture change at www.pioneernetwork.net/Consumers/ Guide. The guide has many key questions, such as:

✔ How is your nursing home involved in culture change?

✔ Do the certified nursing assistants (CNAs) take care of the same group of resident each time they work or do you rotate assignments?

✔ What is your policy regarding food choices and alternatives?

✔ Do you have a rehabilitation team and access to therapists such as speech pathologists, physical therapists, and occupational therapists?

✔ Do you measure the turnover of your staff? If so, what is the turnover rate for your direct care workers? (Any number under 40 percent is good; the national average is 70 percent.)

Responding to Residents' Problems in Nursing Homes

Selecting the best nursing home is critical but your responsibilities do not end there. Since this will be a long stay, it is important to monitor the quality of care and deal with problems that may arise. You and your family member have a right to expect good quality care, respect, and sensitivity to any special issues. Still, the situation that exists when your family member is admitted may change over time. Your family member's condition may deteriorate, her roommate may become agitated, and her favorite aide may leave and be replaced by a competent but not so friendly person. You should be familiar with residents' rights in nursing homes and be a vocal advocate for ensuring that they are enforced. At the same time you have to distinguish between situations that are unacceptable and those that can be the focus of compromise and negotiation. Of course, if the problems involve serious incidents of abuse or neglect, you have to take immediate action.

If the problem does not involve abuse or neglect, is isolated, and can be resolved, your first approach should be a frank but friendly discussion with the staff person who is the source of the problem. For example, your parent doesn't like the shampoo the aide is using because it stings if it gets in his eyes. Maybe a different shampoo or a different technique will solve the problem.

If the problem is more serious, or you see it happening to other residents, but has not risen to the level of abuse or neglect, then speak to the head nurse or the director of the nursing home. Most nursing homes want satisfied residents and family members and will generally try to resolve the problem. Of course, you may encounter some defensiveness or denial.

If these informal approaches fail, then your next recourse is to contact your state's *ombudsman,* a person assigned to investigate complaints in nursing homes, adult homes, and assisted-living facilities. The Long-term Care Ombudsman Program is run by the U.S. Administration on Aging and has volunteers and staff in every state (see www.aoa.gov/aoaroot/Press_Room/Products_Materials/fact/pdf/LTC_Ombudsman_Program_2011.pdf for information). To find your local ombudsman office, call ElderCare Locator (800-677-1116) or your State Health Department. A map is available at www.ltcombudsman.org/ombudsman. In some areas you can call Adult Protective Services. Police should be called if the resident is in imminent danger.

Be prepared to document your concerns with dates, names, and specific violations. Try to take pictures of visible violations to further support your claims.

Get familiar with the very comprehensive list of nursing home residents' rights, which every nursing home is required by law to observe. I tell you more about this list in the nearby sidebar "Nursing-home residents' rights." If you can link the problem to a violation of patient's rights, you will be on stronger ground.

If the problem persists, you can file a formal complaint with your State Health Department. There are other avenues such as private litigation that you might want to investigate.

Another good resource is a booklet by Eric Carlson from the National Senior Citizens Law Center. It presents 20 common nursing home problems and ways to resolve them. You can find it at www.nsclc.org/wp-content/uploads/2011/02/20-Common-Problems-Nov-2010-Final.pdf.

Nursing-home residents' rights

The 1987 federal Nursing Home Reform Law guarantees residents' rights and places a strong emphasis on individual dignity and self-determination. A person living in a nursing home has the same civil rights as someone living in the community. The law states that all nursing homes that participate in Medicare and Medicaid are required to "provide services and activities to attain or maintain the highest practicable physical, mental, and psychosocial well-being of each resident in accordance with a written plan of care that . . . is initially prepared, with participation to the extent practicable, of the resident, the resident's family, or legal representative."

Among the rights listed are: the right to be fully informed of available services and charges as well as the right to receive information in a language they understand; the right to complain; the right to participate in one's own care; the right to privacy and confidentiality; the right to dignity, respect, and freedom; right to visits; and the right to make independent choices. There are also special rights relating to transfers and discharges. For a complete list of the rights, go to: www.theconsumervoice.org. There is no comparable federal statement of rights for assisted living residents, although some states have statements of rights for these residents.

Chapter 16

Moving Toward Advance Care Planning

....

In This Chapter

▶ Being prepared for advanced illness or trauma

▶ Creating an advance directive

▶ Choosing a healthcare proxy

▶ Understanding palliative care and hospice

....

Of all the difficult topics to discuss in planning for the long term, what you want to happen if you or your parent is seriously ill or has an accident is the one most avoided. Other touchy subjects, such as driving problems and money mismanagement, surface on their own. But all too often the discussion of what to do if you become seriously ill or incapacitated and cannot speak for yourself only happens in a crisis — the worst time for thoughtful and well-informed conversations.

Nothing will make these profound discussions easy. But you can lay the groundwork in ways that increase your family's chances of being prepared when decisions about treatment and level of care must be made. This chapter suggests ways to organize your thinking, create legal documents, and understand care options.

Thinking about Advance Care Planning

Advance care planning is not just for people who are elderly or sick. Three landmark legal cases that involved decisions about end-of-life care concerned previously healthy young women in their 20s or 30s — Karen Ann Quinlan, Nancy Cruzan, and Terry Schiavo — who suffered life-threatening traumatic events. Anyone at any age can be in an accident or develop a serious illness.

As a person ages, of course, the likelihood of an event requiring a treatment decision increases. And a quick conversation about a friend's situation or a news report most likely will not be enough to ensure that your own or your parent's wishes are understood and followed. What everyone needs to do is have a series of conversations that involve family, doctors, clergy, or other trusted individuals. In this section I underline the importance of the different aspects of care that you should address in advance. Another good resource is AARP's *The Other Talk: A Guide to Talking with Your Adult Children About the Rest of Your Life* by Tim Prosch (McGraw-Hill).

Realizing the importance of advance planning

No one can predict exactly how and when the need for someone else to make a medical decision for you will arise, what the medical situation will be, and what specific choices will have to be made. That is why a series of discussions is more likely to convey your thinking in depth than a one-time conversation.

Although you and your family members are probably reluctant to have a serious discussion about it, keep in mind that talking about the possibility of a serious injury or illness does not make it happen. In fact, everyone will probably feel better afterward. However, wishes may change, so it is important to review any documents you have created at least every few years and more often if warranted to make sure that they still reflect your current thinking. The results of the conversations can then be incorporated in a variety of documents, which I describe in the following sections.

If you do not have a documented advance care plan, state law will determine who makes decisions for you. Most states have a priority list of family members who will be chosen to speak for you when you can't make a healthcare decision. The person you may have chosen to speak for you may be far down on the list, or not on it at all. And if family members cannot agree, a court may be called upon to make the decision.

Making wishes known with advance directives and living wills

An *advance directive* is a general term for a document that tells healthcare providers the kinds of medical treatment you do or do not want. For example, you may refuse tube feeding or ventilators or antibiotics if, in your view, they will not provide you with sufficient benefit, even if they may prolong your life. You have a right, which is well established in law and medical ethics, to refuse any treatment for whatever reason. You can also say that you want all treatments that offer any possibility of prolonging your life, even if they will be painful or burdensome. (But you do not have a right to demand any particular treatment, because healthcare providers may not be willing to provide it for reasons of conscience or because they consider it *futile,* a vague term but one that carries some weight in medical and legal circles. In such cases, they must refer you to another provider.)

A *living will* is another name for the part of an advance directive that sets out your wishes. You can follow the legal form for your state or write a more detailed expression of your personal philosophy. (See Chapter 12 for more on living wills.)

Advance directives typically name the person who you want to make healthcare decisions on your behalf if you are unable to speak for yourself. The choice of your healthcare proxy (sometimes called a durable power of attorney for healthcare, surrogate, or agent) is especially critical, precisely because the decision may not be clear-cut and may require interpretation of what you have expressed in the advance directive (see later in this chapter for information on choosing a healthcare proxy). Did you mean, for example, no antibiotics ever or just when they would prolong dying? Would you have agreed to a trial of a therapy to see if it improved your condition? Talking about these questions ahead of time, even in hypothetical ways, gives your healthcare proxy some guidance.

An advance directive comes into play only when the person is unable to make healthcare decisions. If, for example, you and your parent disagree about whether surgery is advisable, and you are the healthcare proxy, you cannot decide in favor of surgery without your parent's consent. Usually the point at which the healthcare proxy takes over is coma, unconsciousness, or a doctor's determination of inability to make healthcare decisions.

Dealing with the Rules of Advance Directives

As with everything in long-term care, it seems, paperwork is involved to make your wishes known. When you plan ahead and make your wishes clear, all parties involved will have a set roadmap to follow and transitions will be smoother. Take a look at the following sections to put advance directives into motion.

Finding the forms for advance directives and living wills

To start the ball rolling for putting together your advance directives, your first (but not only) option is a state-approved form that tells your doctors, in either general terms or with specific detail, your wishes regarding treatments. They often include a section on organ donation.

Caring Connections, an arm of the National Hospice and Palliative Care Organization, has a list of state-by-state forms for advance directives available at www.aarp.org/advancedirectives. Each state's form is preceded by Caring Connection's general suggestions about completing an advance directive. These forms must be signed and witnessed. Although other forms can be legal if signed and witnessed, doctors are more likely to pay attention to the state-approved forms.

If you or your parent spends a lot of time in more than one state, it's a good idea to complete both (or all) state's advance directives.

You do not need a lawyer to create an advance directive or a living will, but you do need to follow your state's requirements about signing and witnessing these documents. Many online kits provide a template for an advance directive. If you use one of these, make sure you complete it following your state's rules. If you are unsure of whether you have met your state's requirements, it is wise to consult a lawyer or other trusted professional.

Putting your wishes down on paper

A popular form of advance directive is the *Five Wishes* document. This document, written with the help of the American Bar Association's Commission on Law and Aging, gives you the opportunity to convey your personal, emotional, and spiritual needs as well as your medical wishes. In 42 states and the District of Columba, it substantially meets the legal requirements for an advance directive. Check the website www.agingwithdignity.org to see if your state is included. Even if it isn't, you can complete the Five Wishes to accompany your state's approved advance directive.

Here are the five categories of wishes:

- ✔ The person I want to make care decisions for me when I can't
- ✔ The kind of medical treatment I want or don't want
- ✔ How comfortable I want to be

✔ How I want people to treat me

✔ What I want my loved ones to know

Each of the sections contains an extensive list of things to consider. For example, the document describes four situations — close to death, in a coma and not expected to wake up and recover, permanent and severe brain damage and not expected to recover, and in another condition in which I do not wish to be kept alive — and lists the choices that may apply.

You can access and fill out the Five Wishes form online at `https://fivewishesonline.agingwithdignity.org`.

Choosing a healthcare proxy

One of the most important decisions you can make is the choice of *healthcare proxy:* the person who will make healthcare decisions for you when you are unable to do so yourself. This person should be someone you trust to put your wishes ahead of his or her own feelings. A calm, careful approach to problem solving is an asset, as is the ability to listen to other points of view and mediate differences of opinion. The ability to absorb medical information and ask clarifying questions is a valuable skill. Disagreements often stem from poor communication about the person's medical condition, and sometimes doctors are reluctant to give bad news in a clear way. The proxy may have to read between the lines or ask very direct questions.

Location is another factor; although your healthcare proxy does not need to live with you or even in the same town, it is not a good idea to pick someone far away in case decisions have to be made quickly. Another good idea is to name an alternate as a backup.

A family member is usually the first option, but you may want to choose a friend instead. (Your doctor cannot be your healthcare proxy.) If you have siblings or more than one child, think which one best meets these personal characteristics, regardless of birth order, age, or profession.

Make sure your healthcare proxy understands your wishes. Many people chosen as healthcare proxies (or not officially named as such) may ask a doctor, "What would you do if this were your mother?" This is not a good question because it assumes that your mother and the doctor's mother have exactly the same history, beliefs, and wishes. The doctor's mother may have wanted something very different from what your mother expressed. Many experienced doctors deflect this question by saying, "Tell me a little more about your mother." That conversation can lead to a better understanding of the options.

Be sure to discuss this responsibility with the person you think is best suited for the job and ask if he or she is willing to take on this responsibility. It should never be a surprise to that person. Make sure you tell all other family members who will be involved whom you have selected to make medical decisions for you. They should not be surprised, either. Some will be relieved not to have this responsibility; others may resent your choice. If you are the healthcare proxy, make sure you keep other family members informed about what is happening and what is likely to happen. Many deathbed family conflicts arise because of lack of communication, which leads to lack of trust.

Once you have a signed and witnessed advance care directive, make sure your doctors, healthcare proxy, family members, clergy, and any others you want involved in your care have copies. Keep the original in a safe and easily accessible place should you be hospitalized and your regular doctor is not available. The document does not need to be filed with any agency, and you can write a new one whenever you choose.

Adding do not resuscitate (DNR) orders

Do not resuscitate orders are a special kind of advance directive. They tell doctors, nurses, emergency medical technicians, and others that a person has decided not to undergo CPR (cardiopulmonary resuscitation) if his heart stops beating or he stops breathing. A doctor must sign the DNR order for it to be active. In a hospital or other healthcare facility, staff will start CPR if there is no DNR in the medical record.

Why would anyone not want CPR if it could restore a heartbeat? Certainly this decision is weighty. Success rates for CPR vary, but much depends on the person's overall medical condition. CPR may not be effective for older people with serious chronic conditions. And unlike the portrayals of CPR on television, these interventions can be quite brutal, leading to broken ribs and other injuries, especially for an older person.

Most state laws authorize a doctor to enter a special DNR order that will be honored outside the hospital. This is important because when emergency medical technicians respond to a 911 call at home, they are legally required to start CPR unless there is an out-of-hospital DNR order.

Even with the proper documentation, in the panic of the moment, sometimes DNR orders are ignored. At home the DNR order should be easy to find, not something that has to be hunted down in a crisis. You can post the DNR order on the refrigerator door, for example, or on an easy-to-see bulletin board.

Since a DNR is a doctor's order, you will need to ask your doctor to fill out the form. If he is reluctant to do so, ask why. It may be a good way to start an important conversations about your wishes.

Keeping your advance directive accessible

A carefully completed advance directive is useless if no one knows where it is when you are seriously ill or in an accident. A safe deposit box is great for precious jewelry; for advance directives, not so much.

Discuss your advance directive with your doctor(s), and tell them the name and contact information for the person you have selected as a healthcare proxy. You should provide a copy of the document, which can then go into your medical record. In a hospital, your regular doctor may not be in charge of your care, so it is essential to have the advance directive as part of your hospital record. When you are admitted to a hospital or other healthcare facility, you will be asked (it's a federal requirement) if you have an advance directive. If this is a planned admission, be sure to bring the document with you.

Your healthcare proxy should have a copy of your advance directive as well as any supporting material that documents your wishes. You should review the advance directive every few years, or more often if your health condition changes. The document should have a relatively recent date. A document created 15 years ago is likely to cause someone to ask, "But what if he or she changed his or her mind?"

You can register your advance directive online at `www.uslivingwill registry.com`. It will then be available to all providers. Be sure to update the registry if you change the document.

Choosing Physician' Orders for Life-Sustaining Treatment (POLST)

A recent development in advance directives is the Physician Order for Life-Sustaining Treatment (POLST). POLST started in Oregon but has spread to many states. In New York, it is called MOLST (Medical Orders for Life-Sustaining Treatment), and in Iowa, IPOST (Iowa Physicians Orders for Scope of Treatment). Programs in other states have their own names. See `www.polst.org/programs-in-your-state` for a state-by-state listing of POLST Paradigm programs.

Although the forms vary by state, the basic idea is that legally completed advance directives, living wills, Five Wishes, even having a healthcare proxy are insufficient to guarantee that your wishes will be followed. You need a medical order signed by a physician. Even though an advance directive is legal, hospitals and nursing homes and clinical staff may be wary of following anything but a physician's order.

POLST is intended for people with serious advanced illness who may be expected to face major treatment decisions within a foreseeable time. The POLST form (with variations) lists medical interventions ranging from comfort care to full treatment, artificially administered nutrition (tube feeding), and a place for additional orders. The patient (if able) must sign, as must the legally recognized decision maker (if there is one). Obviously, the physician's signature is essential.

The POLST form is intended to be sent with the person whenever he or she is transferred or from one healthcare facility to another. For instance, if a person is transferred from hospital to nursing home, the POLST form describes to the nursing-home staff the treatment plan that should be in place. An EMT can follow a POLST directive if 911 is called.

Although the POLST program addresses a common problem of medical staff failing to follow a person's wishes even when documented in an advance directive, it does not take into account the fuller range of choices recognized in, for example, a living will or Five Wishes. In the most common situations in which POLST is used, the discussion preceding the physician's signing of the order is brief and limited to the items on the checklist. And hospital staff may not have training or experience in discussing the options with the patient, healthcare proxy, and family. POLST addresses a serious shortcoming in medical practice, but it is not intended to take the place of more traditional advance directives.

Understanding Care Options for Serious Illness: Palliative Care and Hospice

While much of advance care planning focuses on what you don't want to happen, it is equally important to consider the positive options. "There is nothing more we can do" is one of those phrases that should be erased from the medical vocabulary. Something can always be done to keep a person's pain and symptoms under control and to support the emotional and spiritual needs of a person with advanced illness and the family that experiences distress and loss.

Two options that stress holistic management of serious, life-threatening illness are palliative care and hospice. They are different but related. Both suffer from misperceptions that choosing either means giving up, as if serious illness were something that can be cured by will power or yet another last-ditch effort. Some people do not want to die in full battle mode but are urged on by doctors and family to try one more round of chemotherapy or a drug that is still being tested and has nasty side effects. Hospice and palliative care provide other, more peaceful options.

Both palliative care and hospice are voluntary choices. No one can force you or your parent to accept this type of care if you don't want it.

Palliative care

Palliative care is a relatively new medical subspecialty practiced by specially trained physicians, nurses, physician assistants, social workers, clergy, and others. Most palliative care is delivered by hospital teams, but some outpatient services are available through clinics and home care agencies.

Palliative care offers services that improve how individuals function in everyday life, even as they undergo active treatment for a serious illness. Care focuses on pain relief, symptom control, and improving quality of life. Palliative care can be time-limited or ongoing. The ill person and family members are considered part of the palliative care team.

Palliative care can be provided along with treatments intended to cure. It can be started at any point in an illness. In fact, palliative care specialists urge people to consider palliative care at an early stage because the kinds of treatments offered can make it easier to go through the rigor of a chemotherapy regimen, for example.

Palliative care is covered by most health plans, including Medicare and Medicaid, as a regular medical service. However, there is no special Medicare benefit for palliative care as there is for hospice.

If, in a hospital setting, you feel that more needs to be done to control pain or discomfort, ask for a consultation with the palliative care team or specialist. This request does not mean changing doctors; it is asking for special expertise to deal with the problems.

For more information about palliative care, go to the Center to Advance Palliative Care at www.getpalliativecare.org. The website includes a listing of palliative-care resources that you can search by state and city.

Hospice

Hospice is a comprehensive service that focuses on controlling pain and symptoms and improving the quality of life for people with a life-threatening illness who have a short life expectancies (six months or less). Hospice is a form of palliative care for people who are not being helped by active treatment or for whom the burdens of treatment outweigh the benefits. People choose hospice when they want to spend their remaining time without aggressive treatments and with care that focuses on comfort and quality of life. Entering hospice requires forgoing treatment intended to cure.

Hospice is a team approach that utilizes the skills of different medical and nonmedical specialists to create an environment of comfort and emotional and spiritual support for both the patient and the family.

Hospice services may include, in addition to doctors and nurses, physical and occupational therapists, social workers, volunteers, and clergy. Other services are

- Medications to relieve nausea, pain, shortness of breath, agitation, and other symptoms
- Medical supplies such as a hospital bed or a wheelchair
- Support for the family, including counseling and teaching how to do certain healthcare tasks
- A short hospital stay if the person's symptoms cannot be managed at home
- Short-term respite care — time off for the family
- Volunteers to provide companionship
- Bereavement counseling for the family for a year after the person's death.

Sometimes doctors recommend hospice, but in other cases a family member has to begin the discussion. If you ask about hospice and are criticized by a doctor or nurse, ask why they are opposed to the idea. If you are not satisfied, ask for a second opinion.

Hospice is not right for everyone. Some people want to pursue aggressive treatments to the very end. Home hospice may also require a considerable amount of caregiving by the family. Having new people involved in care may seem overwhelming at a time of great emotional stress. But hospice offers an opportunity for care that sees the whole person and the family as the unit of care and works with them to achieve the best quality of life possible.

Hospice at home or in a facility

In the United States, most hospice services are provided at home, but they can also be provided in nursing homes and assisted-living facilities, which may contract with a local hospice to provide the care. There are, in addition, inpatient hospices in some hospitals and free-standing hospices.

Although a team of professionals, as well as volunteers and aides, provides home hospice services, much of the care is provided by family members. Only in the last few days of life is there likely to be constant care by a member of the hospice team. However, one of the benefits of hospice is that you have a 24-hour number to call if an unexpected problem occurs. A hospice nurse can offer advice and make a home visit if necessary, which can reduce unnecessary and stressful visits to the emergency department (ED).

Hospice: From volunteers to corporations

In the Middle Ages, a *hospice* was a shelter for weary travelers (the term comes from the same root as *hospitality*). In London after World War II, Dame Cicely Saunders created St. Christopher's, the first modern hospice, to care for terminally ill people in a holistic, compassionate way. Volunteers provided most of the care. She introduced the concept in the United States during a 1963 visit to Yale University. In 1986, Medicare created a special hospice benefit. Since then the number of people enrolled in hospice has increased. In 2011, an estimated 1.65 million people received hospice services, accounting for about 44 percent of all deaths in the United States. Some people become ineligible for hospice because of improvements in their condition, and some choose not to continue. Still, most people are in hospice for a very short time; under a third had three or more days of hospice services. The average length of service was 19 days. There are now more than 5,300 hospice programs in the United States. The majority (57.5 percent) are free standing/independent hospices, while 20.3 percent are part of a hospital system, 16.8 percent are part of a home health agency, and 5.2 percent are part of a nursing home. They range from small all-volunteer agencies to large, national corporate chains that serve thousands of people daily. Just over a third (34 percent) are nonprofit organizations, and 60 percent are for-profit companies, and that percentage is increasing. The Medicare hospice benefit is the primary payer, accounting for 84 percent of the payment.

Hospice benefits under Medicare and Medicaid

Hospice is a benefit under Medicare Part A and is included in Medicare Advantage plans. All other Medicare benefits under Parts A and B continue, including the attending physician's fees. You can continue to get services for conditions that are not related to the terminal illness. Although it is not a required service under Medicaid, most states and the District of Columbia offer hospice services. The services may vary, so check your state's Medicaid agency. Most private health insurance plans follow Medicare guidelines on hospice.

To be eligible for the Medicare hospice benefit, for example, a doctor has to certify that a person has a six-month or less life expectancy. Some diseases, such as cancer, follow a more or less predictable course. But others, like Alzheimer's disease, do not, and it is much harder to say how much longer a person with Alzheimer's is likely to live. As a result, hospices have been criticized both for taking patients with only a few days to live, when they cannot get the full benefit of the services, and taking patients with an unpredictable disease course, which results in higher costs.

Tips for choosing the right hospice

Choosing a hospice, like choosing a home care agency, requires some research on your part. You certainly want to find out if the hospice is certified by Medicare, which means that it meets federal and state guidelines. You also want to ask about 24-hour phone availability, how the hospice manages medical emergencies, and what kinds of medical equipment will be provided.

Although accepting hospice means giving up treatments intended to cure, many medical interventions such as chemotherapy to relieve symptoms and anti-nausea medications are important adjuncts to hospice care. What is the hospice policy on these kinds of treatments?

You can find out about hospices in your area by asking the doctor, hospital, or state health department or by going to www.hospicedirectory.org and other websites. The hospices listed in this directory indicate whether they are Medicare- and Medicaid-certified.

You can find a list of state hospice associations at www.hospicedirectory.org/cm/about/state_hospice. Make sure you check several sources to get a complete list, as some websites only list hospices with which they are affiliated.

Ending hospice care

A person in hospice care has the right to discontinue the services at any time for any reason. Perhaps your parent is getting better because of the extra attention (some studies show that people on hospice live longer than those who don't get this care). You can always cease hospice care for a while and start again when necessary. But be aware that the hospice can also discharge the patient. This happens rarely, but usually the reason is that the person no longer meets hospice criteria or wants to pursue treatments intended to cure. The hospice may also say that the home is not safe for its workers, or that the family refuses to cooperate with hospice rules. Hospice programs cannot discharge persons because their care is inconvenient or too expensive.

Some hospices have been forced to close because Medicare auditors determined that they were keeping people for extended periods and their claims were denied. So hospices may be wary of taking persons who have unpredictable courses of illness.

Part V
Special Populations

How to Know if You're a Family Caregiver

Do you:

- ✔ Take care of someone who has a chronic illness, disability, or disease?

- ✔ Manage medications or talk to doctors or nurses on someone's behalf?

- ✔ Help bathe or dress someone who is frail or disabled?

- ✔ Take care of household chores, meals, or bills for someone who cannot do these things alone?

- ✔ Accompany someone who is ill or frail to a doctor's appointment?

- ✔ Provide emotional support to someone who is ill or frail?

Getting to know your own strengths and limitations as a family caregiver is an important step in creating a long-term care plan for your parent or other relative. The bonus article at www.dummies.com/extras/planninglongtermcare leads you to some tools to assess your own needs.

In this part...

✔ Get prepared for the special challenges you may face if you or your aging relative is lesbian, gay, bisexual, or transgender (LGBT). Although social acceptance is growing and the legal context is shifting, there are still areas of concern, such as hospital and nursing home visitation and varying state laws on same-sex marriages.

✔ Look at a range of long-term care options available only to veterans of military service who are enrolled in VA healthcare (and their caregivers). I guide you through the eligibility requirements for various forms of in-home assistance and care in VA or state-sponsored veterans homes.

✔ Take advantage of resources to help family caregivers, who provide most of the long-term care and are an essential element in long-term care planning.

Chapter 17

Services for LGBT Older Adults

*L*esbian, gay, bisexual, and transgender individuals (LGBT) face all the same problems of planning for long-term care as their heterosexual and non-transgender counterparts but with additional complicating factors. Although American society has in general become more accepting of LGBT individuals, stigma and discrimination persist in many settings, including healthcare and long-term care. Even when nondiscriminatory laws and policies are in place, institutions and individual staff members may not follow them.

If you are an LGBT older adult or a family member, you should have all possible legal protections in place to help alleviate problems in obtaining long-term care services that are delivered in respectful and sensitive ways. You can also look for LGBT-friendly service providers and can investigate some housing options that welcome LGBT residents. This chapter offers an overview to planning for long-term care for LGBT older adults. It is intended as a supplement to other chapters that deal with specific subjects such as assisted living, nursing homes, home care, and advance directives.

Recognizing LGBT Aging and Health Issues

Older LGBT individuals are at risk for the same kinds of chronic physical and mental health conditions that affect all older adults as well as specific health issues related to sexual orientation and gender identity. Although lesbian, gay, bisexual, and transgender individuals are collectively called LGBT, each group of men and women (and subgroups by age, race and ethnicity, and other characteristics) has distinct features. Still, they share some characteristics that make them particularly vulnerable.

In addition to dealing with certain increased health risks, which I cover in the following section, many LGBT individuals have had difficult experiences with healthcare encounters. In a study called "The Aging and Health Report: Disparities and Resilience among Lesbian, Gay, Bisexual and Transgender Older Adults," a comprehensive report funded by the U.S. National Institute on Aging, 13 percent report being denied healthcare or having received inferior care. More than 20 percent do not disclose their sexual or gender identity to their physicians, which forecloses discussions of related health risks. Although discrimination in healthcare is unacceptable at any point, it is particularly problematic for older adults, who have more contacts with the healthcare system, who may need more assistance from professionals and paraprofessionals, and who may be more vulnerable on all counts. Fear of discrimination, based on past history, may deter some older LGBT individuals from seeking the help they need and may limit their options for long-term care.

Physical conditions

If you are an LGBT person, or a family member or friend, you know how experiences with discrimination, or perceptions that discrimination will occur, can be a barrier to good medical care. While understandable, it is important to recognize that LGBT persons are at the same risk — and in some cases even higher risk — than their heterosexual counterparts for chronic illness and disability. You may have to be extra vigilant.

That is the sobering finding of the National Institute on Aging study. The authors reviewed data from the U.S. Centers for Disease Control and Prevention's Behavioral Risk Factor Surveillance survey from Washington State, supplemented by a national survey of LGBT adults aged 50 to 95. They found higher rates of disability among lesbian, gay, and bisexual older adults than among heterosexuals of similar ages. LGBT older adults experience higher rates of mental distress and are more likely to smoke and engage in excessive drinking than heterosexuals. Lesbians and bisexual older women report higher risk of cardiovascular disease and obesity than heterosexual women, and gay and bisexual older men are more likely to have poor physical health than their heterosexual counterparts. Some of these higher rates of disability might be prevented with good primary care, so it is important to recognize early signs and take preventive action.

Here are some of the key findings of the report:

- Nearly half (47 percent) of older LGBT individuals had a disability that limited their physical activities or required the use of assistive devices like canes or wheelchairs.

- A quarter reported visual impairments, even while wearing glasses or contact lenses, and 19 percent experienced acute hearing impairment. Nearly a quarter reported dental problems, which increase the risk of poor nutrition and poor health.

- Obesity is a serious problem in the LGBT population, as it is in the general population.

- Other reported health conditions include high blood pressure, high cholesterol, cataracts, asthma, diabetes, hepatitis, and osteoporosis.

- Approximately 13 percent have some cardiac condition.

- Nine percent in this survey were living with HIV disease, and among gay and bisexual men, the percentage with HIV disease was 14 percent.

In this survey, women reported poorer physical health than did men. They had higher rates of disability, arthritis, obesity, asthma, and osteoporosis. Men, however, had higher rates of HIV disease, hepatitis, high blood pressure, cardiovascular disease, diabetes, cancer, and hearing impairment.

As might be expected, risks of disability and chronic disease increased with age, and participants with lower incomes and lower educational levels had increased risks of poor physical health. A positive finding, however, was that nearly all (91 percent) engaged in some form of wellness activities. There are also strong indications of resilience as LGBT persons dealt with discrimination.

If you want to find out more, the complete report is available at `http://caringandaging.org/wordpress/wp-content/uploads/2011/05/Full-Report-FINAL-11-16-11.pdf`.

Mental health risks

Mental health risks are higher among LGBT older adults than among comparable heterosexual age groups. The study from the U.S. National Institute on Aging also reported on mental health issues that affect the LGBT population. Following are some of the findings:

- Nearly a third (31 percent) of the respondents reported depression, with transgender individuals reporting the highest rates (48 percent).

- Almost a quarter (24 percent) had been diagnosed with anxiety.

✔ Thirty-nine percent had seriously considered suicide at some point in their lives, including 35 percent of lesbians, 40 percent of bisexual women, 37 percent of gay men, 39 percent of bisexual men, and 71 percent of transgender older adults. Among those who considered suicide, 39 percent reported that their suicidal thoughts were related to their sexual orientation or gender identity.

✔ Not surprisingly, many LGBT individuals reported stress in their lives, but it is reassuring that a high percentage (69 percent) felt confident that they could handle their personal problems. Again, transgender adults were more likely to report high levels of stress, regardless of age, income, and education.

✔ In a related finding, 59 percent of the LGBT older adults reported feeling that they lack companionship, are isolated from others (53 percent), and feel left out (53 percent).

LGBT individuals have the same sorts of workplace, financial, and relationship stresses in their lives as other older adults, but to these are added a history of victimization and discrimination. Eight-two percent in this survey reported being victimized at least once because of their perceived sexual orientation or gender identity; 64 percent had experienced this three or more times. Many LGBT older adults have experienced discrimination in housing and employment.

Knowing Legal Protections and Their Limits

Legal protections in health and long-term care for older LGBT adults consist of a patchwork of federal and state laws and regulations. Even when they promote equality, federal policies and rulings may not be implemented aggressively by states, much less by individuals working in care settings. Still, two federal actions in the past few years are important steps toward fair and equal treatment for LGBT adults.

U.S. Supreme Court and DOMA

In June 2013, the U.S. Supreme Court ruled, in the case of *Windsor v. United States,* that Section 3 of the federal ban on recognizing same-sex marriages in the Defense of Marriage Act (DOMA) was unconstitutional. The section that was struck down defined *marriage* as "between one man and one woman as husband and wife, and *spouse* as "person of the opposite sex." In a separate case, the Court let stand a lower court's decision to strike down California's ban on same-sex marriage. These decisions have removed the barriers to many rights that were formerly denied to people in same-sex marriages, but certain gray areas still exist. The Supreme Court ruling has to be interpreted and implemented by many federal agencies, and they are doing so at their own pace and with varying degrees of consistency.

Federal rights for same-sex couples

DOMA had barred same-sex married couples from receiving federal marriage benefits. In healthcare these included:

- ✔ **Medicare:** DOMA affected some aspects of Medicare, including eligibility based on a spouse's work record, premium amounts, and delayed enrollment penalties for remaining on a spouses' private health plans. For more information on how the Supreme Court ruling affects Medicare applicants and beneficiaries, go to the National Resource Center on LGBT Aging Center at www.lgbtagingcenter.org/resources/pdfs/Post-DOMA_Medicare.pdf.

- ✔ **Taxation of health benefits:** Health benefits received through a spouse's employer are not taxable, but because the IRS did not recognize same-sex marriages, gay and lesbian couples had to pay higher tax bills.

- ✔ **Immediate coverage rules:** Federal law lets an employee add new spouses to a health plan without waiting for an enrollment period. This protection did not apply to same-sex married couples.

- ✔ **COBRA coverage:** COBRA is the federal law that requires health plans to continue coverage (at the employee's expense) for an employee and family members for a temporary period if the person loses a job. Under DOMA, plans could provide this coverage to same-sex partners but were not required to.

- ✔ **Family and Medical Leave Act:** Under this law, employees in companies with 50 or more employees are entitled to up to 12 weeks of unpaid leave to care for a family member with a serious health condition. Under DOMA employees were not required to provide this time off for married gay and lesbian employees to care for their spouse.

- ✔ **Medicaid Managed Long-Term Care Services:** Some states may have protections against spousal impoverishment in these programs.

Some changes are occurring as federal agencies begin to align their policies with the Supreme Court ruling. A fact sheet prepared by a group of advocacy organizations estimates that federal law cites *marriage* in more than 1,000 places as a basis for legal protection. Agencies may have different rules about which state to consider when deciding whether a marriage is valid.

Before the Supreme Court ruling, the IRS, for example, looked to the state where a couple lives (place of domicile/residence). In August 2013, in a major decision, the IRS announced that it will recognize as married for tax purposes same-sex couples married in any state that recognizes their union as legal (the *place of celebration* standard). This decision affects not only filing of federal income taxes, but also federal estate and gift taxes, retirement plans, and other financial arrangements. (Couples will still have to file separate state tax returns in states that do not recognize same-sex marriages.) Accountants and lawyers will be busy in the next few years sorting out how to help their clients take advantage of the decision or, in some cases, minimize the costs of filing as a married couple.

The Department of Health and Human Services (HHS), which oversees Medicare, announced that married couples who are enrolled in a Medicare Advantage plan that permits couples to choose the same nursing home will be allowed to do so based on a national standard, not the law in the state in which they live. While this is a narrow ruling, it suggests that HHS will issue more comprehensive guidelines along the same idea.

The federal Office of Personnel Management's new policy is that legally married same-sex spouses of federal employees are eligible for health insurance coverage, no matter where they live. Since the federal government is a major employer, this decision will affect many people.

For veterans, a federal court ruling in August 2013 may lead the VA to broader recognition of the rights of same-sex married veterans to benefits. The case involved a legally married veteran with multiple sclerosis whose application for her spouse's rights to survivor benefits was rejected by VA. The court ruled that same-sex spouses are entitled to the same benefits as heterosexual spouses. The Department of Defense had earlier announced that same-sex spouses of active duty troops are entitled to equal benefits.

The U.S. Immigration and Citizenship Services, part of the Department of Homeland Security, already uses a *place of celebration* standard for determining the legality of marriages.

Limitations of the Supreme Court ruling

Despite its positive aspects, the Supreme Court ruling has several limitations. It applies only to the federal government's benefits and its agencies, and does not change discriminatory state laws excluding married LGBT couples from state-provided benefits. If you live in a state that does not recognize same-sex marriages through statute, court decision, or its constitution, the ruling does not change your status. And, obviously, the ruling applies only to LGBT individuals who are legally married. (Lambda Legal has a map of state-by-state laws that recognize same-sex marriage at www.lambdalegal.org/states-regions.)

The Social Security Administration has still not issued a definitive statement on how it will administer benefits for married same-sex couples, but the Social Security Act is clear that in determining whether a marriage is valid the Administration must apply the laws of the state where the worker lives and died when the spouse applies for benefits. If the spouse applies from abroad, the Administration must apply the law of the District of Columbia.

Presidential memorandum on hospital visitation

The right to choose one's visitors in a hospital or other care facility is particularly important for LGBT older adults, who may not have children or other biological family members to advocate for them. They rely on families of choice or friends to accompany them to the hospital, ask questions that they may not be able to articulate, and to be their representatives in navigating the complex health care and long-term care systems.

A second federal ruling has a more direct link to health and long-term care, particularly with regards to visitation. On April 15, 2012, President Obama issued a memorandum instructing the Secretary of Health and Human Services to

✔ Initiate appropriate rulemaking to ensure that hospitals that participate in Medicare and Medicaid respect the rights of patients to designate visitors, and those hospitals may not deny visitation privileges on the basis of race, color, national origin, religion, sex, sexual orientation, gender identity, or disability.

✔ Ensure that all hospitals participating in Medicare and Medicaid are in full compliance with regulations that guarantee that all patients' advance directives, such as durable powers of attorney and healthcare proxies, are respected, and that patients' representatives have the right to make informed decisions regarding patient care.

This ruling recognized the problem encountered by many LGBT spouses and partners, even those with valid advance directives and healthcare proxies, to visit their hospitalized loved ones and to be involved in decision making. The memorandum is available at www.whitehouse.gov/the-press-office/presidential-memorandum-hospital-visitation.

New rules for visitation

In May 2011, the Centers for Medicare & Medicaid Services (CMS) issued new rules implementing the memorandum. The rules require hospitals to have written policies detailing visitation rights as well as the circumstances under which the hospital may restrict access based on patient needs. The rules require hospitals to explain to all patients their rights to choose who may visit them, regardless of the relationship, as well as to determine who they do not want as visitors. The rules are available at www.hhs.gov/news/press/2010pres/11/20101117a.html.

In June 2013, CMS issued a reminder to state survey agency directors, who coordinate inspections of skilled nursing facilities, to check with residents and family members to make sure that they have been informed about non-discriminatory visitation policies. Residents must be notified of their "rights to have visitors on a 24-hour basis that could include but are not limited to spouses (including same-sex spouses), domestic partners (including same-sex domestic partners), other family members, or friends." The Nursing Home Reform Act of 1987 does not mention sexual orientation or gender identity specifically but its broad descriptions of rights to be treated with dignity and respect prohibit verbal and physical harassments by staff.

In addition to the federal policies, several states have laws requiring hospitals and other healthcare facilities to have nondiscriminatory policies regarding visitation.

Limitations of formal visitation policies

Formal policies can only go so far in ensuring rights, including hospital or nursing home visitation rights. The legal cases that brought this issue to public and presidential attention, and ultimately to the formal CMS ruling, were not instances in which hospitals had policies of deliberately discriminating against LGBT individuals. They arose because staff members used their own judgments and prejudices to determine who should be allowed to visit a patient. They denied visits to people whose relationships they did not approve of, with tragic results.Some hospitals, especially those involved in lawsuits, have taken steps to improve their care and to prevent outright discrimination. Others may not have given this action a high priority.

A 2013 survey of hospitals in New York State found that many hospitals have improved communications about patients' rights to decide who may be at the bedside. Even so, nearly one in five large New York hospitals still have statements on their websites with language directly contrary to the federal regulation and New York State law. These statements limit visitors to, for example, "immediate family." Some of these hospitals may have formal policies that comply with the federal regulations but have failed to update their websites.

In today's world, however, most people go to websites for their initial information and not to formal policies that may or may not be publicly available. (The survey results are available at www.nypirg.org.)

The Human Rights Campaign has a map of state hospital visitation laws, including states that extend equal hospital visitation rights to

✔ Same-sex couples or partners through marriage equality or statewide relationship recognition (19 states and the District of Columbia)

✔ Same-sex spouses or partners through specific provisions as part of a limited relationship recognition statute (one state)

✔ Designated visitor statute (five states)

✔ Healthcare agent statute (two states)

✔ No statutes (23 states)

The map, updated as of June 2013, is available at www.hrc.org/files/assets/resources/hospital_visitation_laws_062013.pdf.

The inconsistency in state laws, erratic compliance with federal regulations, and difficulty in changing long-standing attitudes and behaviors means that you need to be prepared to establish your rights as a patient and to have the people you designate be recognized as visitors, healthcare proxies, and, if need be, as decision makers.

It is a good idea for caregivers of LGBT individuals who are hospitalized to bring copies of all relevant legal documents, including advance directives and the presidential memorandum and the CMS ruling, to respond to any hospital challenge.

Keeping Legal Documents at the Ready

Be prepared. You should have legal documents that you update periodically and keep in a safe but easily accessed place. You should give copies to all the people who may be involved in your healthcare, especially your physicians and the person named as a healthcare proxy. Having these documents in the right hands is especially important for LGBT older adults, whose nonbiological family representatives are more likely to be challenged about their authority to make healthcare decisions on your behalf. Despite the troubled family history experienced by many (but certainly not all) LGBT older adults, about a third of the LGBT older adults surveyed in the report cited earlier in this chapter did not have a durable power of attorney for healthcare or a will.

Here is a list of documents that relate to your rights to determine your medical care, especially in advanced illness. You may not need them all, but an advance directives and a healthcare proxy are essential.

- ✔ **Advance directive:** *Advance directive* is the generic term for the advance planning documents in which you outline your wishes for treatment and name the individual you wish to act as your spokesperson if you are unable to speak for yourself. See Chapter 16 for more information on advance directives.

   If you spend time in more than one state, you should have a valid advance directive for each state. Caring Connections, an arm of the National Hospice and Palliative Care Organization, has state-specific forms you can download at www.aarp.org/advancedirectives.

- ✔ **Healthcare proxy:** This designation names the individual you want to act as your representative, sometimes called a durable power of attorney for health care. Make sure you have discussed this responsibility with this person and that he or she understands your wishes. See Chapter 16 for information on choosing a healthcare proxy.

- ✔ **Living will:** This is a generic name for a document in which you specify the end-of-life treatments you do or do not want to receive.

- ✔ **A list of hospital visitors you approve:** This shouldn't be necessary but could be helpful just in case the hospital tries to restrict who can visit you.

- ✔ **HIPAA release stating the names of people you want to receive your health information:** Some advance directive forms include this listing. Federal law does not require a HIPAA release, but it may be required by hospital policy.

- ✔ **Do not resuscitate order:** If appropriate, a do not resuscitate order (DNR) entered by your doctor in your medical record (see Chapter 16) tells hospital personnel that you do not want to have cardiopulmonary resuscitation (CPR) performed if your heart stops beating. If you're receiving care at home you may want to talk with your doctor about creating an out-of-hospital DNR order. Without this document available, emergency medical technicians are required to perform CPR.

- ✔ **POLST form:** You might also consider a POLST (Physician Order for Life-Sustaining Treatment) form, which goes by different names in different states. This form is most appropriate for people with advanced illness, especially if they're being transferred from one care or treatment setting to another. The POLST goes into more specific detail on life-sustaining treatments that are or are not to be provided during the end of life. Chapter 16 provides more information on preparing a POLST document.

In drawing up these or any legal documents, it is advisable to consult an attorney who has expertise in elder or healthcare law and who has worked with LGBT clients before. There are many nuances in state laws that need to be considered. A guide to legal issues, including healthcare documents and organizations that can help you find an attorney, is at www.nclrights.org/site/DocServer/PlanningWithPurpose_Web.pdf?docID=6121.

Finding LGBT-Friendly Providers and Facilities

With something as important and intimate as healthcare, it is essential to have healthcare providers you can talk to and who understand your needs and concerns. In today's rushed and fragmented healthcare world, that's not easy for anyone, especially older adults who often need more time to absorb information and to ask questions. It is particularly a challenge for LGBT older adults, who may not have disclosed their sexual identity to a physician or who have experienced discrimination if they did.

Finding healthcare providers

The changing organization of healthcare also means that if you need more than occasional primary care, you will probably see a variety of healthcare providers, most of whom you will not know your personal history beforehand. In a hospital, for example, hospitalists — doctors specially trained to provide acute care — not your primary care physician, will take care of you. Some staff will be sensitive to you and your visitors, some may be hostile, and some will not care one way or the other.

Location may play a role. LGBT individuals who live in big cities generally have more choices than those who live in small towns or rural areas. But wherever you live, you should try to find healthcare providers who will be comfortable with you and with whom you will be comfortable.

You can ask LGBT friends or a local community organization that serves LGBT clients for referrals. The Gay and Lesbian Medical Association (GLMA) has an online referral system of providers who have made a commitment to nonjudgmental care of LGBT patients at http://healthfinder.gov/FindServices/Organizations/Organization.aspx?code=HR3450. Another resource is Center Link, which is the national organization representing all of the LGBT community centers in the United States Go to www.lgbtcenters.org to access their wealth of information.

The Human Rights Campaign has a list of organizations that meet its four criteria of the Healthcare Equity Index. These criteria are patient nondiscrimination, equal visitation, employment nondiscrimination, and training in LGBT patient-centered care. In 2013, 464 healthcare facilities met these standards and were designated Equality Leaders. They're listed at `www.hrc.org/files/assets/resources/HEI_2013_leaders.pdf`. (Only four states — Idaho, New Hampshire, North Dakota, and South Dakota — did not have any Equality Leader.)

Lists of names and places are only a start. You have to ask questions and visit clinics and doctors' offices yourself to determine the level of care and consideration that is provided.

LGBT individuals are sometimes both the people in need of care and their caregivers. Despite many instances of estrangement from their families of origin, because many LGBT individuals are single or childless, they may see themselves or be seen as the most available person to care for an aging parent or other relative or an LGBT friend. A United Hospital Fund/SAGE guide to LGBT caregiving is available at `www.nextstepincare.org/Caregiver_Home/LGBT_Guide/`

Considering independent- or assisted-living and nursing homes

Finding the right independent- or assisted-living facility or nursing home is a challenge for everyone, but again, when the prospective resident is an LGBT older adult there are additional concerns.

In addition to the many general questions you should ask (see Chapter 6) about the facility, its services, and its management and the observations you make on your visits, note whether there are

✔ Posted statements about nondiscrimination

✔ Indications of a LGBT-friendly environment, such as pictures of same-sex couples, rainbows, or other LGBT symbols on marketing materials, signs, or magazines

You can also ask specifically whether the facility has LGBT residents. If the answer is "No," or "We would never ask that," it is likely that the administration is not going out of its way to attract LGBT residents. You can also ask whether staff is trained to be sensitive to LGBT issues and whether residents have a safe way to report unwelcome comments.

Dealing with hostility in a nursing home

Just as you would if you were investigating assisted living, checking out nursing homes should include observations about the setting and whether there are gay-friendly materials available, questions about whether staff have been trained about LGBT issues, and whether there are any specific LGBT groups or activities. You can glean as much from the style of the responses (staff discomfort, avoidance, vagueness) as from the content.

When an LGBT person lives in a nursing home, hostile and disparaging remarks can come from staff, other residents, residents' families, and other visitors. Some residents have dementia and say things that they would not say in their nondemented state. But understanding the reasons for these remarks does not make it any easier to tolerate.

There are different ways of dealing with hostility. If the offending resident is a roommate, you can ask for a change of rooms, or if possible, a private room. If the hostility is more systematic, which suggests that the administration has not done a good job of training staff and giving them appropriate ways to handle this problem, you can discuss this with the long-term care ombudsman in your area. The ombudsman can work with the administration to alleviate the problem. To find the ombudsman in your area, go to: www.ltcombudsman. org/ombudsman. If the problem leads to poor quality of care, such as neglect by staff, you should complain to the regional Quality Improvement Organization (QIO), a private agency under contract to CMS. The QIOs are listed at www. qualitynet.org/dcs/Content Server?c=Page&pagename=Qnet Public%2FPage%2FQnetTier2& cid=1144767874793. If all else fails, you may have to consider moving to a different nursing home.

There is no federal statement of rights for assisted-living residents as there is for nursing homes, but several states have some statement of residents' rights. Check your state's health department or aging agency. Of course, the existence of a state policy on residents' rights is no guarantee that it is honored. Discrimination in nursing homes has been well documented, and it is one reason many LGBT older adults do not want to even consider this option.

The California Advocates for Nursing Home Reform, an advocacy organization, has prepared a ten-page guide on how to deal with problems when a nursing home restricts visits. Much of the guide, available at www.canhr.org/ reports/VisitationRightsGuide.pdf, is applicable in any state.

Looking at LGBT-specific options

Some LGBT older adults would like to live in a community of their peers. Others want more diversity. For now, the options for special LGBT facilities or communities are limited, but in the past few years, several retirement communities and assisted-living facilities have opened to serve LGBT residents.

Some have both LGBT and straight residents. These niche communities are hoping to appeal to a relatively affluent segment of the LGBT community, although a few are geared toward low-income residents. Some new developments encountered financial difficulties in the poor economy. If you are considering one of these facilities, make sure you investigate its funding and business plan.

The Assisted Living Directory has lists of gay-friendly facilities at www. assisted-living-directory.com/content/gay-friendly-facilities.cfm. After filling out a questionnaire, the site will direct you to facilities in your area. And as the website notes, some facilities that welcome LGBT residents do not want to be listed for fear that it may deter potential heterosexual customers.

Another organization, Gay and Lesbian Elder Housing (GLEH) has a Senior Resource Center and a Housing and Services Center. You can fill out a form at http://gleh.org/housing-and-services www.lgbtagingcenter.org/ to be referred to housing options. Another good, comprehensive resource is the National Resource Center on LGBT Aging at www.lgbtagingcenter.org/.

Chapter 18

Planning for Veterans

. . . .

In This Chapter

▶ An overview of the healthcare and long-term care through the U.S. Department of Veteran Affairs (VA)

▶ Long-term services and support at home or in the community

▶ Care in a residential setting or nursing home

. . . .

*V*eterans of United States military service have an additional set of options beyond whatever form of healthcare or long-term care insurance other people may have. But they also have to navigate another large bureaucracy with its own complex rules, requirements, and delays.

Many options for both long-term services and supports at home or in the community are available to veterans enrolled in VA (Department of Veterans Affairs) healthcare. These benefits are usually more generous than those available through Medicare or private insurance, and less stringent in terms of financial eligibility than Medicaid. This chapter describes the basic way the VA system works and its options for long-term care.

Getting into the VA System

The Veterans Health Administration (VHA) is the largest integrated healthcare system in the United States, with more than 1,700 sites of care — hospitals, clinics, community living centers (another name for nursing homes), domiciliaries (mental-health and rehabilitation homes), readjustment counseling centers, and other facilities. About 8.3 million veterans are enrolled, and close to 6 million use the system each year. Although the VA healthcare network is extensive, it's not distributed equally across the nation, so veterans in some areas, particularly rural areas, may not live close to a VA

Medical Center or Community-Based Outpatient Clinic. You can find a map of VA facilities by state at www.va.gov/directory/guide/map_flsh. asp?isflash.

If you are enrolled in the VA system, you can continue to use private or public healthcare insurance and see doctors outside the VA. This arrangement is called Co-Managed Care or Dual Care, and over 70 percent of veterans are enrolled in this program, many of them enrolled in Medicare.

Comparing VA to other healthcare systems

In many ways, the VA system is unlike other systems with which you are probably more familiar:

- ✔ Unlike Medicare, Medicaid, and private insurance, which only pay for care, the VA provides healthcare as well as pays for it.

- ✔ Unlike Medicare, there is no age, work history, or specific disease requirement for eligibility. Eligibility is based solely on military service, but there are many categories of eligibility and priorities for healthcare services.

- ✔ Unlike some private healthcare insurance, there is no exclusion for pre-existing conditions. In fact, if a veteran has a pre-existing condition that is service-related, he or she may be given a higher priority to receive services.

- ✔ Like Medicaid, there is a means (financial status) test; but unlike Medicaid, it is not based on poverty guidelines.

As with most insurance and healthcare programs, you must be enrolled in VA healthcare to be eligible for long-term services and supports. Many older veterans enroll in VA healthcare when they need long-term care. Just being discharged from active service does not enroll you in the VA healthcare system. You have to apply. You can do this online, in person at a VA facility, by mail, or by phone (1-877-222-8387). Go to http://www.va.gov/healthbenefits/apply/application_process.asp for details on the application process for healthcare benefits. There is an additional step when you apply for long-term care, also described on the site.

A helpful 2013 report from the Congressional Research Service answers many questions about healthcare for veterans, including a diagram of the several steps in the enrollment process (p. 6). Go to: https://www.fas.org/sgp/crs/misc/R42747.pdf.

Eligibility for VA healthcare

Eligibility for VA healthcare is a tiered system, and you may need some help from the VA to figure out just where you fit. The three basic eligibility considerations for VA healthcare are military service, type of disability, and financial need. The following sections give a brief explanation of each.

Military service

If you served in the active military, including Army, Navy, Marines, Coast Guard, or Air Force, you may qualify for VA healthcare benefits. Reservists and National Guard members may also qualify for the VA healthcare benefits if they were called to active duty (other than for training only) by a federal order and completed the full period for which they were called or ordered to active duty.

Veterans who were dishonorably discharged are not eligible for VA healthcare, but veterans who had "other than honorable" discharges, often for drug abuse or behavior problems, can still apply. In June 2013, the VA issued a statement that outlined how veterans in these "in-between" categories can apply. Eligibility is determined on a case-by-case basis, but a tentative approval may be granted in emergencies. For details, see http://www.va.gov/healthbenefits/resources/publications/IB10-448_other_than_honorable_discharges_0613.pdf.

Type of disability

You may believe that you have to have a service-related injury to be eligible for VA healthcare services. That's not true, although sometimes service-related injuries show up years and years after discharge, as has occurred with some veterans of the Korean and Vietnam conflicts. And you don't have to establish a disability rating (a number that quantifies the extent of your disability from 0 to 100 percent) before you start to get care.

Being 100 percent disabled is not necessarily a permanent condition. You may recover sufficiently to have your disability rating changed.

The VA has eight priority groups that determine the ranking of eligibility and financial contributions. The key point here is that the most serious disabilities get priority and their financial status is assessed more leniently. As you move down the scale toward less serious conditions, you have to show greater financial need.

Group 1 has the highest priority and includes veterans with the most serious service-related disabilities, and Group 2 includes those with less serious service-related disabilities. The priority continues down to groups of veterans who have non-service-related disabilities and can demonstrate financial need. (I discuss the income consideration more in the following section.) For a complete list and description of the priority groups, go to www.va.gov/healthbenefits/resources/priority_groups.asp.

Financial considerations

You don't have to be poor to qualify for VA healthcare. If you meet the financial threshold, your care will be free. The income thresholds for 2014 are available at: www.va.gov/healthbenefits/cost/income_thresholds.asp. But even if your income exceeds these limits, and you are eligible based on other criteria, you can get care and pay copays for whatever isn't covered. There are lower financial thresholds for veterans with service-related injuries than for those with non-service-related health problems. The VA has a financial calculator at www.va.gov/healtheligibility/apps/enrollmentcalculator/. You have to document financial need every year, and the thresholds may change.

You can use the VA online Health Benefits Explorer as a first step in determining your eligibility (http://hbexplorer.vacloud.us). However, eligibility for specific healthcare services may depend on several outside factors, including the amount of money Congress appropriates for the VA every year. In some cases your priority status also affects the services for which you qualify or the level of copays.

In 2012, the VA relaxed some of the requirements for Group 8, the lowest priority, which means that some veterans who previously would have been denied because their incomes were too high may now qualify. To find out about income thresholds, go to www.va.gov/healthbenefits/cost/income_thresholds.asp. There are also geographical adjustments based on the cost-of-living in different regions (info is available at www.va.gov/healthbenefits/resources/gmt).

Veterans enrolled in the VA for healthcare coverage have completely satisfied the requirement to have healthcare coverage under the Affordable Care Act. An estimated 1.3 million veterans under the age of 65 are uninsured. States that have opted into the Medicaid expansion part of the Affordable Care Act will provide access to healthcare coverage for low-income veterans, making Medicaid an additional option under the Co-Managed or Dual Care Program. Medicaid would pay, for example, for living in a medical foster home for veterans. Veterans who are eligible for Medicaid do not have to pay VA copays. Even if the state has not opted into the Medicaid expansion program, as of October 2013 every state opened a Health Insurance Marketplace that has information on Medicaid as well as other options.

Supporting Veterans and Their Families

The VA's motto is "To care for him who shall have borne the battle, and for his widow, and his orphan." Taken from Abraham Lincoln's stirring second Inaugural Address, delivered one month before his assassination, these words emphasize the VA's moral obligations not only to veterans but also to their families. In today's less stirring but more precise vernacular, the motto might add, "and to his or her caregiver."

Shared decision making

Shared decision making in the VA is an integral part of patient-centered care. It is a process in which the veteran, close family members, social worker, and healthcare team collaborate to make healthcare and long-term care decisions. For long-term care the goal is supporting veterans at the highest level of independence achievable by exploring home- and community-based options that address their health conditions, values, and preferences, as well as family support needs.

Shared Decision Making is introduced, along with videos, at `www.va.gov/ GERIATRICS/Guide/LongTermCare/Shared_Decision_Making.asp`. The site provides two decision aids: a worksheet for veterans and a caregiver self-assessment:

- ✔ The Shared Decision Making worksheet guides veterans in thinking through their needs, resources, and preferences; exploring services and settings; and involving caregivers, social workers, healthcare providers, and others in the process of making long-term care choices.

- ✔ The caregiver self-assessment worksheet encourages family members and others who help the veteran to explore their own needs and resources, in addition to those of the veteran, and to become informed about long-term care options so that they can more accurately assess their ability to support the veteran's needs and choices. It includes sections on the veteran's needs, who helps now, where the veteran wants to live, long-term care options he or she would consider and why they are important. Final sections include the opinions of people who help the veteran make decisions.

Although the shared decision-making process and the accompanying decision aids are intended for veterans and their caregivers, the basic structure and most of the questions are useful to anyone investigating long-term care.

Caregiver support

The VA has many programs and policies that support family caregivers, including some programs that are focused on women's health and family needs. The most significant advance in this area came through federal legislation, which in 2010 provided a monthly stipend to primary caregivers of veterans injured in military conflict after September 11, 2001. These caregivers may be spouses but also may be parents or other relatives. Other benefits include travel expenses to facilities where the veteran (or before discharge, the soldier or other service member) is being treated, access to healthcare insurance, mental-health services, and respite care of 30 days a year.

Caregiver support throughout the system is described at www.caregiver. va.gov, or you can call the toll-free hotline at 1-855-260-3274.

Noting VA Options for Older Veterans

As the veteran population ages, along with the rest of the country, the VA system has had to deal with increasing numbers of older veterans who need in Medicaid terminology, long-term services and supports. Enrolled veterans can obtain all standard benefits and several long-term care benefits. These long-term care services and supports are described in a comprehensive VA guide on geriatrics and extended care available at www.va.gov/geriatrics. Throughout this chapter I refer to specific sections of this guide.

Included services are:

- ✔ **Geriatric evaluation:** Older veterans can receive a comprehensive assessment of their ability to manage independently, including physical health and social environment. Based on this evaluation, a plan of care can be created that includes treatment, rehabilitation, health promotion, and social services. These evaluations are performed by Inpatient Geriatric Evaluation and Management (GEM) Units at VA hospitals, geriatric primary care clinics, or other outpatient settings.

- ✔ **Adult day healthcare:** This therapeutic day-care program provides medical and rehabilitation services to disabled veterans (www.va.gov/ GERIATRICS/Guide/LongTermCare/Adult_Day_Health_Care.asp).

- ✔ **Skilled home healthcare:** Skilled care requires the services of a nurse or other professional and is provided by the VA and contract agencies to veterans who are homebound with chronic diseases. Skilled care includes nursing, physical and occupational therapy, and social services (www.va.gov/GERIATRICS/Guide/LongTermCare/Skilled_Home_Health_Care.asp).

✔ **Homemaker and home health aide services:** Trained assistants who can help the veteran with personal care in the home are available to all enrolled veterans with a clinical need. There is no time limit on the services and the aide is supervised by a nurse (www.va.gov/GERIATRICS/Guide/LongTermCare/Homemaker_and_Home_Health_Aide_Care.asp).

✔ **Home Telehealth:** This service can be used to track blood pressure, blood sugar level, weight, blood oxygen level, and heart and lung sounds. Information is transmitted to a care coordinator by landline or cell phone or by video. Equipment is provided by the VA, and the service is available to all enrolled veterans as long as they meet the criteria for clinical needs. There is no copay for Home Telehealth, although there may be a copay for video visits. (Find out more at www.va.gov/GERIATRICS/Guide/LongTermCare/Telehealth_Care.asp.)

✔ **Hospice and palliative care:** These programs provide pain-management, symptom control, and other medical services to veterans in the late stages of their diseases. Services include respite care and bereavement counseling to family members. There are no copays for hospice care in any setting (www.va.gov/GERIATRICS/Guide/LongTermCare/Hospice_and_Palliative_Care.asp).

✔ **Respite care for family caregivers:** Short-term respite services are provided to give caregivers relief from the physical and emotional demands of caregiving. Respite can be provided at home or in another non-institutional setting (www.va.gov/GERIATRICS/Guide/LongTermCare/Respite_Care.asp).

Receiving pensions

Pensions are funds paid to veterans of disabled veterans of wartime service who have low incomes and are no longer able to work. Finding out whether you or your parent is eligible for a VA pension is important because it can provide needed income and is the key to additional benefits for long-term care in the Aid and Attendance and Homebound programs that I discuss in the next section. VA pensions are available to surviving spouses as well as veterans.

Following are the basic requirements for eligibility for a pension:

- ✔ At least 90 days of active duty service, with at least one day during a wartime period. For those who entered active duty after September 7, 1980, the basic requirement is to have served at least 24 months or the full period for which he or she was called, with at least one day during a wartime period.

- ✔ In addition, the veteran must meet **one** of the following requirements:

  - 65 years of age or older

  - Totally and permanently disabled

  - Resident in a nursing home receiving skilled nursing care

  - Receiving Social Security Disability Insurance (SSDI)

  - Receiving Supplemental Security Income (SSI)

  - Annual family income must be less than the amount set by Congress to qualify for the Veterans Pension Benefit

For more information, go to http://benefits.va.gov/ PENSIONANDFIDUCIARY/pension/vetpen.asp.

Pensions are different from compensation, which is a monthly amount awarded to a veteran based on the extent of a service-related disability. Some disabilities and conditions that may arise after service ends but were aggravated by service also count. You can check out www.benefits.va.gov/ compensation for a schedule of compensation benefits. Note that Veterans of the Korean and Vietnam conflicts who were exposed to Agent Orange and other herbicides on land or on ships may be eligible for compensation on that basis. See www.publichealth.va.gov/exposures/agentorange.

Using Aid and Attendance and Homebound programs

Veterans and survivors who are eligible for a pension may also be eligible for additional services at home. Even some who are not eligible for a pension based on income may be eligible for these services. These programs have been available for many years but are not well known.

The Aid and Attendance (A&A) Pension provides benefits for veterans and surviving spouses who need the daily assistance of another person to remain at home. A physician must certify that you cannot function completely on your own.

Veterans and survivors may be eligible for the Aid and Attendance (A&A) pension if they

✔ Require the aid of another person to perform activities of daily living (ADLs), adjust prosthetic devices, or for safety (Oddly for an agency dealing with people who have experienced the harsh realities of wartime, the VA primly includes "attending to the wants of nature" as one of the ADLs.)

✔ Are bedridden because of disability

✔ Live in a nursing home due to mental or physical incapacity

✔ Are blind or have very low vision

The Homebound program is similar to Aid and Asisstance in that it provides aide and other services in the home but there is an additional requirement. To be eligible for the Homebound program, you must be substantially confined to home because of permanent disability, which is not a requirement for Aid and Attendance. The Homebound program is an enhanced or special monthly pension benefit paid in addition to a basic pension. You may not receive enhanced or special monthly pension without first establishing eligibility for a basic VA pension. However, because enhanced pension is based upon a higher income limit, a claimant ineligible for basic pension due to excessive income may be eligible for enhanced pension benefits.

You can receive an additional pension benefit only for the Aid and Attendance or Homebound program, not both. When applying for either benefit, you have to give sufficient detail to make a strong case that you need Aid and Attendance or are homebound. In addition, the financial assessment is rigorous and includes the value of liquid assets like cash, stocks, IRAs, 401(k) plans, other tax-deferred income, bonds, mutual funds, art, coins, stamps, and collectibles. The A&A pension regulations consider whether some or all of the veteran's estate should be used to pay for care, including whether the assets can readily be converted into cash, life expectancy, number of dependents, and the potential rate of depletion of the assets, including unusual medical expenses.

As an example of the possible benefits, for a single veteran with a yearly income of $12,465, the regular monthly pension benefit would be $1,038; the Homebound benefit would be $1,269, and the A&A benefit would be $1,732. For a surviving spouse, the comparable benefits would be $698, $851, and $1,113. A veteran with one dependent could get $2,054 if accepted into the A&A program.

 Don't give up if your application for the A&A benefit is turned down on the first try. The VA often has long delays in processing disability claims in general, which it acknowledges. Because the application is complicated, many people make mistakes or leave out important information. Then they have to

Veterans can be vulnerable, too

Never underestimate the persistence of scammers who prey on older people. One variety is a *pension poacher,* who finds older veterans and convinces them to submit an application for a pension supplement to receive additional benefits for care at home. These poachers (including some financial advisers) then use the opportunity to sell annuities and trusts, which they claim will shield the veteran's assets (and, incidentally, enrich themselves with hefty fees). Unlike Medicaid, the VA does not have a look-back period that will be examined for asset transfers. If the application is denied, as it well may be, the veteran may not be able to get access to the money in the trust or annuity. And it may well disqualify the veteran for eligibility for Medicaid. Legislation has been introduced to institute a look-back period, but although this safeguard may discourage pension poachers, it would also create a barrier to immediate access to care.

appeal, maybe more than once. The VA does not allow you to pay someone to help fill out the application from the outset, although it does allow you to pay for a VA-accredited professional to handle an appeal. But not all these people have sufficient training or expertise to handle appeals. VeteranAid, a nonprofit organization, recommends that instead of filing a substantive appeal, as the VA suggests, but which can take up to three years to reach a resolution, you can file a statement in support of claim, including new information or older information presented more clearly. If the claim is still denied, you can file a notice of disagreement, and explain the reasons. Then, and only then, will the VA tell you why your application was denied. A full-scale substantive appeal may be the last-ditch attempt, but be prepared to wait. Go to www.VeteranAid.org for more information on the A&A program.

For more information on the A&A and Homebound programs in general, go to www.benefits.va.gov/pension/aid_attendance_housebound.asp.

Finding the Right Residential Setting or Nursing Home for Veterans

The VA has a range of options for long-term care outside the veteran's home. The following sections cover five possibilities.

Veterans' medical foster homes

Medical foster homes are private homes in which a trained caregiver provides long-term services and support to people who need round-the-clock care but don't need to be in a nursing home. The residents may be veterans or nonveterans. The VA inspects and approves all the medical foster homes in its system, and needed medical care is provided by a VA home-based primary-care team. This program is quickly expanding across VA. For more information, see `www.va.gov/GERIATRICS/Guide/LongTermCare/Medical_Foster_Homes.asp`.

The VA does not pay for medical foster care homes. The charge is generally about $1,500 to $3,000 a month, based on income and level of care. You will have to pay out of pocket or use other insurance such as Medicaid or long-term care insurance.

Community living facilities (Nursing homes)

The VA operates 132 community living facilities (which used to be called nursing homes) across the country. Most are on or close to the campus of a VA medical center. Most community living facilities provide 24-hour skilled nursing care, restorative care, access to social-work services, and geriatric evaluation and management. Some also provide mental-health services, special care for veterans with dementia or other cognitive deficits, respite care, and palliative and hospice care. The VA's new name for nursing homes reflects its goal of making these residential settings more homelike and offering veterans more independence and flexibility.

To qualify, veterans must meet specific eligibility requirements, and the VA will pay if you meet certain criteria concerning service-connected status, level of disability, and income. You may still have copays of up to $97 a day depending on income. Veterans eligible for Medicaid can apply to that program.

Some veterans can receive nursing-home care in non-VA facilities in the community under contract to the VA if there is a compelling medical or social need. Generally these are short-term placements — not longer than six months — while longer-term arrangements are made. Of course, veterans with significant assets can pay out of pocket to live in a non-VA home.

In general, care in a community living facility is like care in a community nursing home with one exception: Most of the residents in a community nursing home are women, whereas in a VA facility they are men. Some male veterans prefer a VA facility for this reason; it is easier for them to build rapport with other men who have served in the military.

State-operated veteran homes

Every state has at least one nursing home designated for veterans. Many states have more; for example, Oklahoma has seven. The majority of these homes offer nursing care but some may offer assisted living or domiciliary care. These homes started after the Civil War, when many states created them to provide shelter for homeless and disabled veterans. Unlike the community living facilities I discuss in the previous section, the VA does not manage state veterans' homes, but it does formally review and certify the facilities each year to make sure they're following VA standards.

Eligibility is based on clinical need and available space. Each state establishes its own eligibility and admission criteria. Some state homes may admit nonveteran spouses and Gold Start parents (who have lost a child in the military). Others admit only veterans.

The cost varies by state, and the veteran is expected to pay a share of the costs. Certified state veteran homes receive some funding from the VA to cover some of the costs for veterans residing in the state home, but it does not pay for care for nonveterans. Space is limited, and an application may not result in an immediate placement. Because of costs and location, as well as a shortage of beds, a Medicaid-certified nursing home may be a better immediate choice. However, qualifying for Medicaid would require the veteran to "spend down" and go through a look-back process to see if assets were transferred to become eligible. At this time, the VA does not require either as a condition of eligibility.

State veteran homes fall under the category of niche housing described in Chapter 6 in the sense that the residents share a history of military service that may enhance their community living experience. This sense of camaraderie is one reason veterans may prefer to go to a state veterans' home farther from their family than a nearby community nursing home. For a list of state veterans homes, go to www.nasvh.org/StateHomes/statedir.cfm.

Domiciliary program

The domiciliary program is the VA's oldest healthcare program. Established in the late 1860s, the domiciliary purpose was to provide a home for disabled volunteer soldiers of the Civil War. The Domiciliary has evolved from a Soldiers' Home to become an active clinical rehabilitation and treatment program for veterans, especially those with mental-health or substance-abuse problems or who are homeless. Domiciliary programs are now integrated into the Mental Health Residential Rehabilitation and Treatment Programs (MH RRTPs).

The program offers both short-term rehabilitation and long-term health maintenance care. It also provides a clinically appropriate level of care for homeless veterans whose healthcare needs don't require more intensive levels of treatment. You can find out more about the care program at www.benefits. gov/benefits/benefit-details/301.

Eligibility requirements for these programs include income, need for a structured residential environment, and ability to participate in treatment as well as the ability to independently manage activities of daily living. The goal is to return to the community.

TRICARE For Life

The Department of Defense maintains a system of military hospitals and medical centers in the U.S. and overseas. TRICARE is the healthcare insurance program that covers healthcare for active-duty personnel, their families, retirees, and members of the National Guard and U.S. Army Reserve. It was formerly called CHAMPUS (Civilian Health and Medical Program of the Uniformed Services).

TRICARE For Life (TFL) offers secondary coverage to Medicare beneficiaries who have both Part A and B coverage (see Chapter 10 for more on Medicare coverage). It is available worldwide. In the U.S. Medicare is the primary payer, but overseas, TRICARE is primary. TFL has no enrollment fees, but you must pay Medicare Part B monthly premiums. For services covered by both Medicare and TRICARE, there are no additional out-of-pocket costs. For more information, go to www. tricare4u.com/apps-portal/tricareapps-app/static/pdf/ TRICARE_For_Life_Fact_Sheet_2011_Lo.pdf.

Using Other Resources to Navigate the VA System

Navigating the VA system may take time and persistence, just as it does with health insurance in the private sector or Medicare and Medicaid. In addition to the specific tips throughout the chapter, a good place to get information and assistance is a local Veterans Service Organization (VSO) for VA-specific services and a state or county office for the aging for non-VA services. VSOs are private organizations. Some serve all veterans, such as the American Legion, and some serve specific groups of veterans such as veterans of the Navy or Air Force or African-American veterans. A VA list of VSOs can be found at: `www.va.gov/vso/VSO-Directory_2012-2013.pdf`. Part I of this listing includes VSOs that have been approved to prepare and present claims to the VA on veterans' behalf.

If you still have unresolved problems, enlist your Congressional Representative or Senator's office. They have staff experienced in assisting veterans and their families.

Whatever route you take in navigating the system, be prepared with good information, thorough documentation, and patience.

Chapter 19

Services for Family Caregivers

In This Chapter

▶ Looking at who family caregivers are

▶ Preparing yourself for the responsibilities of the role

▶ Finding resources for information and support

An estimated 80 to 90 percent of long-term care in the community is provided by unpaid family members. Even when an older adult lives in an assisted-living facility or a nursing home, family members continue to play an important, albeit different, role. Despite the changes in family structures that exist today and the vastly different healthcare system that makes caregiving different from earlier eras, family ties are still central to most people's lives. And at no time does this become more meaningful than in times of illness or need.

If you are or may become a family caregiver for a parent or other relative, you will encounter many challenges as well as potential rewards. And if you are the person needing assistance, you too may face challenges in acknowledging your need for help and adapting to a new relationship.

Each family and each caregiving situation is different. Yet there are some common themes. This chapter stresses both these ideas. It is intended as a supplement to other chapters that address issues of importance to family caregivers, such as aging in place, Medicare and Medicaid, home care, and nursing homes.

Defining Family Caregivers

Family caregiver is a relatively new term. It refers to a person who provides or manages assistance for a relative, domestic partner, or friend who needs help because of illness, disability, or advanced age. It is a broad term, intended to include people in nontraditional relationships as well as people related by blood or marriage. A caregiver may or may not live with the person needing assistance. Although caregiving traditionally has been considered a woman's role, and women still make up the majority of caregivers, men are increasingly taking on this responsibility.

One distinguishing feature is that family caregivers for the most part are unpaid. They take on this role because of love, duty, or religious or cultural beliefs. Most have no training for this role, and even many of those who are healthcare or social-service professionals find that their training does not prepare them for the emotional impact of caring for a person close to them.

Some researchers and policy makers call people in this category *informal caregivers* to distinguish them from paid or formal caregivers such as nurses and physical therapists. Other people prefer the term *care partner* or *caretaker*. The term *carer* is used in the United Kingdom and some other countries. In this chapter, I use the term *family caregiver,* recognizing that you may come across other terms.

Family caregivers by the numbers

How many family caregivers are there? Estimates vary, depending on how the question is asked and the research method used to come up with the answer. The broadest answer is that one in five Americans is caring for an adult over the age of 18.

The AARP Public Policy Institute estimates that in 2009 about 42.1 million Americans provided care to an adult with limitations in daily activities at any given time, and about 61.6 million adults provided care at some point during the year. The estimated economic value of their unpaid contributions was approximately $450 billion in 2009, a figure that is greater than the total of institutional care and community-based care combined. (If you're interested to learn more, you can see the report "Valuing the Invaluable: 2011 Update" at www.aarp.org/relationships/caregiving/info-07-2011/ valuing-the-invaluable.html.)

In a 2013 report based on 2011 data, the Congressional Budget Office estimated the economic value of informal caregiving at $234 billion. This figure is lower than the AARP estimate because it includes only unpaid care for people 65 years and older. The ratio of unpaid care to institutional and community-based care mirrors the AARP estimates.

Are we in the golden age of caregiving?

The AARP Public Policy Institute has warned that the *caregiver support ratio* — the number of potential caregivers for each older adult — is now at a peak level. In 2010, the United States had more than seven potential caregivers aged 45 to 64 for every person aged 80 and older. By 2030, as the baby boomers age, that number will have dropped to four to one; and by 2050, when all baby boomers will be in the high-risk years of later life, it will fall even farther to less than three to one. These numbers simply give broad population data indicating the number of *potential* caregivers per care recipient. In reality, many caregivers carry the burden alone, and as the care ratio lessens in the future, the chances of being a lone caregiver will be even greater. For the full report, go to www.aarp.org/home-family/caregiving/info-08-2013/the-aging-of-the-baby-boom-and-the-growing-care-gap-AARP-ppi-ltc.html.

These numbers are so big that they may not seem relevant to you as an individual. To put it into perspective, if you are a family caregiver, you are one of millions of people who are having the same problems and the same experiences. Even though you may feel isolated, you are not alone. And in addition to the assistance you are providing to a family member or more than one person, you are an unpaid part of the elder care workforce. Family caregivers are often called the foundation or bedrock of long-term care, and these statistics back up that designation.

Although caregivers are found in every age group, including children and teenagers and people in their 70s and 80s, the average age is 49. Unsurprisingly, given the burden the role can place on them, family caregivers may experience serious mental-health consequences. As many as 70 percent may experience depression and anxiety. These strains are most common among women, older caregivers, low-income caregivers, and those with a high level of burden. An estimated 17 to 35 percent of family caregivers rate their own health as poor. Studies have shown that family caregivers tend to neglect their own health, do not see their own doctors, or take their own medications. They are more susceptible than non-caregivers to poor immune-system responses, back and muscle problems, and worsening of chronic conditions.

However, many caregivers feel rewarded by their caregiving, usually because of a deeper relationship with the person needing assistance, or because caregiving offers spiritual or emotional growth.

What family caregivers do

If I were to create a comprehensive and detailed job description for family caregivers, it would take up the rest of this chapter and more. Basically, family caregivers do whatever needs to be done. For a succinct list, the AARP report "Valuing the Invaluable" outlines what the new normal in caregiving entails:

- Providing companionship and emotional support (often overlooked but an essential element in the relationship)
- Helping with household tasks, such as preparing meals
- Handling bills and dealing with insurance claims
- Carrying out personal care, such as bathing and dressing
- Being responsible for nursing procedures, such as IV infusions and wound care, in the home
- Administering and managing multiple medications, including injections
- Identifying, arranging, and coordinating services and supports
- Hiring and supervising direct-care workers
- Arranging for or providing transportation to medical appointments and community services
- Communicating with health professionals
- Serving as advocate for their loved one during medical appointments or hospitalizations
- Implementing care plans
- Playing a key role of care coordinator during transitions, especially from hospital to home

Not every family caregiver is required to do all these tasks all the time, but family caregiving is a dynamic process. New challenges, requiring new skills, can arise on short notice.

The conventional way of describing caregiver tasks is to divide them into ADLs (activities of daily living) and IADLs (instrumental activities of daily living). ADLs include bathing and dressing, and IADLs include shopping and transportation. While important, these categories do not cover the wide range of medical/nursing tasks that family caregivers are expected to perform at home. An AARP/United Hospital Fund national survey found that nearly half (46 percent) of the caregivers performed one or more tasks like managing complex medications, changing surgical dressings, and operating medical equipment such as feeding tubes. They also helped with ADLs and IADLs. Being a family caregiver today is more than chicken soup and fluffy pillows. The report is available at www.aarp.org/homealone.

What family caregivers find hard to do

In the AARP/United Hospital Fund "Home Alone" survey, caregivers who performed medical/nursing tasks were asked to name two tasks that they found hard to do. Following were the top responses:

- Using incontinence supplies and administering enemas

- Caring for wounds or treating pressure sores or postsurgical wounds

- Managing medications

- Preparing food for special diets

- Operating medical equipment

- Helping with assistive devices for mobility

- Using meters, monitors, test kits, and telehealth equipment

- Operating durable medical equipment

The majority of respondents had no formal training to do these tasks and said they learned at least in part on their own how to do them. As medical care at home becomes more complex, new training and support programs are needed to assist family caregivers with these challenging tasks and others.

Family caregivers' rights and obligations

Although some family caregiver advocates have developed lists of caregiver rights, these are mostly statements about how caregivers should be treated and what they should expect from others. They are aspirations rather than actual rights that can be enforced.

Regrettably, the list of actual family caregiver rights is quite small. Even so, caregivers may have significant legal rights related to some aspects of their responsibilities. For example, if you have been named the attorney in fact (or agent), you have the right to manage the financial matters specified in the document. Or if you have been named your parent's healthcare proxy, you have the right to make healthcare decisions if he or she is unable to do so.

One important right comes from the Health Insurance Accountability and Portability Act (HIPAA), a 1996 federal law that protects the privacy of a patient's medical information. According to the law, unless the patient objects, healthcare professionals can share relevant information with a family member or other person directly involved in the patient's care or paying for care. This is especially important in hospitals and other facilities where staff may be reluctant to share information, even with the patient. For more information about HIPAA, see the United Hospital Fund's guide at www.nextstepincare.org/Caregiver_Home/HIPAA.

The other side of rights is, of course, obligations. Your primary obligation is to advocate for your family member and ensure that he or she receives adequate, appropriate, and good quality care, including protection from abuse. If you have a power of attorney for financial affairs, you have a legal duty to act in the best interests of your family member and to avoid conflicts of interest. That means, for one thing, that you cannot use the money for your own expenses, even if you fully intend to pay it back, unless there is an explicit agreement that allows you to do this.

Unless adult children have been legally designated a parent's guardian, they do not generally have financial obligations to their parents. However, 30 states have so-called *filial responsibility* laws, mostly dating from the 1800s, that establish this responsibility, except in extreme cases of hardship or prior abuse. Although these laws are rarely enforced, they do exist and you should be aware of them.

Protecting your family member from abuse and neglect

Abuse may be physical, verbal, financial, or sexual. These problems can arise at home as well as in nursing homes and assisted-living facilities, so it is particularly important to be aware of the potential for abuse when hiring workers to help you. Background checks and references are helpful but only a start. Frequent monitoring is essential.

Sometimes family caregivers are unaware of neglect by home care or nursing-home workers because they see only their family member's clean face and combed hair and not the underlying problems of bedsores or other warning signs. Although you may feel intrusive and uncomfortable, it is important to check for these problems. If left untreated, bedsores can lead to serious infections and hospitalizations.

Neglect is in some ways harder to deal with than outright abuse. Most cases of neglect among older adults are self-neglect when the person fails to bathe, change clothes, eat regular meals, and keep the kitchen and bathroom clean. He or she generally falls into a pattern of being disheveled and dirty and living with hoards of papers and junk. Often when someone gets to this state of inability to care for herself, there is some underlying dementia or mental illness. If not addressed (and it is not easy), these problems can lead to removal from the home. If you live with the person, you might be considered abusive because you did not take preventive action. Neighbors might complain and call the police or Adult Protective Services. To avoid these drastic and upsetting actions, it is important to involve outside assistance, such as a social worker or psychologist, early on.

Lawsuits are most likely to be initiated by nursing homes when the resident has not applied for Medicaid or has been turned down. In a 2012 Pennsylvania case, a son was held liable for more than $92,000 in nursing-home costs incurred by his mother while she was waiting for Medicaid approval, which was eventually denied. The judgment was upheld on appeal. On the other hand, a Montana court ruled in favor of a son who was being sued for $15,000 for his mother's nursing-home costs. Legislators in some states, including Pennsylvania, are trying to repeal their filial responsibility laws. New Hampshire, for example, repealed its law in 2013. AARP has an interactive map of states showing those with and without filial responsibility laws and a snapshot of the state's law at `www.aarp.org/politics-soci-ety/rights/info-09-2011/who-pays-nursing-home-costs-inter-active-map.html`.

Spouses are legally responsible for each other's bills and other obligations. Medicaid statutes vary, but most allow spouses of Medicaid recipients to retain some funds for their own use.

Becoming a Family Caregiver

Taking on the role of family caregiver is a big and even life-changing event. You may even be performing many of the duties without even recognizing that you're actually being the caregiver. This section helps you identify the role of caregiver and discusses the importance of negotiation skills in this role.

Identifying yourself as a family caregiver

Even family caregivers themselves often do not recognize that they are doing anything beyond what a daughter, son, spouse, domestic partner, or friend should do for someone who is ill or needs assistance. In the jargon of caregiving, they do not *self-identify*.

Even when they do recognize themselves in the description of what family caregivers do, they may worry that identifying themselves as family caregivers means in some way giving up the primary relationship. My response to this concern is that *family* is who you are in relation to the person needing assistance, and that never changes; *caregiver* is your job description, and that does change over time and as the person improves or becomes sicker.

Here is a quick family caregiver identification test: Do you regularly or occasionally

✔ Take care of someone who has a chronic illness, disability, or disease?

✔ Manage medications or talk to doctors or nurses on someone's behalf?

✔ Help bathe or dress someone who is frail or disabled?

✔ Take care of household chores, meals, or bills for someone who cannot do these things alone?

✔ Accompany someone who is ill or frail to a doctor's appointment?

✔ Provide emotional support to someone who is ill or frail?

If you answered yes to any of these questions, you are a family caregiver. Chances are that if you're reading this book because of your concern for another person, you are or will become a family caregiver. And if you think about your own needs in these areas, you may need a family caregiver.

Readying yourself for negotiation

In addition to the managerial, technical, and organizational skills it takes to be a family caregiver, add negotiating skills. As a family caregiver, you have to navigate the tricky shoals of a changed and sometimes rocky relationship with your family member. That person may be resistant to help, uncooperative, and even aggressive or hostile. Perhaps this behavior is an exaggeration of qualities that existed before the illness or disability; perhaps it stems from depression or dementia. Whatever the cause, it takes extreme patience and new ways of communicating to work out caregiving routines that are less stressful for both of you.

Another form of negotiation is required when dealing with healthcare professionals on whom you and your family member depend for treatment, advice, and support. They may or may not recognize your deep knowledge about the person in front of them, and they may not include you in decision making, even though the decision affects you as well as the patient. Being an advocate for your family member at times means being an advocate for yourself. This is particularly important when caregiving requires understanding complex medication regimens, performing procedures, and other technical tasks. Sometimes professionals describe something as *simple,* which it may be for them, but not for you.

Managing the financial aspects of care, including dealing with insurance companies, banks, transportation services, and government agencies, can also require persistence and negotiating skills.

Finally, you need negotiating skills to deal with other family members who may or may not be involved in caregiving. In several earlier chapters I stress the importance of transparency in money matters, living arrangements, and all the details that go into long-term care. Some families are brought closer by an illness and share the responsibilities equitably, which means that each person does the best that he or she can, given their financial, familial, and employment circumstances. Sometimes, however, illness tears families apart. The situation may eventually turn into a crisis, usually over money or end-of-life decisions. If reasonable efforts to share information and responsibilities are not working out, then an objective family or eldercare mediator may be needed.

Checking Out Different Types of Family Caregivers

Family caregivers come in all ages, and from different backgrounds and cultures. Some may be employed and perform caregiver duties in addition to their daily job; others may have cultural differences that make caring for an elder person even more challenging. The next few sections help you navigate the trials that many caregivers face.

Family caregivers who are employed

The 2009 National Alliance for Caregiving/AARP survey of family caregivers found that more than half (59 percent) of all family caregivers are employed full- or part-time in a position other than as a caregiver. In addition to their full- or part-time job responsibilities, they spent on average 20 hours a week caring for a family member. In addition to the conventional measures of caregiving — doing ADLs and IADLs — a separate analysis of the "Home Alone" survey respondents described in the previous section found that employed caregivers are also performing the same range of medical/nursing tasks as their nonemployed counterparts.

Employed family caregivers who managed medications considered it one of their two hardest tasks, because it took soo much time, was inconvenient, or both. Employed family caregivers who performed medical/nursing tasks were more likely than nonemployed caregivers to report that juggling the demands of caregiving with their other responsibilities cause them stress (61 percent versus 49 percent). The number of tasks they performed also increased the levels of stress. The report is available at `http://www.aarp.org/home-family/caregiving/info-11-2013/employed-family-caregivers-providing-complex-chronic-care-AARP-ppi-health.html`.

Beyond the stresses of daily life, employed caregivers may give up opportunities for travel or advancement, and they may fear disclosing their caregiving role to employers.

Keeping caregiving a secret is hard to do in a busy workplace. If you're constantly distracted and not paying attention to your job, people will notice, and it will likely be attributed to poor work habits or a bad attitude. It is better, if possible, to discuss your caregiving situation frankly with your employer and your coworkers and try to reach reasonable accommodations. Your caregiving affects them as well. This is easier in some jobs than in others. Try to keep any caregiving responsibilities you need to do during your working hours to a minimum and do everything you can to keep your family member's home situation as stable as possible.

Well-meaning friends and other family members may urge you to quit your job, or even expect that you will. Think very hard before you make this move. Although it may seem the only way to manage, it is a big step. Family caregivers who leave their jobs or go to part-time status make a financial sacrifice, not only in terms of lost income at the time but also in future benefits such as Social Security or contributions to retirement plans. Many caregivers find that their caregiving tenure lasts a lot longer than they anticipated and that it is very hard to return to the workplace at the same level at which they left, if they can find employment at all. And many caregivers gain much more than money from their jobs; it is a meaningful and necessary part of their lives.

When the Families and Work Institute asked employed family caregivers for their top wishes for the way in which workplaces could better support them, their responses were

- ✔ Greater flexibility

- ✔ More options for managing time

- ✔ Time off for elder care, especially time off without having to use up vacation time

- ✔ More understanding of their situation from management

For now, these wishes are only partially fulfilled and only for some employed caregivers.

AARP has a free e-book for caregivers, Amy Goyer's *Juggling Work and Caregiving* available at www.aarp.org/caregivingbook.

Following are a few programs designed to help employed family caregivers:

- ✔ **Family and Medical Leave Act (FMLA):** This 1993 federal law guarantees up to 12 weeks a year of unpaid leave for workers to take care of their own health needs or to take care of family members. The leave does not have to be taken all at one time. This is an important right but it only applies to people working in businesses with more than 50 employees, and it limits the family members needing care to spouses, children, or parents. Grandparents and siblings, for example, are not covered. FMLA has most often been used when a period of leave time can be planned, for example, by new parents. Family caregiving for an older adult is more episodic, and it is more difficult to arrange short times away from work. And, of course, FMLA is unpaid leave, which makes it hard for even those who are eligible to take advantage of the law. For more information, go to the U.S. Department of Labor at `www.dol.gov/whd/fmla`.

Some employers have leave policies even if not required by law. Check with your manager or HR representative to find out your company's policies. Employed caregivers should always find out what FMLA policies are, regardless of the size of the company.

✔ **Paid family leave insurance:** In July, 2013, Rhode Island became the third state in the nation to offer paid family leave insurance to eligible working caregivers. California and New Jersey already have this policy, which offers full or partial income replacement while a worker is at home taking care of a personal health condition, adjusting to a new child, or taking care of a family member with serious health needs.

✔ **ReACT (Respect a Caregiver's Time):** ReACT, begun in 2010, is a coalition of corporations and organizations dedicated to addressing the challenges faced by employed caregivers. AARP and the National Alliance for Caregiving created a toolkit and resource guide for employers that describes how many companies have created more caregiver-friendly workplaces. Although intended for employers, the toolkit is helpful for caregivers as a way to assess their own workplace and suggest better policies. Go to `http://www.aarp.org/ReACT`.

Long-distance family caregivers

The U.S. National Institute on Aging defines long-distance caregivers as those who live an hour or more away from the person and estimates that as many as 7 million people may fall into that category. Family caregivers who live with the person needing assistance are constantly on the job, but family caregivers who live at a distance from the person needing assistance face a different source of stress: relying on episodic visits to evaluate the situation and on reports from the person or others about what is needed. They also face the additional costs of travel and phone calls, and perhaps the need for paid help for their parent or other relative or to care for pets. A long-distance caregiver who is also employed and has children to take care of has a triple dose of stress.

Protecting family caregivers from workplace discrimination

Family caregivers may experience discrimination (real or perceived) in the workplace because of their need to take time off to attend to their family member. A patchwork of federal, state, and local laws attempts to address this problem, but policies and enforcement are inconsistent. The U.S. Equal Employment Opportunity Commission (EEOC) in 2007 issued guidance to employers intended to prevent discrimination on the basis of pregnancy, parenting, and caring for aging parents or ill or disabled spouses of family members. The most common forms of employment protection today for employed family caregivers caring for older adults are local laws. According to the University of California's Center for WorkLife Law, at least 67 localities in 22 different states have laws that prohibit discrimination against employees with certain family responsibilities. For a list, see www.aarp.org/content/dam/aarp/research/public_policy_institute/health/protecting-caregivers-employment-discrimination-insight-AARP-ppi-ltc.pdf. Of these, more than half cover only child care. Only seven laws explicitly recognize employed caregivers with eldercare responsibilities. In 2013, Vermont and San Francisco passed laws that create a formal mechanism for workers to inquire about altering their work schedules. While neither law requires employers to agree to the request, they both protect caregivers from retaliation or discrimination.

Some long-distance caregivers react to the constant stress by thinking that the only solution is to move the parent or other relative into their own home, or even to pull up stakes and move to the parent's location. Yet this may not be the best solution, either for the older adult or for the caregiver and his or her family. See Chapter 7 on multigenerational households for more information and advice if this is something you are considering.

AARP has a helpful list of tips to manage long-distance caregiving at www.aarp.org/relationships/caregiving-resource-center/info-09-2010/pc_tips_for_long_distance_caregiver.html. They include

- ✔ Create a contact list of address and phone numbers of all the people who are in regular contact with your parent or other relative, and include at least one person who can (and is willing to) check in daily.

- ✔ Collect important information before a crisis, including medication lists, names and numbers of regularly seen doctors, health-insurance information, utility information (including cable, phone, and Internet), and relevant financial and legal details.

- ✔ Make your visits productive by planning ahead to take care of priority items like visiting doctors, shopping for essentials, and checking for safety hazards.

✔ Gather information on community services that can help with transportation, adult daycare, home-delivered meals, counseling, and other services.

At some point you may decide you need a geriatric care manager or social worker to help coordinate care, especially if your parent needs in-home help.

The U.S. National Institute on Aging's report, "So Far Away: Twenty Questions and Answers About Long-Distance Caregiving," has extensive lists of resources and stories about people in similar situations. It is available at www.nia.nih.gov/health/publication/so-far-away-twenty-questions-and-answers-about-long-distance-caregiving-0.

Multicultural caregivers

Family caregivers from ethnic, cultural, and religious minorities may face special challenges as they try to integrate their family traditions and beliefs into a healthcare system that is not well suited to recognizing and adapting to these differences.

In some families, perhaps in yours, English is not the primary language, even for the family caregiver. Getting accurate information from professionals is difficult, even when a professional interpreter is available. In extended immigrant families, there may also be differences in the degree to which some members have adapted to American society. Sometimes these relate to gender roles. Other differences include willingness to accept help from people outside the family or community.If you are a family caregiver from a multicultural family, you can do a few things to help your parent or other relative and yourself, in addition to following general advice given to all caregivers about reducing stress and asking for help. Start close to home. Try to find a local community group with staff that speaks your language and is familiar with your traditions. Some religious groups have outreach programs for older adults that can act as a bridge to healthcare professionals.

In your dealings with healthcare and social-service staff on behalf of your family member, explain how culture affects your relative's understanding of illness, including

✔ What are his concepts of personal space and contact — how close is too close? Is physical contact, such as handshake or an embrace, taboo?

✔ What is the appropriate way to address the person?

✔ Who counts as family? Are there specific decision makers (who may or may not be the people who carry out the daily tasks of caregiving)?

✔ What are customs and taboos around food?

✔ What is understood as the cause of this disease? What treatments are acceptable? What kinds of alternative treatments are being used?

Dementia has different meanings in different cultures. Ethnic Elders Care, a network devoted to information and resources about dementia in multicultural older adults, has tips for caregivers at http://ethnicelderscare.net/.

A useful discussion of caregiving from different cultural perspectives is available at www.matherlifewaysinstituteonaging.com/wp-content/uploads/2012/03/Supporting-Caregivers-of-All-Cultural-Backgrounds.pdf. This paper was created by Mather LifeWays, a non-denominational nonprofit organization devoted to creating ways for older people to age well by providing housing and community services. It stresses the importance for caregivers of being able to communicate their cultural values and practices to professionals.

As a family caregiver in these situations, you have the additional responsibility of making it easier for your family member to accept the help that is needed and to advise staff on how to provide respectful and appropriate care.

Looking for Help

Family caregiving should not be a solo performance. But where do you find the supporting players? For some caregivers, asking for help isn't easy, and the help that is available may not be what is needed. The following sections can help you on your search.

Family and friends

This may seem obvious, but it is not always easy to ask for and get help from those who are the closest to you. Sometimes caregivers are asked why they don't get their family to help out more, but this deceptively simple question steps on a huge emotional landmine. Some families cooperate without any hesitation or difficulty; in others, sharing responsibility is fraught with emotional traps. Some caregivers choose, for their own reasons, not to rely on other family members; others would like the help but either don't get it or find it comes with too many conditions. A trained professional (such as a family or eldercare mediator or perhaps a geriatric care manager or social worker) can mediate and perhaps work out an acceptable division of labor. You can find a certified geriatric care manager in your area by going to the National Association of Professional Geriatric Care Managers at `www.caremanager.org/`. Some health systems have social workers on staff, and you can find the local chapter of the National Association of Social Workers at `www.socialworkers.org/chapters/default.asp`. That office may be able to refer you to social workers who specialize in geriatrics.

On major issues like housing, finances, and medical decisions, early, ongoing, and honest discussions with close family members can reduce the likelihood of tension and perhaps result in more equitable caregiving arrangements. But there is no guarantee.

When some family members are not closely involved in care, they may say things like, "I don't see what you're complaining about. Dad seems fine to me." Elderly dads and moms have an uncanny ability to marshal their resources for the occasional visit of the out-of-town or uninvolved child, making the caregiving child's accounts of their behavior seem unreasonable. This statement has many variations: "Dad has always gotten lost and driven too fast"; "Mom never could balance a checkbook"; "I forget things too." Less-involved siblings should make a point of dropping in unannounced and staying for a long enough time to see how Mom or Dad acts under everyday circumstances.

Sometimes friends will say, "Just call me if you need some help" or "I wish there were something I could do to help." Most caregivers have learned that imprecise, indefinite, offhand offers of help are expressions of goodwill but that it may be up to the caregivers to nail down an offer. Many people may want to help but don't know exactly what is needed, so it's up to caregivers to think about specific ways others can help.

Friends or other family members who really want to help should make specific offers such as, "I'm going to the farmer's market; can I bring you some vegetables?," "I can stay with Mom on Saturday so you can do some shopping or go to a movie," or "I know it's hard for you to get out for dinner, so I'd like to bring dinner to you one night this week." These acts of assistance are small things; the list could get progressively more complex and demanding. But whatever the offer, it should be firm and nonrefundable.

Federal programs

Two federal programs provide help to family caregivers. The first, the National Family Caregiver Support Program (NFCSP), established in 2000, provides grants to states and territories, based on their share of the population aged 70 and over, to fund a range of supports that assist family caregivers to care for their loved ones at home for as long as possible.

The NFCSP offers:

- ✔ Information to caregivers about available services

- ✔ Assistance to caregivers in gaining access to the services

- ✔ Individual counseling, organization of support groups, and caregiver training

- ✔ Respite care (time off from caregiving)

- ✔ Supplemental services, such as home modification, on a limited basis

The following people are eligible for NFCSP services:

- ✔ Adult family members or other informal caregivers age 18 and older providing care to individuals 60 years of age and older

- ✔ Adult family members or other informal caregivers age 18 and older providing care to individuals of any age with Alzheimer's disease and related disorders

- ✔ Grandparents and other relatives (not parents) 55 years of age and older providing care to children under the age of 18

- ✔ Grandparents and other relatives (not parents) 55 years of age and older providing care to adults age 18 to 59 with disabilities

The NFCSP is implemented at a local level through Area Agencies on Aging. To find your local AAA, call Eldercare Locator at 1-800-677-1116 or go to www.eldercare.gov/Eldercare.NET/Public/Index.aspx.

The NFCSP's assistance is limited by a lack of funding, which has been stuck at around $153 million since 2008.

The second federal program, the Lifespan Respite Care Act of 2006, provides ways for caregivers to have some time off, whether that is a few hours, a day, or longer. The program provides for:

- ✔ Lifespan respite programs at the state and local levels

- ✔ Planned and emergency respite for family caregivers

- ✔ Training/recruitment of respite workers and volunteers

✔ Provision of information to caregivers about respite/support services

✔ Assistance for caregivers in gaining access to these services

✔ Establishment of a National Resource Center on Lifespan Respite Care–the ARCH (Access to Respite Care and Help) National Respite Network and Resource Center

The program is administered through state coalitions. To find respite services in your area, go to `http://archrespite.org/search-for-respite` for an interactive map.

Respite is probably the most often requested service by family caregivers, and yet one of the least utilized. Many caregivers are reluctant to leave a family member with strangers, and many family members make it difficult for the caregiver to leave. If you use a respite service, ask about the background and training of the workers, how they handle emergencies, and how they match workers with clients. Sometimes other family members can take over while the caregiver takes a break. Unless these family members are well acquainted with the routines and there is a good relationship, it may not be a good experience for all.

State programs

Most states have their own programs of caregiver support and services. Some of them are under the broad heading of *home and community-based services,* in which caregiver services are an adjunct to the primary purpose of assisting an older person or someone with a disability, who generally has to be eligible for Medicaid. Some states have respite programs for caregivers whose family member is enrolled in the basic Home and Community-Based Services program.

Some states have *cash and counseling programs* that allow a person on Medicaid and eligible for home care to hire and pay family members to provide the care. If this is an option you want to explore, check with your local Medicaid office. The National Resource Center for Participant-Directed Services has a map of state programs at `http://web.bc.edu/libtools/insights-publications.php`.

Community-based organizations

Organizations in your community are an important source of assistance. Although the services are directed toward the person needing assistance, they also benefit the family caregiver. These organizations may be religious groups, senior centers, or disease-specific organizations or be organized around some other characteristic. They typically offer services like transportation, friendly visiting, minor home repairs, snow removal, yard work, and similar chores. Home-delivered meals and homemaker services may also be available. Many enlist volunteers from the community.

Senior centers often have caregiver events and informational sessions. They may have exercise and fitness programs, nutrition advice, counseling on legal and financial matters, and other useful programs. Adult daycare programs are also valuable resources for people who are able to attend.

Usually the most comprehensive and up-to-date source for your community is the Area Agency on Aging (AAA), which you can find via www.eldercare.gov.

Internet resources

Search for the phrase "family caregiver" on the Internet, and you can spend hours going through the options. Many websites are valuable sources of information, and many are marketing tools (which can be valuable if you are in the market for one of their products). You'll find a lot of repetition, which can be reassuring or annoying. You will also find a heavy dose of cheerleading, which you may appreciate or dislike. After a number of forays into this world, you will figure out which sites are useful to you and which you can skip.

With apologies to all the excellent online resources I am not listing, I recommend that you start with these four:

- ✔ **AARP Caregiving Resource Center** (www.aarp.org/caregiving): This site has a wealth of topics, blogs, advice, and a call-in number (1-877-333-5885) with extended hours (7 a.m. to 11 p.m. ET Monday – Friday, and 9 a.m. to 5 p.m. Saturdays).

- ✔ **The Alzheimer's Association** (www.alz.org): This site has information for caregivers in many different categories and an interactive map of chapters at www.alz.org/apps/findus.asp. Local chapters of the organization have their own websites.

- ✔ **Family Caregiver Alliance** (http://www.caregiver.org/caregiver/jsp/home.jsp): This San Francisco – based organization has guides and fact sheets on many topics related to family caregiving in English, Spanish, and Chinese. The FCA Family Care Navigator has a map of resources by state available at www.caregiver.org/caregiver/jsp/fcn_content_node.jsp?nodeid=2083.

- ✔ **Next Step in Care** (www.nextstepincare.org): This website, created by the United Hospital Fund, has free guides in four languages (English, Spanish, Chinese, and Russian) for family caregivers on navigating the healthcare system, especially during transitions, and a Links and Resources section with categories for national organizations, government agencies, and disease-specific organizations.

No single resource can answer all your questions. But after you understand the territory and know where to go for answers, you will be on a better path as a caregiver.

Part VI
The Part of Tens

Long-term care planning and policy is a global issue. Many other countries are dealing with the same problems of an aging population, limited resources, and the link between healthcare and long-term care. Check out a bonus Part of Tens chapter at www. dummies.com/extras/planninglongtermcare that gives you some insights into how other countries approach long-term care.

In this part...

✔ Discard ten myths that pervade discussions about aging and long-term care. Some relate to aging itself, and others relate to financing and current practices.

✔ Reference a handy list of websites and resources that provide state-by-state information on Medicare, Social Security, and other troves of information about long-term care.

Chapter 20

Ten Myths about Aging and Long-Term Care

There are two kinds of myths. One is a legend or folk tale passed down from one generation to the next to explain a natural occurrence like an eclipse or the creation of a culture. Many people recognize that these types of myths aren't literally true. The second kind of myth is a widely held but largely false belief that people cling to, even in the face of evidence, because it confirms a broader view of the world.

The ten myths in this chapter belong to the second group. They don't involve supernatural beings or explain the phases of the moon. They are widespread beliefs about aging and long-term care, some based on a kernel of truth, that are deeply entrenched in American society. Some are relatively harmless, but others can lead to serious misunderstandings.

Serious Memory Lapses Are Normal in Older Adults

The myth that memory loss is naturally associated with aging is deeply engrained in societal attitudes toward older adults. Sometimes the link is made in a condescending way, and sometimes even as a joke at the older person's expense. But these so-called *senior moments* are also experienced by younger people. Who hasn't been challenged from time to time to recall the name of a movie or book or person? In an era of information overload, some facts or figures go astray. In these cases the lost information comes back without too much delay.

Although some physiological basis explains the tendency of older people to experience temporary and occasional memory lapses, serious memory lapses are *not* normal. Some of the joking about memory loss may be displacement of anxiety about dementia. Alzheimer's disease is one of the most feared disease of our era, arguably more dreaded than cancer.

Forgetfulness can be distinguished from early signs of Alzheimer's disease or other forms of dementia. The Alzheimer's Association says that a typical age-related change involves sometimes forgetting names or appointments but remembering them later. On the other hand, a common sign of Alzheimer's is forgetting important dates or events, asking for the same information over and over, and needing to rely on notes or other memory aids for things they used to handle on their own.

Similarly, many people (of all ages) make occasional errors when balancing a checkbook, but a more worrisome problem is a change in the ability to follow a familiar recipe or keep track of monthly bills.

Some problems associated with dementia may actually be due to other causes. For example, difficulty reading, judging distance, and determining color may be due to cataracts or other vision problems, not a sign of Alzheimer's. Medications can cause delirium, which is a temporary condition that may be confused with dementia.

Bottom line: Not everyone who grows older loses his memory, and not every incident of memory loss is a sign of dementia. However, regular and problematic memory loss is not normal and should prompt a checkup with a doctor.

Older People Fall: Not Much You Can Do about It

Falls are the primary cause of injury among older adults and often lead to serious consequences, including death. In spite of the dire statistics, the belief is prevalent even among older people themselves that falls are bound to happen and are not all that big a deal. Many think it won't happen to them even though one in three older adults — about 12 million people — fall each year in the United States.

Some people believe that if they limit their activity or stay at home they won't fall. In fact, the reverse is true. Doing strength and balance exercises to build flexibility and ordinary walking are important in preventing falls. And over half of all falls take place at home, including falls that involve head injury and hospitalizations.

Reasonably simple home modifications (removing throw rugs, installing grab bars, improving lighting) can prevent falls. Other measures include asking a physician about side effects of medications, having vision checks, and using mobility aids like canes or walkers after being trained by a physical therapist on how best to use them.

Falls are a serious risk to health and function, not a normal part of aging.

All Over-the-Counter Drugs Are Safe

Most older people take a lot of medications — five or six or many more, a concept known as *polypharmacy*. Some of these medications are prescribed by physicians, but many are available at a local pharmacy or natural food store without a prescription. They are called *over-the-counter* or *OTC* drugs and are used to treat pain, headache, constipation, colds, allergies, and many other common complaints. Some are herbal or "natural" preparations. Because they don't require a doctor's approval, many people assume that they are safe to take.

The reality is quite different. Some OTC preparations are dangerous by themselves, especially if taken in large doses or by people with certain medical conditions. The second problem is that the OTC drug may interact with a prescribed medication, another OTC, or alcohol, and cause problems. Aspirin, for example, is probably the most common OTC but can lead to internal bleeding, especially in large doses or in combination with blood thinners like warfarin. Other drugs in the same category of nonsteroidal anti-inflammatory drugs (NSAIDS) that are often used to treat joint pain and inflammation can cause problems as well.

Rather than assume an OTC is safe, you should assume it is not until you have checked with your doctor or pharmacist. The Food and Drug Administration (FDA) requires that every OTC drug has a label called *Drug Facts* that can give you some basic information. It includes active ingredients and purposes, which tell you what part of the medicine makes it work, what it does, and how much of the active ingredient is in each pill or capsule. Especially review the warnings section, which tells when the medicine shouldn't be used, when to call a doctor, and what symptoms you may experience. The directions on the label tell you how many doses to take and what limits may apply.

Note that these Drug Facts labels do not apply to dietary supplements, which are regulated as food products and are labeled with a Supplementary Facts panel.

OTC products can be helpful, and many people swear by them but they also have the potential for great harm. They should be used with caution and with a doctor's approval.

Americans Dump Their Older Relatives in Nursing Homes

The use of the word *dump* in the formulation of this myth suggests that Americans get rid of their older relatives like so much garbage by leaving them at the nursing home door and ignoring them from then on. Often there is a comparison to other countries and cultures, where older people are presumed to live at home and are treated with great deference and respect.

This belief about other cultures also has mythic aspects. As more traditional cultures experience demographic changes that include aging and fewer children, more participation of women in the labor force, and urbanization, older patterns of caregiving are also giving way. In 2013, for example, the Chinese government felt it necessary to make visiting an older parent at least twice a year a legal requirement, not just a cultural tradition.

These are the facts: About 1.5 million people, or 4.5 percent of the U.S. population over 65, are residents in one of the nation's 15,000 nursing homes. Nursing homes are not overflowing: They operate at about 85 percent capacity, and very few if any new ones are not being built. The percentage of older adults in nursing homes has been steadily declining even as the older population increases; in 1990 it was 5.1 percent. This decline may be related to an increase in home- and community-based services, consumer demand for in-home care, or nursing homes' focus on enrolling short-term rehab patients (paid for by Medicare and private insurance) as opposed to long-stay residents (paid for largely by Medicaid). Even adding in the million or so people in assisted-living facilities (which do not provide nursing-home level care), this is hardly a picture that supports the myth of abandonment.

Rather than ignoring their relatives, many family members play an important role in residents' lives, and most nursing homes have both resident and family councils. Why then does this myth persist? All it takes is one news story or anecdote about an older person being placed in a nursing home against his or her will or being ignored by family to strengthen the belief that this occurrence is common.

Many people look back to the "good old days" through a fog of nostalgia, often for a past that never really existed. Believing that Americans abandon their older relatives fits into a worldview that fears changing social structures and family relationships. That may be understandable, but this myth demeans nursing-home residents by portraying them as unloved and unwanted and their family members by suggesting they're selfish and uncaring.

Medicare Pays for All Long-Term Care

No matter how many times people are told that Medicare does not pay for long-term care, the assumption that it does persists. Unlike the myth about abandonment of older people, this myth is more of a wish than a criticism. Everyone wants it to be true; therefore, it must be. Confusion about what counts as long-term care may also be a cause of this false belief. People who need assistance with personal care and other nonmedical care — the conventional view of long-term care — also need doctor and hospital and other services, especially because many of them have multiple chronic conditions as well as difficulties functioning independently. These medical services *are* covered under Medicare; the nonmedical aspects are mostly not, even when they are as essential to the person's survival as drugs and doctor visits.

And when people hear that someone has gone to a nursing home and Medicare paid the bill, the belief is reinforced. The difference is that the person was in the rehab unit of the facility for a short-term stay, not a resident in a long-stay unit.

Many chapters in this book and other resources explain in detail just what Medicare pays for and what it doesn't, but it seems as though nothing brings this home as much as actually taking the first steps to create a long-term care plan. This myth is also quickly dispelled when home care agencies, assisted living facilities, or other providers refuse to provide services not covered by Medicare unless the person or family pays. However, this is a rude awakening. Better know from the outset that — dare I say it again? — Medicare does not cover long-term care, and the failure of a majority of Americans to take long-term care seriously and make other financial arrangements is a serious problem for many families.

Hospice Is Just a Place Where People Go to Die

Most people say that they want to die at home without "all those tubes and monitors," yet end-of-life care continues to be dominated by aggressive interventions and high costs. Medicare costs for people in the last month of life are heavily weighted toward hospital inpatient stays, including intensive care units (ICUs).

Many policy experts say the reason is Medicare's fee-for-service structure, which incentivizes technological interventions and expensive tests. But another reason relates to the myth that *hospice* is a place where people go to die. This remains a barrier for physician referrals and patients' acceptance of hospice as an alternative approach to a hospital. Hospice is often seen as giving up and abandonment. The modest proposal in health reform legislation that would have encouraged physicians to engage in voluntary end-of-life discussions with their patients (so that individuals' wishes could be known and respected), which would have included discussions of hospice and palliative care, went down in flames under the politically charged label of *death panels.*

In fact, most hospice care is given in the place the person calls home, whether that is a residence, an assisted-living facility, or a nursing home. There are some inpatient hospices as well. And hospice is a philosophy of care, not a specific course of treatment, that emphasizes the whole person, quality of life, and relief of symptoms. Hospice is a team approach, with many different professionals providing services and a strong volunteer component as well. Much hospice care is provided by families.

Although the numbers of people opting for hospice services has increased steadily (approximately 1.5 million people received hospice services in 2012), it is still often very late in the course of their disease. According to the National Hospice and Palliative Care Organization, in 2012 the median length of service was 18.7 days, a decrease from 19.1 days in 2011. This means that half of hospice patients and their families received services for less than three weeks, while half received services for more than three weeks. Very short stays do not permit the patient and family to receive the full benefits of hospice care, such as understanding the dying process, controlling pains and symptoms, and receiving counseling. Under the Medicare hospice benefit individuals can receive care for up to six months, and sometimes even longer. Studies have shown that people enrolled in hospice live longer with a better quality of life than those who choose more aggressive options.

Other myths around hospice include the idea that one's regular physician can't be involved, which is not true, and that active treatments have to be discontinued (true only of treatments intended to cure, not those intended to treat symptoms). Hospice focuses on the immediate needs of the person and the family by addressing all their spiritual, emotional, and physical needs.

For more information, see AARP's "Facts about Hospice" at `www.aarp.org/relationships/caregiving-resource-center/info-08-2010/elc_facts_about_hospice.html`.

Millionaires Take Advantage of Medicaid

You've heard this myth many times: A millionaire or zillionaire — a film star, a CEO of a Fortune 500 company, or a highly paid athlete — could legally transfer all his or her assets and after a five-year look back period become eligible for Medicaid nursing-home care at taxpayer expense. Lots of people believe that the ranks of Medicaid recipients are full of rich people who have done just that.

This myth is bolstered by the occasional news story about a person who defrauded Medicaid by concealing assets. Sometimes people assume estate planning is Medicaid planning. There is no shame in estate planning, and rich people do it all the time but without ever intending to become eligible for Medicaid. The rules for transferring assets are rigorously applied in Medicaid applications, and most people who eventually become eligible for Medicaid have exhausted all their resources.

In reality, there is little evidence that people with substantial incomes or assets are improperly transferring them to become eligible for Medicaid. An Urban Institute study showed that people with disabilities who need Medicaid assistance not only had lower incomes and assets when they needed assistance but also were at a disadvantage during their peak earning years. Half of those who received Medicaid assistance for nursing-home care had less than $10,000 in nonhousing assets ten years or more before entering the nursing home. The report concluded, "Among people who spend down, few are asset rich and income poor." (For more detail, see the AARP blog at `http://blog.aarp.org/2013/08/15/do-the-rich-benefit-from-medicaid/`.)

Who among the 1 percent — our nation's richest and most privileged — would really want to go through the legal process of losing control of their assets to be eligible for Medicaid? Medicaid does not provide the kind of special treatment and considerations that they expect. Nursing homes do not have suites and special restaurant food and other luxuries for the formerly rich. In Medicaid, formerly rich does not get you anything better than always poor.

Most people look on Medicaid as a last resort. It is a safety net and not a velvet cushion.

Long-Term Care Means a Nursing Home

Surveys consistently show that only a third of American adults think that they will need long-term care, when in reality about 70 percent of people over age 65 will need at least some form of long-term care during their lifetimes. Part of the reason for this discrepancy is that many people link long-term care to nursing home care, and they say firmly, "I don't want to go there."

In fact, as noted in earlier chapters, nursing homes are now the last resort, not the first option, in long-term care. Many more options exist to remain at home, with assistance and perhaps home modifications. Long-term services and supports — the new terminology for community care — are alternatives to nursing homes. So are assisted-living facilities, although they do not provide the level of nursing care that may be required for someone who is very ill or has dementia.

Still the myth persists. Because of its staying power, some people are reluctant to engage in long-term care planning because they find the prospect of being in a nursing home not only distasteful but also hugely expensive.

What will they do if they become ill or disabled? Here the answers get a little murky. Some say, "My family will take care of me." Others say, "I won't stay around long enough to find out," suggesting that they will commit suicide at the first sign of debility. This is largely bravado, but it does suggest the depth of anxiety about dependence and illness.

More exposure to alternatives to nursing-home care might help dispel this myth, as would information about changes in nursing homes that create a more inviting environment. The message could be: This is not your Grandma's long-term care.

Assisted-Living Facilities Are Regulated Like Nursing Homes

Nursing homes are highly regulated by both federal and state governments. It would seem obvious that assisted-living facilities, promoted as an alternative to nursing homes, would also be regulated in similar ways, but this is not the case.

There are no federal regulations for assisted-living facilities, which vary widely in the population they serve, services, management, and location. In January 2014, however, CMS issued a rule allowing states to include assisted-living facilities in their home- and community-based waiver programs. There will be a transition period while states ensure that facilities follow the required standards. States do regulate assisted-living facilities but license them under different categories and call them by different names.

Generally, state regulations are concerned with assisted-living facilities as congregate housing sites. Fire safety, evacuation procedures, and structural soundness are examples of common standards. They may or may not set requirements for a minimum level of staff training. There may or may not be a nurse on site at all times. They may or may not require CPR training. State surveyors may visit just once a year or even less often.

More regulation does not necessarily mean better care, but regulations set a baseline. Anyone considering a move to an assisted-living facility should find out what the state regulates and what it doesn't. It won't answer all your questions, but at least it's a start.

Long-Term Care Insurance Covers All Your Needs

The myth that all your long-term needs will be covered by insurance comes with some qualifications. If you have a very comprehensive long-term care insurance policy with a highly reliable company, the policy has built-in options for all the possible variations on what kinds of long-term care you may need, and it has protections for inflation, then it is possible that all your long-term care needs will be covered. But that kind of policy is costly, and the amount you have contributed over a number of years may not justify the benefits you will receive. It is more realistic to expect that a long-term care insurance policy will cover about 60 to 70 percent of expenses.

Long-term care policies are priced by the age of the applicant, the benefit period (the length of time you expect to need long-term care), the setting of care (nursing home, assisted living, home), and other factors. Long-term care insurance can be a valuable asset but has limitations.

Chapter 21

Ten Resources with State-by-State Information

. . . .

In This Chapter

▶ Checking out websites that offer state-by-state maps or guides

▶ Keeping track of your state's information

. . . .

*W*ouldn't it be nice if there were just one place where you could get all the information you need about long-term care? Although many resources exist with lots of information, the way long-term care is organized means you have to use a range of different resources.

In the U.S. federal system, much of the responsibility for healthcare, nonmedical services such as personal care and homemaker services, and social services falls within the jurisdiction of the states, even though there is federal oversight and funding. And states have different ways of dealing with these issues. To make the process of getting the information you need a little easier, several websites offer state-by-state information, either through an interactive map in which you click on your state or an alphabetical listing where you enter the location by state, city, or zip code.

This chapter offers a selection of ten of these topics with some background about why they may be useful. The ten topics are organized very loosely into two main categories: resources for housing and community services (assisted living, Area Agencies on Aging, Eldercare Locator, home modification, and family caregiver support) and special topics related to medical care and quality of care issues (Medicaid, cost of care, advance directives, long-term care ombudsmen, and Quality Improvement Organizations).

One way to use this information is to go to the website, find your state, and write down the name of the agency, e-mail address, phone number, and any other relevant data. Keep the notes in a file so you can refer back to the resources whenever needed. You can also bookmark the relevant pages on your computer.

Identifying Local Services through Area Agencies on Aging

A major source of local information is your Area Agency on Aging (AAA) (these are often called triple As, but don't confuse them with the automobile club). AAAs were established under the federal Older Americans Act in 1973 to respond to the needs of Americans aged 60 and over in every local community. By providing a range of options that allow older adults to choose the home and community-based services and living arrangements that suit them best, AAAs make it possible for many older adults to remain in their homes and communities as long as possible.

In 1978, under amendments to the Older Americans Act, Indian tribal organizations that received grants under Title VI of the Act were designated AAAs. These Native American aging programs provide nutritional and supportive services to older American Indians, Alaskan Natives, and Native Hawaiians and provide services to their elders comparable to services offered to other older adults by AAAs.

AAAs also administer the federal National Family Caregiver Support Program, which offers caregiver counseling, support groups, and other services.

The National Association of Area Agencies on Aging (n4a) supports the national network of 618 Area Agencies on Aging and 246 Title VI Native American aging programs. To find the nearest AAA, the website at www.n4a.org/about-n4a/?fa=aaa-title-VI has a two-step process: First, click on your state, and then scroll through the state's listings to find your city, town, or county.

Assessing Assisted-Living and Rehabilitation Facilities

Unlike nursing homes, which are governed by federal as well as state regulations, assisted-living facilities are subject to state regulation, and not every state has regulations in place. There is no handy website to compare all assisted-living facilities and no all-inclusive listing. So you're largely on your own in searching for information about assisted-living facilities. However, some websites do have limited state-by-state information.

✔ **The Assisted Living Federation of America** (www.alfa.org): This website has a list of its member organizations in several categories: assisted-living facilities, independent-living communities, nursing homes, continuing-care communities, and Alzheimer's care communities. You can find member organizations in your community by entering your city, state, and zip code.

✔ **The Commission on Accreditation of Rehabilitation Facilities** (www.carf.org/providerSearch.aspx): This is an independent nonprofit accrediting agency of health and human services in aging services, medical rehabilitation, durable medical equipment, and other areas. It lists accredited providers, including continuing-care retirement communities, by zip code, city, state, name, program type, or keyword. It has special lists for brain injury, stroke, and spinal cord injury.

✔ **Leading Age** (www.leadingage.org/FindMember.aspx): Leading Age, a membership organization of nonprofit organizations and businesses, can guide you to its members who run assisted-living facilities as well as continuing-care communities, home and community based services, nursing facilities, and senior housing.

✔ **The National Center for Assisted Living** (www.ahcancal.org/ncal/resources/Pages/AssistedLivingRegulations.aspx): This affiliate of the American Health Care Association, which is an association of long-term and post-acute care providers, has a list of state-by-state regulations and regulatory changes updated as of March 2013.

Finding Community Services and Housing Options through Eldercare Locator

Nearly every chapter in this book refers to Eldercare Locator, because this website is a basic resource. Funded by the federal Administration on Aging, and administered by the National Association of Area Agencies on Aging (n4a), Eldercare Locator has information on many community services and housing options. The most common inquiries it receives are on general aging resources, financial assistance, transportation, housing options, and in-home services. Go to www.n4a.org/files/about-n4a/community-based-services.pdf for a list of the types of services that you can access through Eldercare Locator.

You can search the Eldercare site by city, state, or zip code; or call 1-800-677-1116. An information specialist is available Monday through Friday, 9 a.m. to 8 p.m. Eastern time. You can also start an online chat with a representative by going to `https://home-c6.incontact.com/inContact/ChatClient/ChatClient.aspx?poc=9801c7c8-84a3-4269-8e5f-51dbf40f9ae9&bu=4593078`. Spanish-speaking information specialists are available.

Eldercare Locator Information Specialists connect older adults and caregivers directly to local Area Agencies on Aging, Title VI Native American aging programs, Aging and Disability Resources Centers, and other pertinent aging resources nationwide.

Getting Support for Family Caregivers

The Family Caregiver Alliance, a San Francisco-based nonprofit dedicated to assisting family caregivers of all kinds, has a Family Care Navigator with an interactive map, updated as of 2012, that lists many resources by state. Some are for support services for caregivers and others are for the family member who needs assistance with housing, legal assistance, and disease-specific support. The site also has a list of common questions, such as "Can I get paid to care for a family member?" Clicking on the question takes you to an answer with further information and other resources. Where available, these resources are listed by state as well. Go to `http://caregiver.org/caregiver/jsp/fcn_content_node.jsp?nodeid=2083`.

Modifying Your Home with Rebuilding Together

Aging in place often requires home modifications. Rebuilding Together is a national network of local Rebuilding Together Affiliates, corporate and individual donors, skilled tradesmen and associations, and almost 200,000 citizen volunteers. Rebuilding Together provides critical repairs, accessibility modifications, and energy-efficient upgrades to low-income homes and community centers at no cost to the service recipient.

To find an affiliate in your area, go to an interactive map with contact information at `http://rebuildingtogether.org/affiliates`. There is also a list you can print out at `http://rebuildingtogether.org/resource/affiliate-list/`. But this list doesn't contain contact information, which you can obtain from the national office at `http://rebuildingtogether.org/contact/`.

Getting Information on Medicaid in Your State

Medicaid, the federal-state program for low-income people, is the primary payer for long-term care services in the community and in nursing homes. The federal rules require some services to be provided (hospital care, for example), but states can choose what additional services they want to offer. The federal website has an interactive map that takes you to your state's Medicaid program and gives information about changes to the Medicaid program under the Affordable Care Act (ACA). Go to www.medicaid.gov/Medicaid-CHIP-Program-Information/By-State/By-State.html. Another site that has state-by-state eligibility information is www.healthcare.gov/do-i-qualify-for-medicaid.

Calculating Costs

Nearly everyone is concerned about the costs of long-term care. You need accurate information about the various options. The U.S. Department of Health and Human Services (HHS), which includes the Center for Medicare & Medicaid Services (CMS), has a website — http://longtermcare.gov/costs-how-to-pay/costs-of-care-in-your-state — that offers two ways to get information about the costs of homemaker services, home health aides, adult day healthcare, assisted-living facilities, and two levels of nursing-home care (semi-private and private room).

The map at this website shows you at a glance by color coding whether you live in one of the more expensive areas of the country (you probably already knew that, but this gives a range of numbers for each type of service). Then you can click on your state to get a more precise estimate. You can change the time frame so that you can look at costs over a short period or 25 years. You can also search for providers in your area. The site also has additional information on paying for care.

Another source is the Genworth Financial annual survey of costs of long-term care at www.genworth.com/corporate/about-genworth/industry-expertise/cost-of-care.html. It has an interactive map of states, including 437 regions, and additional information about how the survey is conducted. The most recent survey was issued in 2013. You can also download the data with an app, which may be handy if you are visiting a number of facilities and want to compare costs.

AARP also has a Long-Term Care Calculator at www.aarp.org/relationships/caregiving-resource-center/LTCC.

Finding Your State's Advance Directives

Advance directives is the generic term for documents that set out the types of medical treatment a person wants or doesn't want if he cannot speak for himself. Advance directives also name the person who is authorized to make healthcare decisions in that situation. Each state has its own legal form for this purpose. In addition, some people want to add documents such as Five Wishes that outline in more detail their preferences. But only the state's official advance directive document has legal weight.

Caring Connections, a program of the National Hospice and Palliative Care Organization (NHPCO), is a national consumer and community engagement initiative to improve care at the end of life. It provides free advance directives and instructions for each state that can be opened as a PDF file. These documents are also available on the AARP website at www.aarp.org/advancedirectives.

If you have any legal questions regarding these documents, contact your state attorney general's office or an attorney.

Caring Connections warns that due to formatting and printing requirements, for some states a blank page appears in the Acrobat Reader as the first page. This does not mean the document has not loaded correctly. Use the navigation toolbar to go to the next page. If you have any questions, you can call Caring Connection's help line at 1-800-658-8898 or send an e-mail to caringinfo@nhpco.org.

If you spend time in more than one state, you should have advance directives that are legally recognized in all these states.

Solving Problems through an Ombudsman

Long-term care ombudsmen are advocates for residents of nursing homes, board and care homes, and assisted-living facilities. Ombudsmen provide information about how to find a facility and what to do to get quality care. They are trained to resolve problems. If you choose, the ombudsman can assist you with complaints. But unless you give the ombudsman permission to share your concerns, these matters are kept confidential. Under the federal Older Americans Act, every state is required to have an Ombudsman Program that addresses complaints and advocates for improvements in the long-term care system.

The ombudsman program is administered by the Administration on Aging. The network has 8,813 volunteers certified to handle complaints and 1,167 paid staff. Most state ombudsman programs are housed in their State Unit on Aging.

A long-term care ombudsman performs the following tasks:

- Resolves complaints made by or for residents of long-term care facilities
- Educates consumers and long-term care providers about residents' rights and good care practices
- Promotes community involvement through volunteer opportunities
- Provides information to the public on nursing homes and other long-term care facilities and services, residents' rights, and legislative and policy issues
- Advocates for residents' rights and quality care in nursing homes, personal care, residential care, and other long-term care facilities
- Promotes the development of citizen organizations, family councils, and resident councils

You can find the ombudsmen in your state through an interactive state map at www.ltcombudsman.org/ombudsman.

Resolving Complaints through Quality Improvement Organizations

If you have a complaint or a problem with medical care — for example, you're a Medicare beneficiary and you want to appeal a hospital discharge that you think is premature — you may turn to a Quality Improvement Organizations (QIO) for help. *QIOs* are private, mostly not-for-profit organizations, which are staffed by professionals, mostly doctors and other healthcare professionals, who are trained to review medical care and help beneficiaries with complaints about the quality of care and to implement improvements in the quality of care available throughout the spectrum of care. The Centers for Medicare & Medicaid Services (CMS) contracts with one organization in each state, as well as the District of Columbia, Puerto Rico, and the U.S. Virgin Islands to serve as that state/jurisdiction's Quality Improvement Organization (QIO) contractor.

By law, the mission of the QIO program is to improve the effectiveness, efficiency, economy, and quality of services delivered to Medicare beneficiaries. The core functions of the QIO program are:

✔ Improving quality of care for beneficiaries

✔ Protecting the integrity of the Medicare Trust Fund by ensuring that Medicare pays only for services and goods that are reasonable and necessary and that are provided in the most appropriate setting

✔ Protecting beneficiaries by expeditiously addressing individual complaints, such as beneficiary complaints; provider-based notice appeals; violations of the Emergency Medical Treatment and Labor Act (EMTALA); and other related responsibilities as articulated in QIO-related law

You can find the QIO for your state at www.qualitynet.org/dcs/ ContentServer?pagename=QnetPublic%2FPage%2FQnetTier2&cid= 1144767874793.

Part VII
Appendixes

 Part of planning for the long term involves basically learning a new language. The bonus article located at `www.dummies.com/extras/planninglongtermcare` navigates the terms, acronyms, and definitions associated with long-term care.

In this part...

- ✔ Check out a glossary of the most commonly encountered terms and gives a brief definition.

- ✔ Reference a compilation of organizations that can give you more information and assistance. The phone numbers and website addresses are up-to-date as of publication date.

Appendix A

Glossary

Accessibility: The characteristics of a home or community environment that make it easy for a person with disabilities to navigate and manage independently. Examples include wider doorways, lower countertops and sinks, grab bars in tubs and showers, and light switches and electrical outlets at waist height.

Activities of daily living (ADLs): Personal care activities and tasks that people typically do on their own, like dressing, bathing, going to the bathroom, moving from bed to chair, and feeding themselves.

Acute Care for Elders (ACE) units: Hospital units staffed by a specially trained interdisciplinary team, which can include geriatricians, advanced practice nurses, social workers, pharmacists, and physical therapists.

Adaptability: Changes that can be made to a home or other building without requiring a complete redesign or the use of different materials for essential features.

Adult day healthcare: A therapeutic daycare program that provides medical and rehabilitation services.

Adult day programs: Social programs that offer activities and meals in a community setting.

Advance directives: The generic term for legal documents that tell family and healthcare professionals what kinds of treatments a person wants or does not want in end-of-life scenarios. Examples include tube feedings, dialysis, pain medication, mechanical ventilation, and other options.

Affinity or niche communities: Housing arrangements designed for people with a common background, usually because of prior employment or other shared interests.

Affordable Care Act (ACA): Often referred to as *Obamacare,* the Patient Protection and Affordable Care Act (P.L. 111-148) and the Health Care and Education Reconciliation Act of 2010 (P.L. 111-152), which aim to provide

Americans with better health security by putting in place comprehensive health insurance reforms that expand coverage, hold insurance companies accountable, lower healthcare costs, offer more choice, and enhance the quality of care.

Age-friendly communities: Places where services, settings, and structures support and enable people to age actively. They recognize a wide range of ability, capacity, and resources for older people, anticipate and respond flexibly to aging-related needs of inhabitants, respect the decisions and lifestyle choices of the aging, protect those who are most vulnerable, and promote their inclusion and contribution to community life.

Agent/attorney-in-fact: A person designated to act on behalf of an individual to manage financial matters.

Aging in place: The ability to live in one's own home and community safely, independently, and comfortably, regardless of age, income, or ability level.

Aid and attendance (A&A pension): In-home support services for veterans who require the aid of another person to perform activities of daily living, adjust prosthetic devices, or for safety.

Americans with Disabilities Act (ADA): Signed into law in 1990 by President George H.W. Bush, the ADA prohibits discrimination and ensures equal opportunity for persons with disabilities in employment, state and local government services, public accommodations, commercial facilities, and transportation.

Annuity: A contract between an individual and an insurance company providing that, in return for a lump-sum payment or series of payments, the company will offer tax-deferred growth and make periodic payments beginning immediately or at some future date. The three general types of annuities are fixed, indexed, and variable.

Assisted-living facility (ALF): A general term referring to a type of congregate living where people share meals and other activities and where individuals can receive personal assistance to maintain their independence.

Assistive technology: Devices and adaptations that are designed to help people who are aging or have disabilities to function independently.

Capacity: A legal finding that a person can understand choices, appreciate the consequences, and act to make certain kinds of decisions such as healthcare decisions; lack of capacity is the trigger for appointing or empowering a surrogate or alternate decision maker.

Cardiopulmonary resuscitation (CPR): An emergency procedure performed when someone has stopped breathing or has no heartbeat.

Caregiver contract: An agreement between a person needing assistance and (usually) a family member that sets out terms for payment for caregiving and defines responsibilities.

Caregiver self-assessment: The process by which a family caregiver reviews personal strengths, limitations, and worries concerning his or her ability to provide care for another person, to more accurately assess the ability to support the family member's needs and choices.

Cash and counseling programs: Medicaid programs allowing a person on Medicaid and eligible for home care to hire and pay attendants, including certain groups of family members.

Certified nursing assistant (CNA): Aides in a nursing home who must meet certain standards and undergo training.

Chronic condition: Persistent or long-lasting illness or disease that may be controlled but not cured.

COBRA (Consolidated Omnibus Budget Reconciliation Act): A federal law passed in 1985 that provides the opportunity for workers who have lost their jobs and health insurance to continue to receive insurance benefits under a group plan; they may be required to pay the entire premium.

Co-housing: An agreement among friends or neighbors who live in separate houses and manage their own finances to work together to manage their own community. Some cohousing projects are started by housing developers. There are entry fees and monthly charges.

Co-insurance: An individual's share of the costs of a healthcare service covered by insurance, calculated as a percentage (for example, 20 percent of the allowed amount for the service).

Community property: Property acquired during a marriage that is shared equally by a married couple, regardless of who earned the money. States have different laws regarding distribution of community property following death or divorce.

Community-based agencies: Organizations and agencies that provide support services in the community that are separate from a medical facility or organization. Examples include social-service agencies, neighborhood houses, and senior centers, which typically offer services like adult day care, transportation, friendly visiting, minor home repairs, snow removal, yard work, and similar chores.

Complex chronic conditions: Conditions involving multiple long-term illnesses or diseases that exist at the same time and require the attention of different healthcare providers.

Comprehensive driving evaluation: Identifies the physical, visual, and cognitive challenges an individual faces when driving. It is often conducted by an occupational therapist but can also be arranged through a state department of motor vehicles.

Consumer-Directed Personal Assistance Program (CDPAP): A Medicaid program that provides services to chronically ill or disabled individuals with a medical need for help with ADLs or a need for skilled-nursing services. Recipients can hire their own caregivers.

Continuing-care retirement community (CCRC): A tiered approach to long-term care services that includes on the same site independent living, assisted living, and nursing-home-level care.

Copayment: A predetermined amount an individual pays for a covered healthcare service usually paid at the time of receiving the service.

Custodial care: Personal care such as bathing, dressing, feeding.

Deductible: The amount owed for healthcare services covered by health insurance or plan covers before the insurance starts to pay.

Delirium: A sudden, acute, often unrecognized but treatable onset of confusion.

Dementia: A general term to describe symptoms such as memory loss, poor judgment, inhibition, and deteriorating language and motor skills. The most common diseases to display dementia symptoms are Alzheimer's and Parkinson's diseases.

Direct-care workers: Paid home-care aides, personal attendants, certified nursing assistants, and others who provide hands-on care to a person.

Disability insurance: Insurance that pays for a portion of lost income if a person becomes disabled and unable to work because of an accident or illness.

Discharge planner: A hospital or nursing-home staff member, typically a social worker or nurse, who organizes the transition from facility to home or to another facility.

Do not resuscitate (DNR) order: A physician's order that states that a person should not be given CPR if he stops breathing or has no heartbeat. A DNR order does not limit the provision of pain medicine or comfort care.

Domiciliary program: An active clinical rehabilitation and treatment program for veterans, especially those with mental-health or substance-abuse problems or who are homeless. Domiciliary programs are now integrated into the VA's Mental Health Residential Rehabilitation and Treatment Programs (MH RRTPs).

Duals (dually eligible): People who are eligible for both Medicare and Medicaid. Medicare is the first payer.

Durable medical equipment (DME): Devices like canes, walkers, wheelchairs, hospital beds, commodes, and other aids that a chronically ill person or someone with a disability needs at home.

Durable power of attorney: A legal document that assigns the authority to make financial decisions to another individual even after the person who appointed the agent is incapacitated.

Durable power of attorney for healthcare decisions: See **healthcare proxy**.

Emergency department (ED): The hospital area that that provides acute care on a walk-in basis to individuals with sudden serious illness or trauma. Often called the *emergency room (ER)*.

Employment or registry agencies: Agencies that provide names of nurses and aides available to provide home care. The workers are contacted and paid directly. Some states maintain a registry through the Department of Health.

Entry fee: The upfront cost of admission to an assisted-living arrangement.

Equal visitation rights: Rules enacted by the Centers for Medicare & Medicaid that protect patients' rights to choose their visitors, including same-sex domestic partners, during a hospital stay.

Estate: All the property and assets a person owns; for example, real estate, life insurance, jewelry, art, antiques, and so on.

Estate recovery laws: State laws that recover the costs a state has expended in Medicaid services for a deceased person by laying claim to the person's property and estate.

Estate taxes: Federal and state taxes levied on the estate of a person before distribution of the estate to the heirs/beneficiaries.

Executor: The person legally responsible for making sure that the instructions in a will are followed.

Extensive- or life-care contract: A type of contract for continuing-care retirement communities that provides housing, services, and amenities, including unlimited use of health care services, at little or no increase in monthly fees as a resident moves from independent living to assisted living to nursing-home care. This type of contract is the most costly but carries the least risk.

Fair Housing Act: Passed in 1968 and administered by the U.S. Department of Housing and Urban Development (HUD), the FHA is designed to prevent discrimination in housing based on race, color, gender, and handicap (disability), among other characteristics.

Family and Medical Leave Act (FMLA): The 1993 federal law that guarantees up to 12 weeks of unpaid leave for eligible workers to take care of their own health needs or to take care of family members.

Family caregiver: A person who provides or manages assistance for a relative, domestic partner, or friend who needs help because of illness, disability, or advanced age. Sometimes called *informal caregiver, caretaker, care partner,* or *carer.*

Federal Commission on Long-Term Care: A commission created to propose financing strategies and changes in delivery services for long-term services and supports; issued report in 2013.

Federal poverty guidelines: The minimum amount of income that a family needs for food, clothing, transportation, shelter, and other necessities. The guidelines are updated each year and vary by state.

Fiduciary duty: The obligation of a person placed in a position of trust to act only for that person's benefit, and to act with good faith in furthering his or her interests in the handling of that person's money or property.

Filial-responsibility laws: Old laws that establish an obligation of an adult child to support his or her parents.

Financial power of attorney: A document signed by one person giving another person permission to take care of different kinds of financial affairs, like signing checks, agreeing to pay a contractor for home repairs, handling bank accounts, and taking care of other tasks. It does not extend to making healthcare decisions.

Fixed assets: Long-term kinds of property that are used to generate income but are not easily or quickly converted into cash, such as real estate or bonds.

Formal home care services: Nursing or aide services provided through an agency and paid for by insurance or privately.

Geriatric evaluation: A comprehensive assessment of a person's ability to manage independently, including physical health and social environment.

Geriatricians: Physicians, primarily internal medicine doctors, who have taken additional training that focuses on the diseases of aging and their treatments. They have been certified by the American Board of Internal Medicine to practice geriatric medicine.

Gerontologists: Researchers who study the mental, physical, environmental, and social aspects of aging. They do research, teach aging in universities, and contribute to the broad knowledge about the impact of aging on individuals and society.

Granny-pod: A self-contained structure on the same property but not attached to a main house that has water, electricity, and plumbing, and may incorporate assistive technology like monitoring vital signs, filtering air contaminants, and many other services.

Group homes: Houses in residential neighborhoods that accommodate a small number of people for a fee. The owner provides meals and assists with some ADLs.

Guardianship/conservatorship: A court process in which a judge appoints someone to make decisions about a person's care and finances after that person is unable to act on his or her own.

Guardianship of the estate: The authority to manage money and other assets; called a *conservatorship* in some states.

Guardianship of the person: The responsibility to make healthcare and other decisions that affect the well-being of a person.

Healthcare proxy: A person appointed to make healthcare decisions if the person is unable to make decisions on his or her own; may be called surrogate decision maker or healthcare agent.

Health Insurance Marketplace/Exchange: Under the Affordable Care Act, a website that offers information on and enrollment in a range of selected private health plans as well as Medicaid.

HIPAA (Health Insurance Portability and Accountability Act): A federal law protecting the privacy of a patient's medical information. According to the law, unless the patient objects, healthcare professionals can share relevant information with a family member or other person directly involved in the patient's care or paying for care.

Hoarding: A compulsion to collect and inability to part with things and animals regardless of their value, utility, or safety risk. Hoarding interferes with everyday life by making it impossible to use space in the home as intended and impedes access in an emergency.

Home- and community-based services (HCBS): An umbrella term for services including case management, home-care aide services, personal care, adult daycare, and respite care, as well as other services, such as home modification assistance. HCBS are intended to keep people at home for as long as possible.

Home care: Various in-home services provided to a chronically or seriously ill person usually by a nurse or aide. It may include, but is not limited to, a physician, nurse, physical or occupational therapist, social worker, home health aide, home health attendant, or medical equipment services.

Home health advance beneficiary notice (HHABN): A written notice that explains the reason for a reduction or termination of home health services.

Home telehealth: A service used by healthcare providers to remotely monitor the condition of patient with chronic diseases. It can be used to track blood pressure, blood sugar level, weight, blood oxygen level, and heart and lung sounds. Information is transmitted to a care coordinator by landline or cellphone or by video.

Hospice: A comprehensive, team-based philosophy that focuses on controlling pain and symptoms and improving the quality of life for people with a short life expectancy; a benefit package under Medicare.

Hospital discharge plan: The plan for a patient transition to home or to another healthcare facility after the hospital stay is completed.

Hospitalists: Doctors trained in critical-care medicine and skilled at handling medical crises that happen to seriously ill patients; they work in hospitals but do not generally see patients in the community.

Hybrid policies: Insurance policies that combine a life-insurance policy or annuity with long-term care insurance benefits.

Improvement standard: The notion that, in order to continue to receive therapeutic services under Medicare, a patient had to show continuous improvement or the services would not be covered; federal court decision ruled it violated Medicare regulations.

Independent living: Any housing arrangement for people aged 55 and over; may be apartment-style living or freestanding homes, subsidized low-income senior housing or high-end retirement communities.

Informal home care services: Unpaid care provided by family members or friends.

In-home DNR order: A physician's order that tells emergency workers called to the home that they should not perform CPR on this person.

Instrumental Activities of Daily Living (IADLs): Tasks that most people manage for themselves, like making phone calls, managing money, managing medications, shopping, and cooking.

Intestate: The term applied to a person who dies without a will. Probate court may be needed to determine how property from the estate will be divided.

LGBT: Lesbian, gay, bisexual, or transgender individuals.

Licensed home care agency: A home care agency that is licensed by the state to provide nursing services and aides who do personal care. Some are contracted through Medicaid to provide long-term personal care.

Life settlement/viatical settlement: A life-insurance policy that is sold to a third party at an amount that is less than the policy's death benefit. The settlement is termed a *viatical settlement* when the seller is terminally or chronically ill and has a short (less than two years) life expectancy.

Liquid assets: Things of value that can quickly be turned into cash, such as bank accounts (checking and savings), certificates of deposit, and money market funds.

Livable communities: Places with affordable, appropriate housing; adequate transportation; and supportive community features and service, where inhabitants can age in place and engage in the community's civic, economic, and social life.

Living trust: A financial asset that a person both owns and controls as both the trustee and the beneficiary while alive and not disabled. The trustee also names the successor trustee who will manage the trust after disability or death and successor beneficiaries who will get the assets in the trust after the trustee's death.

Living will: A form of advance directive that outlines medical treatment wishes; it may be added to the state's official advance directive.

Long-term care insurance: A policy purchased to help provide financial support when assistance is needed at home, in the community, or in a nursing home. Policies vary in coverage, benefit period, and other aspects.

Long-term care ombudsman: An official responsible for investigating complaints in nursing homes and assisted-care facilities in a state.

Long-term care: The spectrum of medical and nonmedical services needed over a long time by a person who is ill or disabled.

Long-term services and supports (LTSS): An umbrella term covering the non-medical services that are intended to meet the needs of an individual living in the community.

Look-back: The period of time during which transfer of assets for less than market value counts against Medicaid eligibility.

Medicaid: A joint federal and state program that helps with medical costs for some people with limited income and resources. Medicaid also covers long-term care in homes, communities, and nursing homes.

Medicaid managed long-term care: Plans run by private insurance companies under contract to the state to coordinate services and supports for people eligible for Medicaid.

Medicaid waiver: An agreement between the federal government and a state allowing the state to use some of its Medicaid funding for specific services to keep people in the community.

Medical day programs: Unlike adult social day programs, these programs provide assistance with healthcare needs as well as social activities.

Medical foster homes: Private homes in which a trained caregiver provides long-term services and supports to people who need round-the-clock care but do not need to be in a nursing home.

Medically Needy Program: A Medicaid program that assists people who have high medical expenses but whose income exceeds the maximum threshold for Medicaid eligibility.

Medicare: The federal health-insurance program for people who are 65 or older, certain younger people with disabilities, and people with end-stage renal disease. Part A covers hospital insurance, Part B pays for doctor bills and outpatient services, Part C is a Medicare Advantage plan, and Part D is prescription drug coverage.

Medicare-Certified Home Health Agencies (HHAs): Agencies approved by the Center for Medicare and Medicaid Services (CMS) and licensed by the state to provide skilled services, primarily nurse visits, but also physical therapy or social work visits, among others.

Medicare Advantage Plan or MA (Medicare Part C): A Medicare plan administered by a health insurance organization or plan. The plan covers all Part A and B benefits; most Advantage plans also cover prescription drug benefits.

Medicare Part D Doughnut Hole: A gap in coverage that begins when the beneficiary and drug plan have spent a certain amount for covered drugs. Scheduled to be eliminated by 2020 via the Affordable Care Act.

Medication administration: The preparing and giving of medications.

Medigap: A general term for supplemental insurance coverage used to pay for additional expenses not covered by Medicare.

Multigenerational living: A living arrangement in which multiple generations of the same family live together. Multigenerational households may include two or more consecutive generations, or include skipped generations; for instance, grandparents caring for grandchildren whose parents are unable to care for them.

Multiparty account without a right of survivorship/convenience account: A type of joint bank account where the agent has the authority to make deposits and withdrawals; but in the event that the primary person dies the remainder of the account goes into the estate and does not pass to the cosignator.

Naturally occurring retirement communities (NORC): Residences or communities in which many people are aging in place and live near others in the same stage of life. They are places that were not specifically built for seniors but now have a significant proportion of older residents. Neighborhood/open/horizontal NORC are arranged across a number of one- and two-family homes in age-integrated neighborhoods; housing-based/classic/closed/vertical NORCs are located in single age integrated buildings, or across a housing complex with the same management.

NORC programs: Programs that coordinate a broad range of social and medical services to support the residents in a NORC designated area.

Nonmedical or companion agency: Agencies that provide companion services, which include reading and conversation, assisting with clothing selection, organizing the mail, and picking up prescriptions from the pharmacy. They are not usually licensed by the state.

Notice of Medicare provider noncoverage: A notice that tells the date covered services will end.

NSAIDS: Nonsteroidal anti-inflammatory drugs.

Observation status/observation service: Hospital services given to a person while the doctor decides if the patient needs to be admitted as an inpatient or can be discharged. In the context of a hospital stay, being on observation may affect the amount an individual on Medicare has to pay for services and eligibility for rehabilitation services in a skilled-nursing facility.

Original Medicare: The traditional, fee-for-service plan of Medicare, in which healthcare providers are paid directly by the government for the services the patient receives.

OTC: Over-the-counter drugs.

PACE (Program of All-Inclusive Care for the Elderly): These programs are open to people who are eligible for Medicare, Medicaid, or both, and who have been deemed to have nursing-home level care needs. The programs provide care primarily in an adult daycare center. Comprehensive services include primary care, hospital care, medical specialty services, prescription drugs, home care, physical and occupational therapy, recreation therapy, nutritional counseling, transportation, and social-work counseling.

Paid family leave insurance: Insurance available to eligible working caregivers, which offers full or partial income replacement while a worker is at home taking care of a personal health condition, adjusting to a new child, or taking care of a family member with serious health needs.

Palliative care: A medical specialty and a range of services that improve how a person with a serious illness functions, even as they undergo active treatment. Care focuses on pain relief, symptom control, and quality of life. Palliative care can be time-limited or ongoing. The ill person and family members are considered part of the care team.

Paratransit: Public transportation service provided for people with disabilities.

Payable on death certificates of deposit: Bank accounts that are payable upon death to a beneficiary designated by the account holder. Sometimes called testamentary accounts.

Personal emergency-response system (PERS): A device, such as a necklace or bracelet, used to call for help in an emergency. It connects the victim with an emergency response center, which then dispatches help.

Physician's order for life-sustaining treatment (POLST): A physician's order that lists medical treatments that should or should not be provided when a person with advanced illness is transferred from one setting to another; called different names in different states.

Polypharmacy: Multiple drugs used by a single individual to treat chronic illnesses.

Power of attorney (POA): Written authorization to act on someone else's behalf. This authorization ends when a person becomes legally incompetent unless the person has signed a **durable power of attorney**.

Principal: The person signing a power-of-attorney document to assign someone else to act on his or her behalf.

Probate: The process of settling an estate. *Small estate probate* is the simplest form of probate that can be used for estates ranging in value from $1,000 to $10,000 depending on state law; *unsupervised or independent probate* is used when the estate has more than the value of a small estate but doesn't require a lot of court supervision; *supervised probate* applies to large estates and wills with complicated provisions where the court plays a major role in approving every action.

Respite: A short period of rest from caregiving duties.

Reverse mortgage: A financial product that gives a homeowner a line of credit, a lump sum, or monthly payments, which are not repaid until the owner sells the home, moves permanently into a nursing home, or dies.

Shared decision making: The process in which the patient, close family members, social worker, and healthcare team collaborate to make healthcare and long-term care decisions; a formal process in VA.

Single-purpose mortgage: A federally insured mortgage for which the proceeds can only be used for a specified purpose, such as property maintenance or repairs.

Skilled care: Care provided by a nurse or a physical therapist or other professional. Some examples of skilled nursing care are IV injections, tube feedings, and wound care.

Skilled-nursing facility (SNF): A facility licensed to provide short-term rehabilitation services by professionals as well as long-stay care.

Special-needs trust: A legal instrument that allows a parent or other person to set aside money for special types of care and support for a person with disabilities without jeopardizing the person's Medicaid status.

Spend-down: The process of using up one's income and assets, usually for long-term care, to meet Medicaid eligibility requirements.

Springing durable power of attorney: A document that sets conditions under which the durable power of attorney goes into effect; for example, when a doctor certifies that the person has become incapacitated.

State Health Insurance Assistance Program (SHIP): Programs that provide one-on-one, personal counseling to guide individuals through their insurance choices.

State Pharmacy Assistance Programs (SPAPs): State programs that help some people pay for prescription drugs based on financial need, age, or medical conditions.

Stranger-originated life insurance (STOLIs): Transactions that usually involve an older person being approached by a licensed life-insurance agent or another party to obtain new life insurance, with the policy being controlled from the start and paid for by a third party. These products carry considerable risk.

Supplemental Security Income: The federal program that pays benefits to disabled adults and children who have limited income and resources, and older adults who are not disabled but who meet the financial limits.

Supplemental transportation programs (STPs): Nontraditional transportation services for older adults who don't drive and others who need assistance. Most STPs provide door-to-door rides, and some arrange for a driver to stay with passengers until they are ready to go home.

Testamentary trust: A trust created with the assets from a decedent's estate or through a will that places conditions on their use.

TRICARE: TRICARE is the healthcare insurance program that covers healthcare for active-duty personnel, their families, retirees, members of the National Guard, and U.S. Army Reserve.

TRICARE For Life (TFL): Part of TRICARE that offers secondary coverage to Medicare beneficiaries who have both Part A and B coverage. It is available worldwide.

Trust: A legal arrangement in which one person gives the rights to another to hold title to property and/or assets for the benefit of a third party.

Universal design: Standards for building of homes, commercial buildings, and public spaces, including appliances, floor plans, and fixtures that are easy for all people to use, flexible, sturdy, and reliable.

Urgent-care centers: Medical facilities that operate as walk-in clinics for people with non-life-threatening illnesses or injuries, such as sprains, cuts, infection, flu, and similar complaints. Waiting time is usually shorter than in an emergency department, and the urgent care center can call an ambulance to take you to an emergency department if warranted.

VA: U.S. Department of Veterans Affairs.

VA health benefits priority groups: The method by which VA prioritizes the enrollment of veterans for health benefits. There are eight priority groups with various eligibility requirements, and eligibility must be verified by the VA before a priority group is assigned.

Veteran's pension: Funds paid to veterans of disabled veterans of wartime service who have low incomes and are no longer able to work.

Villages: Housing arrangements for independent nonprofit organizations with membership dues where members pool resources to leverage buying power and obtain services more cheaply. Services may include home maintenance and repair, home health and personal care, housekeeping, legal, and financial assistance.

Waiting period: The time that must pass before coverage can become effective or benefits begin. Also called a *qualifying period* or *elimination.*

Will: A legal declaration of how an individual wants his or her money and/ or property distributed after death. A *simple will* is a document used for the outright distribution of assets; a *pour-over will* assigns some assets to a trust that has already been established; a *holographic will* is handwritten but not witnessed; and an *oral will* is spoken but not written down.

Appendix B

Resources

• •

*E*very chapter includes resources for further investigation. This appendix brings together some of the major resources in one convenient location and adds a few that are not mentioned elsewhere.

AARP

AARP is a nonprofit, nonpartisan organization that helps people age 50 and over achieve independence, choice, and control in ways that are beneficial and affordable to them and society as a whole. AARP offers consumer-oriented information about long-term care, family caregiving, Medicare, and other programs.

The best place to start is the AARP website, www.aarp.org. For specific topics, see the following area-specific websites:

- ✔ **AARP Caregiving Resource Center** (www.aarp.org/caregiving): This site has a wealth of topics, blogs, and advice. Alternatively, you can use the Caregiving Resource Center's call-in number (877-333-5885) from 7 a.m. to 11 p.m. Eastern Time Monday through Friday and 9 a.m. to 5 p.m. on Saturdays.

- ✔ **AARP Driver Safety** (www.aarp.org/home-garden/transportation/driver_safety): This site has links to register for online or classroom driver safety courses, vision tips for older drivers, and other information.

- ✔ **AARP Housing Options** (www.aarp.org/home-family/caregiving/senior-housing): This site offers help in choosing the right kind of housing and describes independent living, assisted living, and nursing homes. It also has a section on downsizing and moving if that is the option you choose.

- ✔ **AARP Money** (www.aarp.org/money): The "Money" section has news and advice about a range of financial matters from choosing the best cellphone provider to investments and annuities. It has tools that help you calculate a mortgage or credit card payoff.

> ✓ **AARP Public Policy Institute** (www.aarp.org/research/ppi): The AARP PPI has information about federal and state policies regarding long-term care, workforce issues, and many other topics.

> ✓ **Universal Design** (www.aarp.org/home-garden/home-improvement/info-09-2009/what_is_universal_design.html): This site gives recommendations for accessible home design, including appliances, floor plans, and fixtures that are easy for all people to use, flexible, sturdy, and reliable.

Centers for Medicare and Medicaid Services (CMS)

CMS is the federal agency that oversees Medicare and Medicaid. Here are some of the most commonly used resources:

> ✓ **Medicaid** (www.medicaid.gov): This site has information about federal policies and state developments; for individual state programs, see state department of health website or Medicaid office.

> ✓ **Medicare** (www.medicare.gov): You can also call 800-633-4227. This site has material on various aspects of Medicare such as the rules regarding home healthcare eligibility, durable medical equipment, and the ins and outs of Part D for prescription drugs. Two important links are Nursing Home Compare and Home Health Compare, described in this list.

> ✓ **Nursing Home Compare** (www.medicare.gov/nursinghomecompare/search.html): This site allows you to search for nursing homes by location or facility name. It provides information on staffing, training, prevention of abuse and neglect, reporting incidents of poor quality, and other standards.

> ✓ **Home Health Compare** (www.medicare.gov/homehealthcompare/search.html): Home Health Compare is a CMS website that gives you information on specific agencies and how they are doing with meeting federal standards.

> ✓ **Quality Improvement Organizations (QIOs)** (State directory at www.qualitynet.org/dcs/ContentServer?c=Page&pagename=Qnet Public%2FPage%2FQnetTier2&cid=1144767874793): Each state has a designated QIO that is responsible for ensuring and improving quality of care and for reviewing complaints. If, for example, you feel that you are being discharged from a hospital too quickly, you can appeal the decision to the local QIO. Most people don't know about these organizations, but they can be very helpful in resolving problems.

Administration for Community Living

The Administration for Community Living (ACL) is the federal agency responsible for increasing access to community supports for older Americans and people with disabilities of any age. Its general website is www.acl.gov, and the following departments within the ACL provide more specific information.

- ✔ **Administration on Aging** (www.aoa.gov): The Administration on Aging (AoA) is part of ACL. AoA supports what is often called the "Aging Network" of agencies and professionals. AoA was created in 1965 with the passage of the Older Americans Act and provides support services, nutrition services, preventive health services, the National Family Caregiver Support Program, elder rights services, and services to Native Alaskans, Native Hawaiians, and Native Americans.

- ✔ **Area Agencies on Aging (AAAs)** (www.n4a.org/about-n4a/?fa=aaa-title-VI): Part of the AoA's Aging Network, there are over 600 Area Agencies on Aging that provide information and referrals to services such as adult daycare and senior-center programs in their region. Some state associations of AAAs also have maps of their locations within the state.

- ✔ **Aging and Disability Resource Centers (ADRCs)** (http://www.eldercare.gov/Eldercare.NET/Public/About/Aging_Network/ADRC.aspx): A collaborative effort of the Administration for Community Living, Centers for Medicare & Medicaid Services, and now the Veterans Health Administration (VHA), ADRCs serve as single entry points into the long-term supports and services system for older adults and people with disabilities.

- ✔ **Eldercare Locator** (http://eldercare.gov/Eldercare.NET/Public/Index.aspx): The Eldercare Locator, a free service of AoA, is a basic go-to site for locating resources in your community. You can access an online chat forum, or you can call 800-677-1116 for information.

- ✔ **The National Center on Elder Abuse** (www.ncea.aoa.gov): This website offers information on the types of elder abuse and national and state resources on elder abuse.

- ✔ **National Family Caregiver Support Program (NFCSP)** (www.aoa.gov/AoA_Programs/HCLTC/Caregiver/index.aspx): This program is administered through your local Area Agency on Aging. This program offers information and support to family caregivers, including support groups, and (where available) legal and financial advice and respite. Each program has its own set of services, depending on resources.

- ✔ **Long-term Care Ombudsmen (**www.ltcombudsman.org/ombudsman): Ombudsmen investigate complaints and negotiate solutions to problems in nursing homes and assisted-living facilities.

Other Resources

Following are an assortment of links to other agencies and organizations that may be able to assist you in planning for long-term care.

- ✔ **AbleData** (www.abledata.com): A project of the National Institute for Disability and Rehabilitation Research, AbleData has information about assistive devices and resources.

- ✔ **Aging with Dignity** (www.agingwithdignity.org): This national nonprofit organization has the mission of affirming and safeguarding the human dignity of individuals as they age and to promoting better care for those near the end of life. Its "Five Wishes" form gives you the opportunity to convey your personal, emotional, and spiritual needs as well as your medical wishes. In 42 states and the District of Columba, it substantially meets the legal requirements for an advance directive.

- ✔ **Alzheimer's Association** (www.alz.org): At this website you can find links to local chapters, which offer educational sessions, support groups, and other services. The main site has information about Alzheimer's disease and other dementias, including research and treatment.

- ✔ **American Bar Association's Commission on Law and Aging** (www.americanbar.org/groups/law_aging.html): This organization and website examine a wide range of legal issues affecting older persons.

- ✔ **American Diabetes Association** (www.diabetes.org): This website has links to local chapters, information on prevention and treatment, and services.

- ✔ **American Heart Association** (www.heart.org/HEARTORG): The AHA has information about heart disease and stroke, treatments, and prevention.

- ✔ **Banfield Charitable Trust** (www.banfieldcharitabletrust.org/pet-owners): This group offers a number of programs that are designed to help pet owners struggling to care for their pets or facing difficult life circumstances. Help includes financial assistance for emergency and preventive vet care through Banfield Pet Hospitals and local nonprofits across the country, a program for pet owners who are in hospice, a food program for pets through grants to Meals on Wheels programs, and other assistance to pet owners facing financial challenges.

- ✔ **Cancer Care** (www.cancercare.org): Cancer Care's website provides free, professional support services to anyone affected by cancer. The organization has educational programs for patients and caregivers, counseling services, and limited financial assistance. Services are available online and by phone.

- ✔ **Caring and Aging with Pride** (http://caringandaging.org): This is the first national project to study health and wellness among lesbian, gay, bisexual, and transgender older adults and their caregivers.

- ✔ **Center to Advance Palliative Care** (www.getpalliativecare.org): This website offers information about what palliative care is and resources for locating palliative-care providers.

- ✔ **Center Link** (www.lgbtcenters.org): This national organization represents all the LGBT community centers in the United States.

- ✔ **Center for Medicare Advocacy** (www.medicareadvocacy.org): This nonprofit organization is focused on education, advocacy, and legal assistance for older adults and the disabled.

- ✔ **Eden Alternative** (www.edenalt.org): The Eden Alternative is a specific model of nursing home care focusing on small-group residences, control by residents, and inclusion of plants and animals. Its principles can be found at www.edenalt.org/our-10-principles; and state-by-state resources about Eden can be found at www.edenalt.org/resources/eden-resources.

- ✔ **Family Caregiver Alliance** (www.caregiver.org/caregiver/jsp/home.jsp): This organization has guides and fact sheets on many topics related to family caregiving in English, Spanish, and Chinese. The FCA Family Care Navigator has a map of resources by state available at www.caregiver.org/caregiver/jsp/fcn_content_node.jsp?nodeid=2083.

- ✔ **Gay and Lesbian Elder Housing (GLEH)** (www.gleh.org): This advocacy and education organization works on developing affordable housing and providing comprehensive care for LGBT seniors. It has a Senior Resource Center and a Housing and Services Center on its website.

- ✔ **Green House Project** (http://thegreenhouseproject.org/): The Green House Project is a model for creating senior by building or converting residential homes into settings that can provide high levels of care. The site features an interactive map that shows the home operating and in development by state.

- ✔ **Hospice Directory** (www.hospicedirectory.org): This resource directory helps you locate a hospice as well as a list of state hospice associations.

- ✔ **Human Rights Campaign** (www.hrc.org): This organization works for equal rights for LGBT individuals. Its site has a state-by-state map of hospital visitation laws, and its Healthcare Equity Index helps determine whether a healthcare organization is designated as a leader in LGBT healthcare equality.

- ✔ **Medicare Rights Center** (www.medicarerights.org): This advocacy group has online guidance at and trained volunteers available at 1-800-333-4114.

- ✔ **National Association of Professional Geriatric Care Managers** (www.caremanager.org): This organization of trained geriatric professionals assist individuals and families in finding appropriate housing, home care services, medical management, communication, social activities, and legal and financial advice. The website has a database of its members, searchable by zip code.

- ✔ **National Association of Social Workers (NASW)** (www.socialworkers.org): NASW works to enhance the professional growth and development of its members, to create and maintain professional standards, and to advance sound social policies. You can also find lists of licensed social workers and therapists, mostly NASW members, at http://www.helpstartshere.org/find-a-social-worker.

- ✔ **National Association of State Veterans Homes** (www.nasvh.org): This website has a list of veterans' community living facilities by state.

- ✔ **National Center for Participant-Directed Services** (www.bc.edu/schools/gssw/nrcpds.html): You can also find a map of state cash and counseling programs at https://bcweb.bc.edu/libtools/insights-publications.php. Cash and counseling programs (sometimes called by different names) make it possible for Medicaid and home-care-eligible persons to hire their own attendants, including some groups of family members instead of agency workers.

- ✔ **The National Consumer Voice for Quality Long-Term Care** (www.theconsumervoice.org): This consumer advocacy group provides support and training for long-term care consumers and their caregivers. They offer information for residents, including a complete list of residents' rights guaranteed by the 1987 Nursing Home Reform Law.

- ✔ **National Council on Aging** (www.ncoa.org): Through its BenefitsCheckup tool, NCOA has information for older adults on accessing benefits such as help paying for medications or food. The tool is organized by state or zip code.

- ✔ **National Hospice and Palliative Care Organization** (www.nhpco.org): This website has information about end-of-life concerns and links to help you find providers of both types of services. Its Caring Connections program has a list of state-by-state forms for advance directives available at www.caringinfo.org/i4a/pages/index.cfm?pageid=3289.

- ✔ **National Resource Center on Lifespan Respite Care — the ARCH** (Access to Respite Care and Help) (http://archrespite.org/search-for-respite): Here you can find an interactive map of respite services.

✔ **Next Step in Care** (www.nextstepincare.org): Created by the United Hospital Fund, NSIC has free guides in four languages (English, Spanish, Chinese, and Russian) for family caregivers on navigating the healthcare system, especially during transitions, and links to national organizations, government agencies, and disease-specific organizations.

✔ **Pet Partners** (www.petpartners.org): This nonprofit organization provides information about service animals for people with disabilities, animal programs in assisted-living facilities and nursing homes, and research about the human-animal bond.

✔ **SAGE (Services and Advocacy for Gay, Lesbian, Bisexual, and Transgender Elders)** (www.sageusa.org): This group provides services and support, including the National Center on LGBT Aging and the National LGBT Aging Roundtable; SAGECAP (Caring and Preparing) offers counseling and information for people caring for an LGBT individual.

✔ **Social Security Administration** (www.ssa.gov): The Social Security Administration (SSA) administers Social Security benefits, which may be an important part of the financial side of your long-term care plan. The agency's website lets you check or estimate your retirement benefits online and get other information.

✔ **U.S. Department of Veterans Affairs** (http://va.gov): The VA has information for veterans and their families on adult day healthcare, caregiver assessment, geriatrics and extended care, home telehealth, homemaker and home health-aide services, hospice and palliative care, respite for family caregivers, shared decision making, and other topics.

Index

• Q •

• R •

• S •

About the Author

Carol Levine has taken the "road less traveled" on her career path. As an undergraduate at Cornell University, she studied Russian history, literature, and language, and continued her studies at Columbia University, where she received an MA in public law and government. The link to her current position as director of the United Hospital Fund's Families and Health Care Project is not immediately apparent, but she says each step along the way involved honing her skills as a researcher, analyst, and writer.

She was introduced to the world of medical ethics through her tenure at The Hastings Center, where she edited the *Hastings Center Report* and is now a Hastings Center Fellow. Much of her work in the 1980s and early 1990s concerned HIV/AIDS and ethics, and in 1993 she was awarded a MacArthur Foundation Fellowship for that work.

She joined the United Hospital Fund in 1996 to work on issues related to family caregiving, a professional interest that grew out of her personal experience as a caregiver to her late husband who was disabled as the result of an automobile accident. That work has been recognized by her designation as a WebMD Health Hero in 2007 and a Civic Ventures Purpose Prize Fellow in 2009. She serves on many advisory boards related to family caregiving and long-term care.

In addition to publishing many professional and consumer articles, she edited *Always On Call: When Illness Turns Families into Caregivers* (2nd ed., Vanderbilt University Press, 2004), and with Thomas H. Murray, co-edited *The Cultures of Caregiving: Conflict and Common Ground among Families, Health Professionals and Policy Maker* (Johns Hopkins University Press, 2004).

While working on this For Dummies book, she was also compiling an anthology, *Living in the Land of Limbo: Fiction and Poetry about Family Caregiving,* which will be published in 2014 by Vanderbilt University Press. This brings her abiding interest in literature full circle.

Carol lives in New York City, surrounded by books and needlepoint and, as often as possible, by children and grandchildren.

Dedication

To my mother, Betty Solomon, *alav ha-shalom* [of blessed memory], who was a determined long-term care planner.

Author's Acknowledgments

In keeping with this book's broad perspective, a great many people contributed to the various iterations of the text. Each brought special expertise and a collaborative spirit that helped shape the book and make it not only more precise and up-to-date but also more relevant to readers.

Many dedicated AARP staff members reviewed and commented on various sections of the manuscript. They are listed here in alphabetical order, and I am grateful to everyone from A to W: Jean Accius, Debra Alvarez, Jean Anthony, Kelly Bagby, Patricia Barry, Elizabeth Bradley, Mary Liz Burns, Deborah Chalfie, Rita Choula, Elizabeth Costle, Wendy Fox-Grage, Ariel Gonzalez, Amy Goyer, Rodney Harrell, Ilene Henshaw, Sally Hurme, David John, Enid Kassner, Keith Lind, Don Redfoot, Susan Reinhard, Rhonda Richards, Joyce Rogers, Elaine Ryan, Erin Scheithe, Michael Schuster, Lindsay Sena, Dorothy Siemon, Yolanda Taylor, Lori Trawinski, Kathleen Ujvari, Deb Whitman, and T. Ryan Wilson. A special thank you to Jodi Lipson, director of AARP's book division.

Several of my colleagues at the United Hospital Fund reviewed chapters, answered questions, and encouraged me throughout the process: Michael Birnbaum, Greg Burke, David Gould, Anya Nawrocky, and Fredda Vladeck. Kristina Ramos-Callan helped prepare the Appendixes. More generally I have benefited over the years from the thoughtful discussions of health policy and long-term care that have been at the heart of the Fund's mission. One of the privileges of working at the Fund is the opportunity to work with many national experts with a variety of backgrounds. They responded to my requests with their customary skill and precision: Carol Cronin, Institute for Patient-Centered Care; Hillary Meyer, SAGE; Sheri Reder, VA; Carol Rodat, PHI; Catherine Thurston, SAGE; and Ann Wyatt, nursing home consultant. In addition, Ilana Mittleman helped with Internet research.

My devoted daughters Jenny Tuten and Judy Levine and my knowledgeable son-in-law Andrew Pickar read and commented on various sections.

Such a diverse group of experts was bound to bring a variety of opinions and interpretations to their review. While I valued all these comments and incorporated many of them, the opinions and advice expressed in the book represent my views and should be read in that light. They are not formal policy statements from either AARP or the United Hospital Fund.

Sincere thanks to my agent, John Thornton, and to the talented and supportive editorial staff at Wiley: Erin Calligan-Mooney, acquisitions editor; Linda Brandon, project editor; Caitie Copple, copy editor; and Mark Friedlich, technical editor.

Publisher's Acknowledgments

Acquisitions Editor: Erin Calligan-Mooney

Project Editor: Linda Brandon

Copy Editor: Caitie Copple

Technical Editor: Mark Friedlich

Art Coordinator: Alicia B. South

Project Coordinator: Rebekah Brownson

Cover Photos: ©TOPIC PHOTO AGENCY IN/ agefotostock